'This is a time of immense tension in th
secularism, over security and conflict, ov
knowledge and ways of understanding, and
with all of this. Lynn Davies has written a
with crucial theoretical insights and very re
our way in these troubled times. It gives us hope for a better future.

**Michael W. Apple, John Bascom Professor of Curriculum and Instruction
and Educational Policy Studies, University of Wisconsin, Madison**

'Ours is an age of deep uncertainty and concomitant hard certainties. This
important book conveys the turbulence, bursts of hope, historical turns, and
technical revolutions of our times, and suggests that only critical thinking
and secularism can protect our young from dogma and disillusionment, and
enable them to survive our increasingly complex, unpredictable world.'

Yasmin Alibhai-Brown, newspaper columnist

'Equipped with an armada of cases (Afghanistan, Pakistan, Sri Lanka,
Northern Ireland, Rwanda, Palestine-Israel, Kosovo, Angola and many
more), Lynn Davies takes the reader on a near-dizzying postmodern/
postcolonial journey in seven succinct and well-written chapters in which
she searches for the nexus of conflict, security, religion, secularism and
education. Finessing the term 'security', she gives it both a nuanced reading
and complexity that allows the reader to understand core aspects of 'human
security'. Professor Davies isolates a central dilemma – 'that schooling
[which foments doubt and, therefore, unlearning or deradicalization]
appears simultaneously irrelevant to the huge global questions ... and yet
central to the learning of alternative ways to conduct human relations'
(p. 8). One by one, Davies topples the gods such as development and hybrid
identities. She presents us with a fluid, chaotic and turbulent world where
education is one of a vast array of possibilities (at the same time arguably
the possibility) for finding alternative ways of being human. For my own
work in Sudan, a place with all the ingredients of Davies's ethnographic
universe – violence and conflict, radical religion (Islam), neoliberal
development projects, militarization of society, major security issues at all
levels and a school system that serves all of these – the work is invaluable: a
tour de force. She has done much of my work for me!'

Professor Emerita Sondra Hale, Anthropology and Gender Studies, UCLA

Unsafe Gods

Unsafe Gods

Security, secularism and schooling

Lynn Davies

A Trentham Book
Institute of Education Press

First published in 2014 by the Institute of Education, University of London,
20 Bedford Way, London WC1H 0AL
www.ioe.ac.uk/ioepress

© Lynn Davies 2014

British Library Cataloguing in Publication Data:
A catalogue record for this publication is available from the British Library

ISBNs
978-1-85856-525-5 (paperback)
978-1-85856-549-1 (PDF eBook)
978-1-85856-550-7 (ePub eBook)
978-1-85856-551-4 (Kindle eBook)

Every effort has been made to trace copyright holders and to obtain their permission for the use of copyright material. The publisher apologizes for any errors or omissions and would be grateful if notified of any corrections that should be incorporated in future reprints or editions of this book.

The opinions expressed in this publication are those of the author and do not necessarily reflect the views of the Institute of Education, University of London.

Typeset by Quadrant Infotech (India) Pvt Ltd
Printed by CPI Group (UK) Ltd, Croydon, CR0 4YY
Cover images: schoolchildren ©iStock.com/GlobalStock; security cameras ©iStock.com/StudioCampo; mosque ©iStock.com/oversnap; church ©iStock.com/shimmo; barbed wire fence ©View7/Dreamstime.com

Contents

Acknowledgements

I want to thank many people who knowingly and unknowingly have made possible different parts of this book. First, as always, my erstwhile colleagues in the Centre for International Education and Research at the University of Birmingham – Michele Schweisfurth, Clive Harber, Chris Williams and Hiromi Yamashita. Their legacy of support, stimulation and laughs has kept me going over the years. Then my brilliant Preventing Extremism team – Basia Spalek, Zubeda Limbada and Laura Zahra Mcdonald – now forming the organization ConnectJustice, which I am proud to be associated with. Then Andrew Hobbs of RoHo Learning, my critical idealism friend, who read and made profoundly useful comments on the initial chapters. Then my colleagues in German International Cooperation (GIZ) who were responsible for my experiences in Afghanistan and Sri Lanka – Rüdiger Blumör, Ulf Metzger and Elke Krause-Hannak. Their wisdom and insight into conflict and fragility is unübertroffen. Then there are the complexity people – Ritesh Shah and Mieke Lopez-Cardozo, who encouraged me to continue with complexity, and even started the Complexity DropBox, with the University of Auckland complexity group being a great sounding board for what became the first chapter. And then there were the Islamophobia colleagues – Jasmin Zine and Sarah Soyei – who brought such practical knowledge as well as critical edge to the thinking.

Not all of these people and groupings may have actually read the relevant bits of the book, but they are always audiences in my mind. You write for the people you respect and love – so I blame you if this book bombs. But I cannot blame my publisher Gillian Klein who has achieved the miraculous task of sternly making meticulous improvements to the writing at the same time as making me feel good about it. Finally thanks and love to my family – husband Chris, daughter Anna and son-in-law Russell – who keep me sane and the wine glass topped up.

About the author

Lynn Davies is Emeritus Professor of International Education at the University of Birmingham. Her primary research and teaching interests have been in the area of education and conflict, exploring schooling in contexts of fragility and the role of education in extremism and fundamentalism. She has over twenty years' experience in contexts such as Kosovo, Palestine, Angola, Sri Lanka and Afghanistan, as well as in evaluating work in the UK on preventing radicalization. This is all informed by research on student democracy and children's rights.

Professor Davies's books include *Education and Conflict: Complexity and chaos* (Routledge, 2004) and *Educating Against Extremism* (Trentham, 2008), and she has recently co-edited the collection *Gender, Religion and Education in a Chaotic Postmodern World* (Springer, 2013). She is a Research Fellow at UNISA (University of South Africa), a Visiting Professor at the British University of Dubai, and is on the Board of the Africa Educational Trust. The current book builds on some of the thinking in *Educating Against Extremism* to develop a new conceptualization of the nexus between conflict, religion and education.

Chapter 1
Security and complexity

My definition of a free society is a society where it is safe to be unpopular.

Adlai Stevenson

This is a book about risk. As the title implies, our gods, the things we worship or at least hold dear, are not without danger. Religion is not safe, but secularism is not safe either. Education is certainly not safe. In some ways this book is simply about damage limitation. Yet it is also about finding the optimum sorts of security for people to live together and for a society to evolve to better forms.

Two threads weave in and out of the book. One is an argument for secularism – but a particular type of dynamic, inclusive, contextual secularism. The other is a theoretical underpinning to this, derived from complexity theory. I want to show how a dynamic secularism best promotes the sort of complex, adaptive society which can in turn generate security. As an educationist, my interest in this relates to learning – how societies learn and progress, but also the deliberately educational aspects of learning such as schooling. Putting together security, secularism, education and complexity has been a challenge – and is probably hopelessly over-ambitious. But it represents a point in a journey. My interest in security goes back to my work on pupil deviance and gender (Davies, 1984). My work in the comparative education field led to a mistrust of universal solutions to education reform such as school effectiveness (Harber and Davies, 2002). Exposure to different conflict-affected states led to the search for a good theory, and hence to the 2004 book *Education and Conflict: Complexity and chaos*. Then came a particular interest in the role of education in extremism (Davies, 2008) and from there deradicalization. This book returns to complexity theory and joins it with the issues of religion that are a crucial part of analysing how people and countries experience security or insecurity.

Arguing for secularism does not mean this is an anti-religion book in the style of Richard Dawkins or Christopher Hitchens, much as I enjoy their writing. If anything it is more akin to Martin Rowson's perceptive book *The Dog Allusion* (2008), which accepts (albeit wearily) that people need religion, even if, as a universal phenomenon, it has parallels to keeping pets. In both there are transcendental heights of complete, unquestioning and unfettered love, taking time, money and energy, and neither are particularly rational. But religious adherents, any more than pet lovers, will not be disturbed through scientific, logical arguments. Mine is a book about accommodation, not rejection.

Although it is ambitious, putting together security, religion and education is essential. They form a nexus, but one where the intersections come together in complex, messy and unpredictable ways. National security has both a religious and an educational underpinning – yet it would be a mistake to see these two aspects as making separate 'impacts' on security. Not only are they pivotal, but they interact and evolve in highly complex ways. No starker example of this exists than the Nigerian Islamist sect Boko Haram, which in 2012 mounted a series of terror attacks in the largely Muslim north of Nigeria. Boko Haram loosely translates as 'Western education is sinful', and, in its quest to establish an Islamic state, its targets are moderate Muslims as well as Christians. Linking the bogeys of 'sin' and 'the West' to education is a cunning and powerful ploy, able to radicalize disenfranchised and frustrated youth with little experience of schooling. While security forces seek military solutions to conflict, these can be short-lived. In the end it will be the political and ideological solutions that prevail.

The book then attempts something of a new synthesis. The journey of the book itself is not a linear one towards a glorious finale (this would not fit complexity), but a series of parallel accounts which, seen together, aim to justify the prescriptions towards the end. In this introductory chapter I discuss the understandings of security which emerge in different parts of the book, and outline those components of the theory of complex adaptive systems which are relevant to religion, secularism and education. This is admittedly selective, but a comprehensive analysis of complexity is not only impossible but actually not necessary. There are key insights which seem to leap out at you.

The next two chapters (on religion for negative conflict and then on secularism for positive conflict) are broad-based – often at national or global levels. Chapters 4 and 5 relate more specifically to education, looking at secular education and values and then at the practicalities of safe schools. These are about prevention. The final two chapters deal with the more active and intentional intervention – deradicalization, or unlearning, and finally the learning which can foster change that can mean more workable security for all. This leads to the uncomfortable conclusion that security requires a degree of instability or turbulence. Just as one can have negative peace and positive peace, or negative and positive conflict, there can be negative and positive insecurity. The conclusion summarizes the Unsafe Gods which can hinder adaptation and gives illustrations of projects and social movements which provide the most promising sort of turbulence for social evolution.

Security nests, levels and trade-offs: Global versus human security

First I discuss types and levels of security, and the particular interests of this book. The term 'security' has come to be associated mostly with macro-level conflicts, with security forces and security departments being prominent in the public realm. The implication is that solutions to insecurity are based primarily on the military and on intelligence, and are about shooting and spying. Yet the presence or absence of security can be felt at a number of levels, often nested inside each other – personal, local, societal, national and international. More recent is the concern with human security – the way we live our lives. The core aspects of human security – access to social justice, rights and freedom from violence, as well as access to health, water and education – have taken centre stage in development and humanitarian efforts. Paul Stares writes:

> The concept of global or human security represents ... both a *horizontal* extension of the parameters of security policy to include an even larger set of problems, such as poverty, epidemics, political injustice, natural disasters, crime, social discrimination and unemployment, as well as a *vertical* extension of the traditional referent object of security policy to above and below the level of the nation state.
>
> (Stares, 1998: 15)

This raises the key question of who is defining security for whom, and for whose ends, as well as who has the responsibility for the security of others, and in what direction.

Questions about trade-offs also arise. The domination in security studies by the international relations discipline and by analyses of military power implies a simplistic logic that more military power means greater security for all. This is now disputed, especially with regard to human security. The trade-off, especially for a poorer, already conflict-affected state, is that greater spending on the military means less spending on social goods such as education, health or water. The soldier–teacher ratio is always a telling statistic. Also, the militarization of peace or of development may mean that violence becomes normalized. Whether national security inevitably means sacrificing other values is the perennial question.

As Bjørn Møller (2003) points out in the context of the Israel–Palestine conflict, concepts of security resonate with concepts of peace – security is not just the absence of threats to national territory and its institutions. Negative peace (equated with the absence of war) is a narrow definition, and an expanded definition means looking for positive or stable peace. Genuine peace and security would presuppose the elimination of what Galtung (1969) calls *structural violence,* that is, of the relative deprivation of large parts of the world population. Thus positive peace is almost synonymous with human security. Nonetheless security studies commonly do not tackle this expanded concept, and the focus is often on counter-terrorism. Ironically this means a securitization of many aspects of human life, including education, as I discuss in Chapter 5. Møller usefully distinguishes three axes: security of whom, the 'referent object'; security of what; and security from whom or what. So for national security, the object is the state and the value at risk is sovereignty or territorial integrity; for societal security the objects are nations and social groups, with the values at risk including national unity and group identity; when the object is individuals or 'mankind' the values at risk are survival and quality of life; and when the object is the ecosystem, the value at risk is sustainability. Our concern is where education might be situated across these axes, concerns and risks.

Yet it is important not to see security simply as a number of levels or even 'axes', but to acknowledge how they are nested within each other. Conflicts, population movements, state collapse, refugees and international criminality associated with the 'permanent emergency of self-reliance' have replaced communism as the main perceived threat to Western security (Duffield, 2010: 56). The now huge literature on 'weak states' or 'fragile states' or 'failed states' is there not just in the interests of those polities or economies, but also reveals how such states may harbour a range of problematic elements which resonate more widely, including, but not confined to, terrorism. A fascinating study of organized crime, conflict and fragility by Rachel Locke (2012) documents the massive reach of transnational organized crime (TOC) across the world in drugs, human trafficking or minerals. Fragile states, with their 'opportunistic' environment, provide more opportunities for such crime to flourish. Half of all the illicit money in the world is estimated to come from developing and transition contexts. Locke's study does not mention education at all, but has potentially interesting points to make with regard to complexity, and why people turn to illegal activity:

> Recent research suggests that individuals change their behaviour
> depending on their expectations of the future ... When the future

is expected to be worse than the present, the incentives move towards living in the present: profligate consumption and reduced infrastructure investment ... Turning down illicit or compromising offers of immediate financial reward may not only be economically challenging, it could also be cognitively irrational.

(Locke, 2012: 4)

The rationality of crime or religion is a recurrent theme of the present book.

The next question is: who 'does' or provides security, and why? Many groups, from Hezbollah in Lebanon to FARC in Colombia, have competed with the government for popular support by providing services to the population. In Jamaica, local 'dons' are considered more legitimate than the state in some areas, taking on roles as varied as settling disputes and providing school fees. When there is a lack of state or institutional legitimacy and a history of state predation, citizens will not only have little incentive to engage with the state, they will have a strong rationale for seeking alternatives. Surveys of gang members show that 46 per cent have economic reasons for joining. But more than half had non-economic motivations – to gain security, gain respect, and react to injustice. Economic solutions do not address these motives (Locke, 2012). And the literature on why people join extremist groups often points to the security of belonging, of being a member of a new 'family' (Davies, 2008).

The other problem of lack of state security is the shift to the privatization of security. Robert Jackson (1990) talks of 'quasi-states', which have a dissonance between the loci of authority and power, and where administrative capacity is inadequate, making the state little more than a hollow shell. Møller claims 'The main security problem in today's developing world may ... not be an excess but rather a deficit in state power' (Møller, 2003: 7). We seem to go back to Weber, and the erosion of the state's 'monopoly on the legitimate use of force' (Weber, 1958: 78). The increase in civil or intercommunal conflict and of crime means that security becomes privatized. People resort to self-help if their families or property are threatened, arming themselves or hiring private security companies. A spiral of amplification ensues, where arms proliferate and violence escalates. This is apparent not just in weak states but in apparently strong ones: after a recent massacre at a school in the US, the call for a law restricting possession of assault weapons led to an *increase* in sales of them, as people stocked up in advance of the ban. The spokesman for the hugely influential National Rifle Association (NRA) made the classic remark: 'the only thing that stops a bad guy with a gun is a good guy with a gun' (Taylor, 2012: 39). The NRA is calling for armed guards in schools, and for teachers to have guns (with parallels to South Africa). But this relates not just to school security but to ideological claims – the constitutional right in America to own a gun.

This is certainly security *below* the level of the nation state, as defined by Paul Stares. The other direction, above the level of the nation state, relates to the justification for the use of arms globally. The two international questions are: who is intervening in whose security, and what is the goal of such intervention? Liotta (2005) argues that in interventions as disparate as those in Somalia in 1993, in Liberia at various stages of disintegration, in the Balkans, and in Iraq in 2003, there emerged an overt increase in US and British hegemonic behaviour, accompanied by uneven commitment to issues involving human security. While British Prime Minister Tony Blair could speak of 'universal values' and American President George Bush could proclaim that 'freedom is the non-negotiable demand of human dignity', foreign policy choices regarding intervention were almost exclusively made when such choices satisfied the narrow, selfish and direct 'national security interests' of more powerful states (Liotta, 2005: 61). As Liotta points out, the blatant failure of the international community to do anything in Rwanda in 1994 illustrated – apart from a collective international decision to do *nothing* – that human security was hardly proving to be the trump card of choice in decisions over whether to intervene in the affairs of other states. Liotta claims that, taken to extreme forms, human security and national security could be conceptually approached as antagonistic rather than convergent identities.

It could be argued that lessons have been learned from Rwanda, and foreign powers are currently weighing up interventions in the Middle East in terms of a role in alleviating human suffering as well as considering strategic power interests. I would argue that especially in terms of intervention and global security, the bottom line is always national interests. With regard to the surrounding interests in the Syrian crisis, I much appreciated the comprehensive analysis in *The Times* (2012a) by seven of its regional specialists, of which a brief résumé is as follows:

- Iran supports Assad and is concerned that Assad's removal will decrease its regional influence.
- Iraq is concerned that Syria provides a base for jihadists and is concerned that the conflict could reignite its own Sunni–Shia fighting.
- Lebanon is split down the middle between supporters and opponents of Assad, and fears sectarian tension between Sunni and Shia could spark its own civil war; Syria is the key geo-strategic linchpin connecting Hezbollah to its patron, Iran.

- Turkey is home to the opposition Syrian National Council, and worries that Kurdish guerrillas will establish bases in northern Syria.
- Israel worries that Assad's chemical weapons could fall into the hands of Hezbollah, and that a new Syrian administration renews claims to the Golan Heights.
- Jordan is concerned that the Syrian conflict could energize domestic opposition to King Abdullah II, and has a growing refugee population increasing stress on its poor economy.
- Saudi Arabia supports the rebels and uses tribal links to exert influence in south and eastern Syria.
- Qatar is also a base for Syrian defectors and exiles; it wants to advance its growing presence on the international stage.
- Further afield, Russia has huge economic and military stakes in Syria and is vetoing the UN resolution on military action against Assad.
- China too is vetoing, and sees intervention as potentially threatening to its own interests in Tibet and North Korea.
- In the US the CIA is working with the opposition to identify the Iranian Revolutionary Guard, Al Qaeda, and Hezbollah further to prevent them exploiting a post-Assad Syria.
- Britain is trying to promote some sort of coalition but is backing the Free Syrian Army, aiming to give Britain some influence in a post-Assad Syria and hoping that supporting them might see off any jihadists or Al Qaeda affiliates. There appears to be a growing number of wannabe British jihadists going to join the Islamic opposition in Syria.

But nowhere in this tangle of interests and influence do analysts talk of education, let alone human security. The thought of doing peace education and 'loving thy neighbour' anywhere in this region would seem laughable. A theme which runs through this book is whether education can do no more than try *not* to cement sectarian, religious-based identities and tribal factions. Education could just exist in a bubble, turning out engineers and plumbers and doctors and accountants and teachers and piano tuners in the way it always has, until things die down. Neither opposition groups nor revolutionaries nor foreign leaders will have learned their stance or their strategy in school (see Chapter 6). Importantly, education could encourage critical dissent once a dictator is overthrown. Any resolution of the ensuing power struggle will demand some awareness of democratic, non-violent procedures of negotiation, compromise, soft power and coalitions, in order to prevent one sectarian leader being replaced with another or by an uncompromising religious ideology. I explore this in the final chapter. At this point the central dilemma has to be acknowledged: that schooling appears simultaneously irrelevant to the huge global questions of security and yet central to the learning of alternative ways to conduct human relations.

Security as unsafe

A final paradox is that efforts to increase security are not always benign. There are three aspects to this: focusing on a country's development in order to foster internal stability and hence avert threats to global security; promoting self-reliance; and enhancing societal security. All could be considered unsafe.

First, development *as* security. The British in Malaysia first coined the term 'hearts and minds' to describe winning the loyalty of the people – a phrase now used in Iraq and Afghanistan. Poverty is 'monotonously rediscovered' as a recruiting ground for the moving feast of strategic threats that constantly menace the liberal order (Duffield, 2010: 61). Internal cohesion and 'good governance' become the key. The 'integrated mission' encapsulates ambitious and complex programmes of disarmament, institutional reform, capacity building, economic development and societal and state reconstruction – including education. Mary Anderson's influential book *Do No Harm* (1996) reflects the sentiments of development as security, advocating using aid selectively to alter the balance of power between social groups and to isolate violent actors. The aim is to foster collective goals and strengthen those local interests that support peace. Yet top-down approaches can be seen as manipulative. They can also be taken over by competing interests: even the Taliban are concerned about winning hearts and minds, as I discuss in Chapter 5.

Second, a different form of dangerous patronage. In an examination of the development–security nexus, Mark Duffield (2010) raises concerns about how Western nations, in worries about their own security, attempt to define security for poorer nations in terms of their 'self-reliance'. This is 'biopolitics' – how life is to be supported and maintained and how people are expected to live. The familiar refrain is that not only is it ethically right to reduce global poverty, but that *not* doing so leads to civil wars, failed states, and safe havens for terrorists. This seems straightforward enough – that alienation is reduced through meeting basic needs. Yet Duffield is concerned about the destabilizing division – that this is the *containment* of the global poor rather than reducing the life-chance divide between the developed and the developing worlds. There is paternalism in the requirement of adding conflict resolution or a conflict-sensitive aspect to aid – an example being making assistance for a school building programme conditional on the teachers first completing cultural-awareness training. But also, there is polarization. There is an unfailing tendency to experience non-Western peoples as somehow incomplete or lacking the requirements for a proper existence. I complained about this in work on capacity development, critiquing the notion that people 'lack' capacity rather than seeing them as having different capacities for survival (Davies, 2009). Development becomes 'moral trusteeship', to make the incomplete life full and wholesome, educated, and gender aware. But the notions of economic security are even more divisive. The 'liberal way of development' championed notions of sustainability based on household and community relations grounded in small-scale ownership of land or property, thus privileging local and adaptive self-reliance. At the same time the ability of the world's poor and marginalized to circulate is outlawed. Duffield (2010) points to the steady erosion of the rights of migrants, refugees and asylum seekers to enter and settle in the global North. While some equate globalization with a borderless world of spaces and flows, for the world's poor there have never been so many frontiers, checkpoints or restrictions – a global lockdown for them. The distinction is between the 'good' circulation associated with business travel, managed migration, student placements and tourism, and the 'bad' circulation associated with escaping from poverty. I return to the issue of polarization and lockdown later when I analyse complexity.

The third unsafe area is the advancement of societal security as a bulwark against the forces of nationalism and globalization. The concept was initially developed by Barry Buzan in *People, States and Fear* (1991), where society was just one aspect of the state that could be threatened. The concept remained state-centric until redeveloped by Ole Waever *et al.* in *Identity, Migration and the New Security Agenda in Europe* (1993). This book emphasized the key notion of ethnic survival. Societal security was defined as:

> the ability of a society to persist in its essential character under changing conditions and possible or actual threats. More specifically, it is about the sustainability, within acceptable conditions for evolution, of traditional patterns of language, culture, association, and religious and national identity and custom.
>
> (Waever *et al.*, 1993: 23)

Here we see the rediscovery of the cultural aspects of international relations. But as Møller rightly asks, does this simply lead to 'rubber stamping' all assertions of threats to national (or ethnic) security as equally valid? His call for an 'objective yardstick' is key for my book, in my advocacy of human rights (Møller, 2003: 5). One conceptual problem is the term 'societal', which can mean anything from the nation state to a minority religious group. For our concerns, does an emphasis on cultural sustainability lead to ethnic or religious divisions which in the end may threaten cohesion? Put bluntly, does societal security actually threaten human security? When a group perceives a threat to its identity, whether real or imagined, a clear defensive strategy is to strengthen its unique societal identity rather than increase its hybridity and complexity. But this is achieved at the cost of differentiation from the wider community. Key identity markers such as language and religion are highlighted. Education can play a part in this, with demands either for separation or for specific cultural inclusion in the curriculum. 'Emergency measures' may be adopted in the face of integrative threats. A clear example is the setting up of the shadow system of education in Kosovo, when its leaders were faced with the assimilationist education structures of the Serbian state. The opening and preservation of religious schools in a plural society is another example of securitization – this time the security of a specific religion. With global pressures on rights, cultural norms may appear to be threatened. This is evidenced in the case of the Roma, where gender inclusivity and equity would appear to threaten their culture. As Martin Levinson (2012) points out, the Roma find security in their own groups. There are benefits to *not* changing with the times. He asks whether 'hybrid identities' really are empowering – something I come back to.

The question of whether seeking security for a religion may threaten other sorts of security is examined in the next chapter. Religion has been extensively politicized, because of its close link to some forms of nationalism. A few nations (e.g. Jews and Bosnian Muslims) are defined in religious terms, as are states such as Pakistan or Iran. In such cases, other religions risk being viewed as threats to national cohesion, and hence are securitized. To the extent that nations or states are defined not in religious terms but as secular, the politicization of any religion at all (even if it is the national one) may likewise come to be seen as a threat, as in modern-day Turkey or in certain Arab states where radical Islamic fundamentalism threatens already Muslim states. So we see threats *to* a religious group identity as well as perceived threats *from* it – as in the securitization of Islam in the West. I look more at Islamophobia and the UK Preventing Violent Extremism (PVE) strategies in Chapters 5 and 6. In theory, human rights conventions such as Article 18 of the Universal Declaration of Human Rights should regulate group expression and identity:

> Everyone has the right to freedom of thought, conscience and religion; this right includes freedom to change his religion or belief, and freedom, either alone or in community with others and

in public or private, to manifest his religion or belief in teaching, practice, worship and observance.

This seems to obviate the need to securitize one's religion in countries that sign up to this. The reality is much more complex.

Summary so far

- Occupying a wider conceptual field than peace/conflict, the present-day notion of security covers not only defence, counter-terrorism and national stability, but also human security, rights and freedoms. These interact in highly complex and context-specific ways.
- While insecurity at one level appears to threaten all levels, attempts to *increase* security at one level or point does not necessarily help others. A focus on global security (militarization) diverts money from human security; securitization of development adds to polarization between rich and poor societies; attempts at group security threaten national or even global security and cohesion.
- Education occupies an uncertain position in all this.

Because of its focus on religion and secularism, this book does have an interest in particular sorts of security, which should be specified and delimited at this point. These are:

- national security in terms of civil conflict and sectarianism
- state and global security in terms of the containment of extremist ideologies
- personal security in terms of safe spaces to learn and develop.

The links between them are fascinating too. We continue to learn about intersections between education and conflict. There is now a massive literature on this, but much (including mine) needs updating. The latest *Human Security Report* (2012), for example, has some intriguing multi-country and extensive trend data on education and war which has been conveniently ignored by aid agencies. It presents a picture that is frequently at odds with core assumptions that underpin the mainstream narrative of the impact of war on education outcomes as being 'devastating' and 'disastrous'. The report found that in a large proportion of cases, indicators for educational outcomes *improve* during periods of fighting, and, even more counter-intuitively, that educational outcomes in conflict-affected countries improve in many cases in regions that are *most affected* by the impact of warfare. While educational outcomes were indeed substantially lower in the worst-affected regions, in most cases these outcomes were low – *or even lower* – in the pre-war periods. 'This indicates, contrary to the assumptions of the mainstream narrative, that the low educational outcomes in war are not driven primarily by warfare but by factors that predate the war' (Human Security Report Project, 2012: 107). It is just such mainstream assumptions about security that this book attempts to unpick.

Complexity and complex adaptive systems

My chosen way of navigating the minefields is through complexity theory. It is exciting to find a fit between such theories and the exploration of religion and secularism. Complexity theory is, of course, an umbrella term for a number of scientific theories around the non-linearity of complex social interactions, whereby causes interact in a non-additive fashion, some factors reinforcing each other, some cancelling each other out, and some creating new unpredicted pathways altogether. The link to evolutionary biology is the phenomenon of adaptation to new environments. The complex adaptive system (CAS) – whether the brain, the immune system, the world economy, or an ant colony – is able to respond to its environment to survive, with redundant features bypassed or dying out and new ones tried out and then developed. The CAS may have to reach 'criticality' or 'the edge of chaos' before emerging into something new. A degree of turbulence is essential, as a CAS exists in a state called 'far-from-equilibrium'. In fact, a stable equilibrium would mean death for a complex system (Davis and Sumara, 2006). This point is crucial to our understanding of conflict and security. The concluding chapter of the book spells out what sorts of turbulence we might want to introduce into a system for evolution and adaptability, rather than seeing security as a comfortable flat plateau. I outline six features of complexity and show how they may help us to understand security and insecurity. Some aspects of how systems become complex and adaptive are conducive to the sort of security we might want, while others represent a danger, a risk to be managed.

1. Non-linear change

The failure of much political, social and educational policy is the result of reductionist thinking of linear cause and effect. School effectiveness strategy is a case in point, where it is assumed that an injection of something in one school will have the same effect in another, that 'best practice' can be transferred. Here we see the notion of inevitability. At another level, large-scale political ideologies are also based on linear thinking – as Geyer (2003) points out, Karl Marx and the inevitability of the overthrow of capitalism is an example of linear thinking, as are many utopian visions. Modernization theories of Third World development are similar, and so are many behaviourist approaches.

While religious organizations can have elements of a CAS, religions themselves are underpinned with linear ideologies. These include notions of the 'end time', the 'path' that humankind will take towards God. They also include many ideas based on linear cause and effect – sin and you will be punished, love and you will be rewarded. In political terms, Geyer (2003) interestingly analyses how Anthony Giddens's Third Way, while appearing to acknowledge complexity and unpredictability as well as 'manufactured uncertainty', has overtones of earlier twentieth-century attempts to create a linear order. This stems from his desire to find a radical 'new way' to give the left back its historical importance. Geyer makes a point which will be central to this book, that (from a meta-theoretical level) beyond creating a stable fundamental order within which individuals can learn, interact and adapt, there is actually little a state can do with any linear certainty.

Not only are linear visions unproductive, at their extreme they can be deadly. Pure communism, where the state dominated every economic transaction, and pure capitalism, where the market determined all social interactions, have been equally unsustainable. It was the pursuit of these extreme forms of order which brought about extreme forms of human suffering:

> ... the repression, death and suffering which the Soviet peoples experienced ... is mirrored in the repression, death and suffering brought on the Third World by World Bank/IMF structural adjustment programmes implementing extreme forms of marketization on their societies.
>
> (Geyer, 2003: 253)

This is not to say that there should be no linear parts of our existence:

> Sometimes, linear approaches make a lot of sense. Each time we fly an airplane, we should be mighty thankful that engineers work linearly. However, to protect us from terrorist attack, security systems must function differently. They need to be able to sense the unexpected and make insightful interpretations from a mass of messy data.
>
> (Woodhill, 2010: 105)

With regard to education and security, the insight about effects not being additive but interactive is critical. We cannot add something into a system (peace education) and predict an impact. Similarly, we cannot subtract something (biased textbooks) and assume this will be even part of a solution. Change in a CAS is not cumulative, not a series of additions of the good nor subtractions of the bad. This does not have to mean we do nothing, but we must approach change in a very different way.

2. Self-organization

The idea that systems self-organize is perhaps most counter-intuitive when thinking about security and images of military command. Complex adaptive systems, like the brain, do not have leaders or master neurons telling the other parts what to do. Wael Ghonim was the 'techie' who fomented revolution in Egypt by unleashing a digital tsunami, starting with the creation of a Facebook page from Dubai in summer 2010. The page was called 'We are all Khaled Said' after the young man who was beaten to death by police in Alexandria. It quickly became an online meeting place for Egyptians inspired by the revolution in Tunisia and was used to organize protests by hundreds of thousands of people in Tahrir Square. Ghonim was eventually arrested on his return to Egypt, but he made a very interesting comment, attributing the success of the uprising to its lack of leadership:

> There was no master plan ... Just people on the streets. Having no leadership was a big plus because the regime had no leader to negotiate with. If we had had leaders we might have ended up with a different kind of dictatorship.
>
> (Campbell, 2012: 2–3)

For a long time he was known to his tens of thousands of Facebook followers only as 'admin', the name under which he posted his messages.

While there are Facebook followers, this sort of interaction is not about singular leaders or heroes. This was well captured by Marc Sageman in his book *Leaderless Jihad* (2008). New technology has enabled the swift movement of ideas across peoples and continents, but most importantly it has enabled self-organization. It is no accident that we talk of 'viruses' in computers, or of something 'going viral': viruses too have no leader, but can spread. Flocks of birds can organize into complex patterns for migration or to escape a predator, yet there is no recognizable leader. They self-organize because each individual is fine-tuned to its immediate neighbours. In a dynamic self-organization, the structure of the system is continuously transformed through the interaction of contingent, external factors with historical, internal factors. One cannot go back to a single origin any more than forward to a known outcome.

The presence or absence of leadership has been a key feature of security studies. The assumption has been that decapitating a movement will cause it to wither, that the killing of Osama bin Laden is a definitive nail in the coffin of Al Qaeda. Yet as Sageman (2008) points out, it is the informal networks which mobilize people. These are fluid, not with 'members' but with 'participants' – as in the Madrid train bombings of 2004. The process of radicalization generates small, local, self-organized groups in a hostile habitat but linked through the internet. If the habitat changes, the network will adapt to its new niche. The same point was made by Locke (2012) with regard to criminal networks – the idea that removing the head of the snake, the head of the Mafia, will kill the body is facile. Criminals simply regroup, find new alliances and new connections. Scott Atran in his indispensable book *Talking to the Enemy* makes a related point, that hierarchical armies whose minions act on their own initiative tend to lose wars, but egalitarian jihad prospers because, like Google, its leadership is distributed over a social network in ways that are fairly fluid and flat: 'As with most forms of violent jihad in the world nowadays, the path to glory and the grace is mostly a self-organizing affair, whether in neighborhoods or chat rooms' (Atran, 2010: 57). Atran says however that it is not entirely a leaderless jihad, for some people more than others are ready to take the initiative to go and others to guide, but it is the fact that it has no formal leadership that really matters. Al Qaeda still inspires, but it has no command or control over the grass roots, where much of the terrorist action now is.

In talking of self-organization in relation to peacekeeping, Philip Darby uses the interesting and important concept of 'self-securing':

> Self-securing unsettles the understanding that security is best handled from 'above', traditionally by the state and now, quite often, by the state acting together with the United Nations. Following the thrust of complexity theory, it challenges hierarchy, centralisation, linearity and separation (borders).
>
> (Darby, 2009: 1)

Darby argues for harnessing 'the social', downgraded since the advent of neo-liberalism, and identifying alternative ways of making relationships with others. This includes neighbourhood practices of self-security, the use of public space, and the role of dissent as a form of community-building. As well as social movements, examples of self-security include popular responses to natural disasters and to financial collapse in various parts of the world. The power of community, of social movements and of networks is picked up again in the final chapter. While Darby and Duffield might possibly disagree on self-reliance, Darby admits that the ruling security and development paradigms cut across the grain of politics; the structural violence of the leading powers and global agencies ensure the continued subordination of the Third World to the First. The World Bank infamously declaimed 'Poor countries – and poor people – differ from rich ones not only because they have less capital but because they have less knowledge' (World Bank, 1998: 1).

I would add that it is important in the challenge to centralization that self-organization is not confused with the neo-liberal belief in the unchecked operation of 'market forces'. Rather, it is concerned with the active 'agents' who create the meanings around any external drivers. I like Steven Johnson's formulation of 'bottom-up':

> In the simplest terms, [these systems] solve problems by drawing on masses of relatively stupid elements, rather than a single, intelligent, 'executive branch'. They are bottom-up systems, not top-down.
>
> (Johnson, 2001: 18)

In his work on complexity, Mark Mason (2008) might prefer the notion of the 'marginal' rather than the 'stupid', but the message is the same. He cautions us that 'unlike the rigid – as intimated by Kuhn – paradigms of scientific endeavour to date, complexity theory makes space for individuality, for the apparently marginal, for the seemingly trivial accidents of history' (Mason, 2008: 38). What may appear to be marginal may well be part of the complexity of a system, and may be a constituent of the critical level above which emergent properties and behaviours become possible. Emergent behaviour from the bottom up is nicely described by Johnson:

> In these systems, agents residing on one scale start producing behaviour that lies one scale above them: ants create colonies; urbanites create neighbourhoods; simple pattern-recognition software learns how to recommend new books. The movement from low-level rules to higher-level sophistication is what we call emergence.
>
> (Johnson, 2001: 10)

Key to emergence is learning and the role of the learner. Davis and Sumara provide this definition: 'a learner is a complex unity that is capable of adapting itself to the sorts of new and diverse circumstances that an agent is likely to encounter in a dynamic world' (Davis and Sumara, 2006: 14). They continue however with the important point that 'learners' are not just individuals, but can include social and classroom groupings, schools, communities, languages, cultures, species – and bodies of knowledge themselves. Every 'system' can learn, and through learning emerge to a higher order. Derk Loorbach (2010) in his work on complexity and sustainable development mentions learning first when he argues:

> Dealing with persistent societal problems in the long-term will require approaches that give special attention to learning, interaction, integration and experimentation on the level of society, instead of policy alone.
>
> (Loorbach, 2010: 164)

But it must be reiterated that learning for self-organization and emergence does not neatly map on to formal education systems as we know them – in some cases quite the converse. Learning in a CAS derives from differently configured sources, which are explored next.

3. Information and connectivity

Everything from bacteria to trees responds to information – whether chemical or other forms of language. The brain has millions of neural connections and information pathways, but it is not just a 'computer made of meat'. In human information there is room for emotion, intuition or appreciation of music as well as information about information – including truth and rumour. Massive connectivity is needed within an organization and outside it for survival. In spite of e-learning, formal schooling has not really caught up with cyberspace and social networking. When I look at social movements and critical action in Chapter 7, I seek to explore the power of networking. Education clearly underpins the literacy needed – not just to read a text or a blog or a tweet, but to understand the ideas, the concepts, and the emotions underlying a revolution. Information gives both the reasons for a protest as well as the mechanisms for alliances and combined power. This book cannot go deeply into social movement theory, but there are interesting parallels with complexity.

The link to security is obvious – in terms of the classic 'war on terror'. This is a war in which information is far more important than the military solution. Bin Laden may have been killed, but Al Qaeda (AQ) was and still is largely self-organizing, with independent cells as well as viral connections. Understanding – and interrupting – their information flows is crucial to preventing attack. Jason Burke (2013), in analysing the chaotic 'if still dynamic' nature of modern Islamist militancy, holds that vastly improved security precautions and competent intelligence services, with collaboration with other agencies, have headed off possible threats. One MI5 official compared their operations to the famously tedious stonewall tactics of the Arsenal football team ten years ago. 'It's boring but it works', he said (Burke, 2013: 4). AQ success will have been through networks, and real lone wolves are rare. But it will be clear that networks are the only way to defeat other networks.

Much is made of the 'information explosion' with global communications, but this is not uniform. In his classic book *Guns, Germs and Steel* (1998), Jared Diamond talks of control of information. Early states had hereditary leaders with a title equivalent to king who exercised a monopoly over information, decision-making and power. Even in modern democracies, crucial knowledge is available to only a few individuals, who control the flow of information to the rest of the government and consequently control decisions. Diamond cites the Cuban missile crisis of 1962, where the information and discussions that determined whether nuclear war would engulf half a billion people were initially confined by President Kennedy to a ten-member executive committee of the National Security Council that he himself appointed; then he limited final decisions to a four-member group consisting of himself and three of his cabinet ministers.

So again, we should not be taken in by the notion of the information explosion, or assume that we all have access to everything because of the internet. There is still a long way to go. And the power of information is not just about counter-terrorism. It affects all aspects of security. Personal security is enhanced when one knows about health risks (even if one chooses to ignore them, using a different information strand). Community security is enhanced when people 'know' each other – what in Afghanistan military analyses is called 'the average connectedness of the population'. I argue in Chapter 3 that this is why segregation, including religious segregation, is dangerous for security. Instead, the connectivity that comes from constant dialogue or encounters enhances security, as people fear each other less and are less easily mobilized for hatred – although this is not foolproof, as was seen in Bosnia. But again, hierarchy is not needed. We know that in complex systems, short-range relationships are key: most of the information is exchanged between close neighbours, meaning that the system's coherence depends mostly on agents' immediate interdependence, not centralized control (Davis and Sumara, 2006). In social science terms, freedom of information and freedom of the press mean greater connectivity. Autocratic regimes fear such freedom, with reason, as it gives people ideas and alternative possibilities – the characteristics of a CAS.

However, short-range information does not have to be between like-minded people; an essential characteristic of a CAS is diversity. It has been found that a diverse bunch of people usually outperforms a homogeneous group in solving a problem, no matter how expert the group is. This relates to the notion of 'the strength of weak ties' – that we learn more from acquaintances than friends, because of the close networks acquaintances have that we are not part of but can get information from nonetheless (Granovetter, 1983). Any segregation – of schools or communities – which prevents people who think differently bumping up against each other is a hindrance to complexity and adaptability.

In examining religion, an adaptive state would also espouse freedom of religious thought, as Walter Clemens found when contrasting Baltic states with the Balkans in transitions from communism. The Baltic republics (Estonia, Latvia, Lithuania) quickly became what Freedom House terms 'consolidated democracies', as did Slovenia. Their political rights and civil liberties, including religious freedom, were ahead of 'semi-consolidated democracies' such as Macedonia or Serbia or of 'semi-consolidated authoritarian regimes' such as Kosovo, and they were higher on the Human Development Index (Clemens, 2010: 247). The central place of rights and freedoms in complex adaptive states – or complex adaptive schools – is explored in Chapter 4.

4. Feedback and feedback loops

Using information is not just about gathering intelligence, but also about utilizing this either to maintain equilibrium or to change it. Thermostats, which use information about temperature to regulate their activity, are the classic example usually given for feedback. In social systems, however, feedback includes learning from mistakes. A physical CAS does not see things as mistakes, but simply as information that triggers a counter-response. As human beings we have difficulty in seeing all feedback and mistakes simply as useful information. As I write, there is a banking and financial crisis in many parts of Europe. Part of the problem of solving the crisis is due to reluctance by the banks or politicians to admit mistakes of their own making, and the preference to blame previous administrations (and continue to pay themselves bonuses). Similarly, both religious and secularist movements have made mistakes. Like politicians, it is difficult for religions or their leaders to admit what we now see as mistakes – whether it be the Inquisition, slavery or child abuse. I argue that an exclusive secularism that prohibits religious expression is also a mistake.

It is interesting how the Taliban are using feedback. They are trying to win the hearts and minds of the people, with a clear switch from military operations towards governance, to capitalize on the unpopularity of the Karzai government. Jeremy Kelly (2012) quotes a 'secret' NATO report (based on 27,000 interviews with Taliban detainees) that says that to garner support, a complex set of checks and balances has been established to ensure its 'simple, value-based administration' runs smoothly. The report says that, in the insurgent equivalent of 'How's my driving?', the Taliban is said to be conducting market research on its commanders:

> In the event the district, provincial or Taleban central civilian commission system fails, the Taleban leadership has now distributed numbers … which can be used to anonymously inform Taleban leaders of internal issues involving corruption, brutality, misdirected military operations, or an inability to solve local criminal, tribal or regional issues.
>
> (Kelly, 2012: 6–7)

Colleagues of mine in Afghanistan dispute this, but certainly the switch to a hearts and minds approach is evident.

Reflexivity is part of using feedback. This is not a new concept, and the notion of the 'reflective practitioner' has been around in education for a long time. Here is a writer on complexity talking about capacity development for innovation focused on reflexivity, signalling the role of education:

> Being self-reflexive means questioning one's own assumptions and beliefs. It means looking inward when problems with others emerge rather than, from the security of one's own prejudices, judging and blaming others. … This is not easy. Western inspired education and training systems have largely excluded such core capacities for self-reflection and introspection from curricula.
>
> (Woodhill, 2010: 56)

There is a significant mention of 'security' here. Being desperate for security is not always good for adaptability. I return to the question of the security of one's prejudices in subsequent chapters.

'Looking inward' does not necessarily refer only to individuals. Can reflexivity be 'managed', so that the system adjusts to changed circumstances and arrives at a higher order of organization and complexity? Loorbach (2010) proposes the 'transition arena', where a small number of diverse and autonomous actors engage in 'envisioning', generating transition images of the future – but including actors from the existing regime with an eye on legitimacy and financing. The notion of envisioning may evoke some cynicism in those continually subjected to inspirational management training, but these transition arenas are said to be different from think tanks in their acknowledgement of uncertainties and surprise, the importance of networks and of self-steering, and the necessity to create space for innovation and experiment across these networks. Transition arenas have apparently had successful operations in terms of environmental, energy, and housing concerns in the Netherlands and Belgium.

The question is whether these strategies would work in transitions in security policy or education policy. An interesting facet is that actors in the transition arena do have their own perceptions of the issue, but participate on a personal basis and not as a representative of their institution or according to their organizational background. I say more about the politics of recognition and representation later with regard to so-called or self-styled religious leaders.

5. Amplification

To progress, a CAS moves in jerky motions, in breakthroughs, so that a small input may have a big impact. And the effect is destabilizing. As we saw earlier, an adaptive organism has to get to the edge of chaos before finding a new, better equilibrium. Schools will make the mistake of returning to the status quo too soon. Whether enabling student voice or negotiating with the Taliban, you have to take risks, to introduce some sand into the machine.

However, one of the problems of working in the area of peace and conflict is that it appears easier to amplify tension than to amplify harmony. It only takes one or two persons to fan the flames of conflict, whereas it seemingly takes hordes of people to put out the fire, to foster or sustain peace. The power of rumour (which is a particular sort of information) is crucial here. Spreading rumours about how nice people are and how they are unlikely to hurt you is much less powerful than the opposite. In fact, it would be treated with suspicion. I treasure a memory of a television sketch about two airline pilots on a long-distance flight who were extremely bored. They decided to liven things up in the cabin. 'Ladies and gentlemen', they said over the intercom, 'there is no cause for alarm'. The more they repeated messages of assurance, the more panic-stricken the passengers became. I am convinced this sketch is not fantasy.

Writers on terrorism agree on the power of amplification. Atran talks of how by amplifying and connecting relatively sporadic terrorist acts into a generalized 'war', the 'somewhat marginal' phenomenon of terrorism has become a primary preoccupation of government and people. 'This transformation questions the constant refrain by our same leaders that "terrorism will gain nothing"' (Atran, 2010: 278). 'In this sense', claims Burke, 'AQ has won, in that the aim of terrorism is to inspire irrational fear, to terrorise' (Burke, 2013: 5). For Sageman, each incident, broadcast through a spreading world media, acted as 'propaganda by the deed' which inspired young people (Sageman, 2008: 32).

Linked to amplification is the concept of bifurcation or polarization, which can act as a 'positive feedback loop'. A polarized pattern of inequality, with the tendency to reward high achievement and penalize failure, intensifies social divisions. Polarization therefore cements elements in the system, rather than (in educational terms) providing mobility. This then amplifies grievance about low opportunities. Combined with illiteracy because of school failure, youth are more easily mobilized into armed groups; payment, drugs, or even just food as a child soldier are sometimes the only form of income. The success of accelerated learning programmes and reintegration of ex-combatants will depend on how such initiatives are nested within the structures of the wider school system. Education reform and improvement may simply mean new polarizations between high and low attainers (whatever the criteria become), between 'good' schools and 'poor' schools.

Sri Lanka, for instance, is worried about the intense competition and frustration experienced by those who fail to get into the few elite schools in the country. It is therefore instigating a programme of a 'Thousand Schools' which will be in disadvantaged areas and will receive special provisions to enable them to be centres of excellence. I remain unconvinced that this policy will address social and ethnic inequality. It is diversity, but an exclusionary diversity, and will not address the problems of connectivity. Spreading rumours about excellence is akin to spreading rumours about war. Left to itself, 'inertial momentum' means that a phenomenon carries on in its path unless stopped by another competing phenomenon which makes it redirect. Hence under bifurcation, 'good' schools maintain and even increase their own momentum, while 'poor' schools do not attract teachers or students and continue to decline. Creating excellent schools means that by definition others are not excellent. What is more, they do not receive the same funding. Some aspects of complexity theory are difficult for the layperson such as me, but amplification and polarization do not seem to be rocket science. Failing schools are not secure schools in any sense.

6. Lock-in, path dependence and frozen accidents

What seems like the opposite to amplification, but is in fact a related phenomenon, is the notion of lock-in and path dependence. To adapt, a system needs to avoid lock-in, when features become so ingrained that it is impossible to move – or think – beyond them. There can be change, but only in a reversal to historical paths. Acemoglu and Robinson in their book *Why Nations Fail: The origins of power, prosperity and poverty* (2012) cite path-dependent change as an explanation for why there are huge differences in living standards across the world. Their theory of divergence is little related to geography, culture or resources, but rests instead on the difference between 'extractive' and 'inclusive' economic and political institutions. Extractive political and economic institutions reinforce each other as the rich seize control, and with it seize resources for themselves. Elites fear creative destruction, any replacement of the old with the new, and will resist it. In contrast, inclusive institutions enforce property rights, create a level playing field, and encourage investments in new technologies and skills. Inclusive institutions have a degree of political centralization to establish law and order, tax systems, health care, education and an inclusive market economy, but political power is widely distributed and in a pluralistic manner.

There is no space here to do justice to their argument, but one interesting idea for my book is the notion of 'critical junctures' which interact with institutions – the Black Death, the opening of the Atlantic slave trade, the Industrial Revolution, the printing press. When a critical juncture appears it may lead to radical divergences. The persistence of the feedback loop between political and economic institutions however creates a vicious circle for extractive institutions. There is no presumption that any critical juncture will lead to a successful political revolution or change for the better – history is full of one tyranny replacing another. There may be path-dependent change, such as the reproduction of old institutions under colonization in Latin America, contrasted with the legislation in the US which gave people wider access to frontier lands. Or there can be 'institutional drift' – two societies will drift apart slowly because of random mutations.

The historical record is not very generous to modernization theory, in that many relatively prosperous nations have succumbed to and supported repressive dictatorships and extractive institutions. It would seem that education occupies a complex role here, being both a cause and a result of economic progress, and yet also a source of indoctrination. Acemoglu and Robinson (2012) point out how both Germany and Japan were among the richest and most industrialized nations in the world in the first half of the twentieth century and had comparatively well-educated citizens. This did not prevent the rise of the National Socialist Party in Germany or a militaristic regime in Japan intent on territorial expansion via war. Modernization theory – that a well-educated populace will naturally lead to democracy, peace, economic progress and civil liberties – is fundamentally incorrect. Too many intersections, too many critical paths, too many existing power interests and too many lock-ins intervene.

A related term is that of the 'frozen accident' – of which the QWERTY keyboard is often cited as the classic example. In the early days of typewriters the keys jammed if someone was typing too fast. The QWERTY keyboard was invented to deliberately distance the most used letters, that is, to slow down the typing. Nowadays, this is not necessary, but it has never been changed. Similarly, trivial reasons, now lost in the remote past, may have lain behind the Sumerian adoption of a counting system based on 12 rather than 10 (leading to the modern 60-minute hour, 24-hour day, 12-month year, and 360-degree circle) in contrast to the widespread Mesoamerican counting system based on 20 (leading to its calendar using two concurrent cycles of 260 named days and a 365-day year). As Diamond (1998) points out, if the QWERTY keyboard had not been adopted elsewhere in the world as well – say, if Japan or Europe had adopted the much more efficient Dvorak keyboard – that trivial decision in the nineteenth century might have had huge consequences for the competitive position of twentieth-century American technology. There are other examples. What predisposed India to a rigid socio-economic caste system, with the grave consequences it had for the development of technology? Why were proselytizing religions (Christianity and Islam) a driving force for colonization and conquest among Europeans and West Asians but not among the Chinese?

A question for us would be whether the formal mass education systems of the West are frozen accidents, barely changed from those needed to provide a differentiated workforce for the beginning of industrialism. They are only just over a hundred years old, and could be seen as a hiccup in history; yet there is severe lock-in around much of their operation and vision.

Interestingly, Caroline Dyer (2012) uses this concept of the frozen accident to describe the colonial legacy in India of criminalizing mobility. Nomadism was officially associated with criminality in the Criminal Tribes Act of 1871, with nomadic groups being listed with wandering singers and acrobats, as if living in forests and leading a wandering life was something only criminals would do. The stigmatization of mobility continued through legislation of the 1959 Habitual Offenders Act, investigating whether a suspect had an occupation 'conducive to a settled way of life'. This Act has so far not been repealed.

I argue even more provocatively that religious belief systems are more in danger of lock-in than secular regimes. To describe religious belief systems as frozen accidents is probably going too far, but some do show signs of lock-in, unable to progress with the times or adapt to new circumstances. Any and all of the religious debates about women priests, gay marriage, family patterns, modesty in dress and inheritance rights display the tension between the path dependence of traditional values and the so-called forces of modernity. Lock-in is more likely because values are seen to stem from the divine and hence the unquestionable. Secular value systems such as human rights could also mean lock-in but, as they are human constructions, they have the possibility to be critiqued, to be more dynamic and to be updated. Crucially, they do not rely on a sense of return to something old and therefore to be valued.

Sageman (2008) talks of Salafism as a 'revivalist ideology' – so termed because it calls for a revival of what people believe the original community was like (Salaf means 'the ancient ones'). Salafis want to reconstruct the original Muslim community under the rule of sharia, the Islamic law based on the Quran, believed to be the actual word of God. Religious terrorism is built on the belief that the world has decayed into a morass of greed and moral depravity – failures in sexual purity, family values, and the rule of the word of God. Islamic terrorists reject democracy, which they interpret as the domination of man over man and instead demand sharia, which is an egalitarian society under the rule of God. Democracy is seen as creating injustice because it leads to men enslaving or exploiting others.

In thinking about path dependence and security, the question is whether to try to shift what appear to be frozen attitudes through education, or to work within them. Atran (2010) argues that the US-inspired 'reconciliation' with the Taliban may be fatally flawed in demanding that Pashtun hill tribes give up the arms that have kept them independent for centuries. Material incentives may not work. While the logical thing for Pashtun conservatives to do is to stop fighting and get rich through narcotics or Western aid, many will not sell out. Newer, fair-weather Taliban may be involved in the drugs trade (as are government allies), but committed veteran Taliban have tended to avoid at least internal trafficking on moral grounds. Producing and selling drugs for consumption by infidels is seen as acceptable or even righteous, which may explain the tolerance of a brewery in Kabul (which I have never understood). To negotiate with conflicting groups means understanding the complex morality of a group as well as the historical sources of attitudes towards arms and violence.

Structures, rules and organization: Is a complex adaptive system moral?

This brief foray into aspects of complexity shows a mixed set of implications for security. Non-linearity in change is good for adaptability but lock-in and frozen accidents are not. Information, connectivity, feedback loops and networks are an essential part of a complex adaptive system, but they characterize successful terrorist and criminal groups as well as benign social movements. Amplification can magnify fear as well as hope. Complexity does not appear to have a moral base, and a more complex system is not more moral than an apparently less complex one. As Trey Menefee succinctly puts it:

> Complexity simply is. It exists the same way gravity exists, and is a causal reason for both good and bad things. Gravity both supports all life on earth and is directly responsible for every plane crash. Neither complexity nor gravity are good or bad, they're just things we move around with. At best, we understand it, at worst we ignore it.
>
> (Menefee, 2012a)

He points out that both Canada and Somalia have complex adaptive systems. The primary difference is that Canada has a system that rewards 'good' behaviour; Somalia has a system that rewards militancy, piracy, and corruption:

> It's difficult to run a business when Al Shabaab might come to town any day. ... I imagine it's also very difficult to keep a school up and running for the poor when there is no government to provide safety, tax revenue or accreditation. This is to say that militancy, piracy and corruption are all adaptations inside an unhealthy system.
>
> (Menefee, 2012a)

This is something I have long argued with regard to attempts at institutional culture change in 'fragile' states – that we have to see features like the 'allowance culture' (officials only engaging in activities if they can claim allowances) not as dysfunctional but as survival (Harber and Davies, 2002, 2003).

In fact, wars themselves exhibit all the common characteristics of complex systems, as Neil Johnson (2008) points out. There is constant feedback yielding a system with memory; agents in the war can adapt their behaviour; the system is open, with both external and internal, self-generated effects. Outside activities, ones that help robustness and self-organization, can include the rich source of 'nutrients' that supply a war in terms of drug trafficking or other criminal activity. One important point relates to the description of outside interests in Syria detailed earlier. Wars involving three or more actors – be they insurgents, guerrillas, paramilitaries or national armies – are far more complicated than those involving just two. 'If A hates B, and B hates C, does that mean that A must therefore like C? Not necessarily. Hate is many sided, just as love can be' (Johnson, 2008: 305). Johnson gives the example of Colombia, where there are many armed groups. A sides with B, B sides with C, but A hates C. Therefore A starts to fight B so as not to favour C – and the whole process becomes a self-driven perpetual conflict.

In spite of the Canada versus Somalia comparison, complex adaptability happens at not only the national level. There are few systems where absolutely everyone is well off or absolutely everyone is incredibly poor. Poverty should be seen as *an* emergent structure inside the system, not *the* emergent structure. Some people are doing quite well inside the system while others fare much worse. And there are no quick fixes. Menefee (2012b) gives an interesting example of farmer education in the rural South. This is supposed to increase yield. The theory is that a farmer who grows more makes more, and this lifts them out of poverty. It also provides more food for the urban poor. Yet Menefee began questioning whether it is really in a farmer's self-interest to raise yields. De Beers, the diamond dealer, uses its monopoly position to create scarcity by stockpiling its diamonds. For the farmer education initiative, the logic is that the poor are not fed because food is not cheap enough. Increasing supply usually means a decrease in prices. 'But why would any producer want to make less money for their product, especially if the margins are getting worse?' (Menefee, 2012b). Increasing yields works better for some farmers than others, given price swings nested in the global economy. The point of the example is that imposing what seems to be incontrovertibly a 'good thing' is not necessarily, in a complex nested system, good for everyone.

Does this mean that we should abandon our notions of 'the good'? It is clear that a CAS is not necessarily more 'moral' in whatever judgement we use, religious or secular; it just survives, reaches the edge of chaos and evolves. Complex systems do not have an 'invisible hand' directing activity. Religions may be complex systems, but not because of a god directing them, rather because they become robust, self-organizing networks, able to beat off the competition. Competition may work sometimes to reward the winner and penalize the loser. Self-organization can vary from corruption to positive change in the community. AQ has evolved and continues to do so – violence has served it well so far. An education project can lead to a self-organized community system, or to rural exodus, or to improvement of livelihoods for some. We do not always know whether behaviour will be linked to perceived cultural and religious rewards or to cash value – that is, what system of rationality people are using.

However, one crucial component of a CAS which does give us traction is its structure. In physical terms these might be molecules or physical laws of gravity. Emergence happens within these frames – although it may alter them. We used to think that genes were immutable, but we now know that these too can evolve and be changed by lifestyle or even diet. In social terms, structures are the building blocks, the frameworks. On top of this is what is usually referred to in complexity theory as 'organization' – the human element, the way people work within these structures, and the values they espouse which condition the way they work. So values do become important in understanding adaptation – or the lack of it.

Sometimes structures are coterminous with what Jim Woodhill (2010) terms 'institutions', in turn to be understood as 'rules' that make ordered society possible, such as language, currency, marriage, property rights, taxation, education and laws. Institutions help individuals know how to behave in given situations. They are critical for establishing trust in a society. As we saw, some institutions, once developed, lock societies into a particular path of development – for example which side of the road to drive on. Others provide a framework for emergence and progress – for example in the earlier comparison between extractive or inclusive economies. A CAS may not be moral in any conventional sense but it does have rules which permit it to operate without complete chaos. As Wade Davis writes in his book *The Wayfinders:*

> All peoples face the same adaptive imperatives. We all must give birth; raise, educate and protect our children; console our elders as they move into their final years. Virtually all cultures would endorse most tenets of the Ten Commandments, not because the Judaic world was uniquely inspired, but because it articulated the rules that allowed a social species to thrive. Few societies fail to outlaw murder or thievery. All create traditions that bring consistency to coupling and procreation. Every culture honours its dead, even as it struggles with the meaning of the inexorable separation that death implies. Given these common challenges, the range and diversity of cultural adaptations is astonishing.
>
> (Davis, 2009: 31)

In terms of religion and secularism, the interest would be the source of these rules and the institutions which control their implementation. This is sometimes portrayed as a key tension between divine and earthly rules. Yet it need not be. My position is that a human rights framework can act as an umbrella for a range of religious value systems. A believer might say that their religious precepts predate human rights conventions and actually incorporate many or most of them. But this is not the point: the point is to avoid static, non-dynamic ways both to respond to change and to generate change. The dilemmas are that a CAS needs sufficient commonality to enable a small change to take root, and yet sufficient diversity to mean creative tension. A common identity of an organization is necessary for restructuring in the face of external shocks or development, and then it can restructure without losing that identity. Otherwise it becomes chaotic because of debilitating conflicts of interest. A functioning CAS is characterized by a large amount of interest-based negotiation. It could be argued that a rights base saves some time in such negotiations, that a return to first principles is not always necessary, and that total chaos is avoided. In the language of complexity, rights would be termed a 'sub-optimal order' necessary for dynamic equilibrium. A rights-based approach is not perfect, but it is probably the best that we currently have. Chapter 4 explores this further when describing the value base to a secular education.

A related concept is that of 'enabling constraints' – sometimes associated with a liberal constitution. These work to guarantee rights, including property rights, to enable individuals to plan their lives and to make long-term investments. There would be guarantees that the government itself would abide by its laws, repay its debts, and therefore borrow at lower interest rates and so on. Ghani and Lockhart in *Fixing Failed States* (2008) explain Singapore's transformation through a number of strategies which seem to map onto complexity. They quote Lee Kuan Yew describing how Singapore 'embarked on a journey along an unmarked road to an unmarked destination' (no linear thinking here), 'that would turn crisis into opportunity through pragmatism and imagination'. Yet this had key democratic control features. Lee pointed out 'we cannot afford to forget that public order, personal security, economic and social progress, and prosperity are not the natural order of things, that they depend on ceaseless effort and attention from an honest and effective government that the people must elect' (Ghani and Lockhart, 2008: 39). Full accountability and transparency became benchmarks. What seems to happen is that a liberal democracy and freedom of public discussion generate new information that makes it more likely that a government will correct its mistakes. Freedom does not come at the expense of power. The final chapter proposes a set of enabling constraints for education.

We could, as humans, dump a semantic label on all this as a form of morality, perhaps the greatest good for the greatest number. There is no space to enter the discussions of whether altruism is simply a functional form that has evolved for people to live together in a reciprocal way or whether it relates to something deeper in the soul. The point of the discussion relates to where we think we might try to intervene in our educational concerns – at the basic structural level of rules and institutions, or the organizational level of human interpretation and creativity, or both.

Conclusion: Education at the periphery or the forefront?

I am aware that complexity theory is not without its critics – nor is it new. But it has huge traction in explaining any contemporary nexus – whether, as for Duffield (2010), development/security or, in my case, education/religion/ security. In the concern for adaptability, there are clearly many types of adaptation and evolution. This is not about the West defining the good society for others, nor indeed positing the good education system. The comforting thing about fears of imposition is that such imposition is impossible. It is like trying to nail jelly to a wall.

But I like M. Mitchell Waldrop's notion of 'perpetual novelty' in a CAS. CASs typically have many *niches,* each one of which can be exploited by an agent adapted to fill that niche. The economic world has a place for computer programmers, plumbers, steel mills and pet shops, just as the rainforest has a place for tree sloths and butterflies. The very act of filling a niche opens up more niches – for parasites, new predators and prey, for new symbiotic partners. In education, we might cite niches for teachers and dinner ladies but also for educational publishers and those who impose qualifications standards frameworks. Whether the last two are seen as predators and parasites or simply symbiotic partners is an open question. The issue at the heart of it is that new opportunities are constantly being created by the system.

> There's no point in imagining that the agents in the system can ever 'optimize' their fitness, or their utility, or whatever. The space of possibilities is too vast; they have no practical way of finding the optimum. The most they can do is to change and improve themselves relative to what the other agents are doing. In short, complex adaptive systems are characterised by perpetual novelty.
>
> (Waldrop, 1992: 147)

The fluidity is exhilarating. As discussed earlier, there is no master neuron in the brain, no master cell in a developing embryo. If there is to be any coherent behaviour in the system it has to arise from competition and cooperation among the agents themselves. No matter what politicians and bankers do, the overall behaviour of the economy is still the result of myriad decisions made every day by millions of individuals. This is both depressing and liberating.

It is liberating in the realization that not everyone can become a banker, but an awful lot of people across the world go to school. There *has* to be a niche there. In my concerns about particular sorts of security outlined earlier, a common feature is violence. I maintain that violence and killing are *not* the hallmarks of a sustainable human CAS. In evolutionary terms, it might seem that they reduce the competition, that they encourage the survival of the fittest. But in social terms this ignores the interactive nature of violence – that there is likely to be retribution, amplifications and escalations, and hence damage to one's own system. Connectivity breaks down when there is an erosion of trust. Knocking off a human competitor is not the same as life and death in the natural world, still less the death of a cloud system. Our complex cultural systems have the power to *interpret* an act of violence and engineer a response. Violence is a form of information, of communication. But it cannot be efficient to kill thousands of people nor to erode their potential for adaptability through the poverty and destruction that results from conflict.

While wars may exhibit features of complex systems, as I have argued, they do not then self-organize into peace. The amplification spirals are too intense. The global set of connections in violence becomes paramount: Samir Rihani (2002) says it is understandable why despotic regimes buy weapons to oppress civilian populations, threaten neighbouring nations, wage war, or just make money. But why do supposedly civilized nations sell, and sometimes give, weapons so eagerly? This relates to the power leverage coupled with the fringe benefits for producers. The Gulf War demonstrated the futility of conflict as a means of resolving problems. There were and are no winners, with the possible exception of arms producers and those who profited from conflict and sanctions:

> Weapons, war and intransigence do not lend themselves to the flexibility and pragmatism required by nations, as Complex Adaptive Systems, to achieve stable patterns that permit leisurely evolution to proceed optimally.
>
> (Rihani, 2002: 230)

They also divert resources from measures that would increase national capability – such as education.

I would like to categorize violence as path dependence – the lock-in to primitive ways of response, not learning from 'the other' but fearing them. The question is whether this lock-in, the knee-jerk response, is diminishing. It is not clear that the world is evolving for the better. Why, given our sophistication in information, have we not evolved to a more peaceful, manageable, cooperative coexistence? The religious answer is because of evil, Satan, original sin, and ignorance. The non-religious answer also includes ignorance (of how to manage the world or distribute resources fairly) but includes something called 'human nature' – power, greed, an excess of, or imbalance between, competition and cooperation.

My question is whether, within the vast 'space of possibilities' about the future, education has an interventionist, triggering function, and how this intersects with the role of systems of belief. Winthrop and Graff (2010) argue that education reform is one of the few policy areas where policy and programme interventions can hope to mitigate the risk of further militancy and promote security. Yet in much security writing, education is seen as peripheral, or not mentioned at all. Could it move more centre stage as an actor, not just be something which is seen to be *affected* by conflict and insecurity? Are we ignoring something powerful? Education systems are not single systems at all, but are part of a mesh of other socializing systems ranging from politics to churches to the family. I would be less optimistic than Winthrop and Graff about education's role in 'mitigation', with their implication that it has some sort of unique role. Formal education systems also learn – but very slowly and not in predictable ways.

As well as the need to be very tentative about the role of education in conflict, there are paradoxes in using complexity analysis. If, as said, a CAS has no fundamental morality, then can one attempt to impose one? There is little point in writing a book such as this without a degree of prescription, yet mine is not a utopian vision. It is about adaptability, not perfectibility. Immune systems are complex and adaptive, but doctors do intervene when they malfunction. I have to admit partiality in what I see as 'functioning' and 'malfunctioning' in education. So I am imprinting my values on a CAS – which appears contradictory if the idea is of self-organization, unpredictability, risk and creativity. There is no guarantee that a CAS in, or as, an educational environment will act to foster world peace, tackle obesity, or win the Eurovision Song Contest. So what I am arguing is more minimalist: that understanding slightly better how CASs work can enable us to avoid making misguided assumptions about change. I do think that a dynamic secularism, with the concept of dynamic borrowed from complexity science, is a better bet for non-violence than other versions – and than theocracy. The difference is that this is not a prescription about the one 'right way', but starts much further back, a prescription about the pursuit of tentativeness, uncertainty and provisionality. If that sounds like an oxymoron it is because it is. As a set of CASs within wider co-evolving CASs, all that education can do is provide the enabling conditions for the small interventions, random mutations and critical junctures which might nudge people to prefer non-violent solutions to conflict.

Chapter 2
Religion and security

Religion is an insult to human dignity. With or without it, you'd have good people doing good things and evil people doing evil things. But for good people to do evil things, it takes religion.

Steven Weinberg, physicist, Nobel laureate

This chapter weaves between the two faces (or multiple faces) of religion in security. The first part, the bad news, analyses why religion is particularly dangerous for national security, while the second part moves to the slightly better news of the place of religion in personal or group security and the role of faith-based groups in picking up the pieces during and after conflict. Complexity analysis enables disclosure of why the particular 'frozen', essentialist aspects of religion present the greatest problems. I look at the growing evidence that conflict is worse and less tractable if underpinned by religious divides. Conflict is not necessarily worse when between two faith groups, but if religion is held as the *cause* of the conflict, then it is more difficult to solve. Battle lines can also be drawn up between religion and secularism, with religious nationalism contesting the secularization of the state.

In a conflict, it is clearly difficult, if not impossible, to specify what is actually about religion in terms of theology, and when this takes centre stage. More often it is about religious identity than about precise beliefs, and then about the link of that identity to power, land, resources or ethnicity. As discussed in Chapter 1, the current geo-political turmoil in the Middle East appears to be underpinned by various Sunni versus Shia divides; yet it is not really an argument about versions of Islam. It is a power argument, with countries, and allegiances, and blocs lined up. The fear of Islamist takeover of government is another spur to so-called neutral nations deciding what to support. Adams (2012) even fears a genocide based on religious and sectarian divides. When the Arab Spring reached Syria, it dredged up animosities that had been lurking for decades. The protest movement was avowedly non-sectarian, attracting Syrians from all communities. But as the civil war intensified, militia groups within Druse, Christian and Shiite areas were being armed by government. This has all but guaranteed reprisals against these communities on the fall of Assad. In addition, growing numbers of foreign Sunni extremist fighters battled not just to rid Syria of Assad, but to religiously cleanse it.

So whether in Syria, Nigeria, or Northern Ireland, religion weaves in and out of politics and conflict in highly complex and sometimes unpredictable ways. Nonetheless, it is possible to isolate features which make conflict particularly obdurate. To do this, we first have to go back in history to see how religions took hold.

Bands, alliances, and our tribal selves

In his book *The Social Conquest of Earth* (2012), biologist Edward O. Wilson explains how everyone has to have a tribe, an alliance with which to jockey for power and territory, to demonize the enemy, to organize rallies and to raise flags. Modern groups are psychologically equivalent to the tribes of ancient history. The drive to join is deeply engrained, a result of complicated evolution which biologists now understand as blending individual selection (individuals competing) with group selection (competition among groups). Group selection favours altruistic behaviour and is responsible for the most advanced level of social behaviour, that attained by ants, bees, termites – and humans. But to play the game the human way required a complicated mix of closely calibrated altruism, cooperation, competition, domination, reciprocity, defection and deceit. The brain's memories have to travel far into the past to summon old scenarios and far into the future to imagine the consequences of every relationship.

Experiments over the years have revealed how swiftly and decisively people divide into groups and then discriminate in favour of the one to which they belong – even when randomly assigned. We always rank the outgroup below the ingroup. Opponents are seen as less fair, less trustworthy and less competent. I love this report on Afghanistan, which talked of mistrust between Afghan soldiers and their supposed allies:

> One group generally sees the other as a bunch of violent, reckless, intrusive, arrogant, self-serving, profane, infidel bullies hiding behind high technology; and the other group generally views the former as a bunch of cowardly, incompetent, obtuse, thieving, complacent, lazy, pot-smoking, treacherous and murderous radicals.

> (Coghlan, 2012: 5)

People are quicker to anger at evidence that the outgroup is behaving unfairly or receiving undeserved rewards. For Wilson, our bloody nature is ingrained because group versus group was a principal driving force that made us what we are. Civilization appears to be the ultimate redeeming product of competition between groups, as we struggle on behalf of good versus evil, punishing selfishness. But if group conflict created the best in us, it also created the deadliest. Wilson talks of this being our greatest, and worst, genetic inheritance.

But our question is, are religious bonds and groups any worse than other bonds – of ethnicity, occupation, social class or educational history? Scott Atran pursues a Durkheimian analysis:

> By instilling tribal trust and common cause, imagined kinships and faith beyond reason, religions enable strangers to cooperate in a manner that gives them an advantage in competition with other groups. In so doing, religions sanctify and incite fear (which is the father of cruelty) but also hope (which is the friend of happiness). Between the Hecatomb and Humanity, religions' polar products, the destinies of civilisations continue to evolve.
>
> (Atran, 2010: 32)

Here we need to examine identity more closely, to see how people internalize an ideology as part of the self. Jeff Haynes (2007, 2009), who has written extensively on religion and conflict, talks of the close link between religion and identity politics. Individuals may feel personally injured when they perceive that others – whom they believe *share* their identity – are being ill-treated. And as we currently see in terms of perceived insults to a god, individuals also state that they feel personally injured when the absolute identity of a god with whom they identify is being ill-treated or mocked.

James Dingley (2009) returns to the debate about whether the conflict in Northern Ireland is really a religious problem. Certainly, no one is or was demonstrating or rioting over the theory of transubstantiation or papal infallibility. Yet he argues that a major part of the problem in Northern Ireland is genuinely religious. Religion is greatly underestimated as a force in contemporary Western society, both in terms of literal belief and in terms of symbolic and metaphorical meaning. Religion is often the only factor that divides an otherwise very similar population (with both groups a genuine mixture of Gaelic, Scots and English). Segregation amplifies, with each group maintaining its own schools and its own social, recreational, news, economic and job networks.

In this, one of the first features of the role of religion in forming group identity can be identified. Wilson (2012) has shown us how each tribe had its own creation myth, and it was these myths that gave each tribe a reason for existence and held the tribe together. A key feature pertaining to lock-in was that each myth 'had to be set in stone'.

But it is not just a myth about creation. A set of exclusive relationships or networks is formed around a religious denomination that includes some in a privileged set of relations, information systems, myths and symbols:

> If relationships or networks are trivial, they can be ignored, but if they pertain to vital aspects of life, such as economic opportunity or security, then they become fundamental and worth fighting for and maintaining as they preserve life and interest. The networks act as communication systems, distributing knowledge and information, and historical memory banks.
>
> (Dingley, 2009: 369)

In our concern about security, this is central. The 'historical memory banks' include an essentialist perspective on other people, and the belief that those others are unlikely to change. Schools can be part of such networks of belief systems and essentialism about good and evil. Atran's research in Jemaah Islamiyah (JI) affiliated schools in Indonesia found that 74 per cent of these students (compared to 7 per cent of the students at other schools) believed that all people 'were born evil but some learn to become good'. Students who believed people are 'born evil' were about 11 times more likely to believe it was their duty to kill non-Muslims. Students were also asked to imagine what would happen if a child born of Jewish parents were adopted by a religious Muslim couple. While 83 per cent of students from other schools thought that the child would grow up to be a Muslim, only 48 per cent of students at the JI school shared that belief:

> This essentialist belief that a child born of another religion could never fully become a Muslim correlated strongly with support for violence. Students with this belief were about ten times more likely than other students to believe it their duty to kill non-Muslims.
>
> (Atran, 2010: 308)

Sageman (2008) gives more detail on how essentialist beliefs turn to murder. He discusses how *Takfiris* view themselves as the only true Muslims and believe that only they understand Islam. They reject traditional imams, whom they view as lackeys paid by the state or a corrupted mosque. They also reject various traditional interpretations that evolved over fourteen centuries because they think they have been corrupted by Greek philosophy. Those who do not belong to the global Islamic terrorist movement do not deserve the label of Muslim, as they have degenerated into a state of barbaric unbelief (*jahiliyya*). Therefore you can kill them (contradicting the Quran which prohibits a Muslim from harming another Muslim).

However, this justification for the killing of evil people is not just *takfiri* Islamic. Chris Kyle in his book *American Sniper* recounts how he has killed 255 people yet feels no guilt. After six years as a US sniper in Iraq, he writes:

> Every person I killed I strongly believe that they were bad. When I go to face God there are going to be lots of things I will have to account for, but killing any of these people is not one of them.
>
> (quoted in Gillespie, 2012: 9)

But protecting others also justifies the killing. Here the rationale that the victims were bad has to be extended. One sniper who watched through his telescope as a family mourned the man he had just shot says 'Here is someone whose friends love him and I am sure he is a good person because he does this out of ideology'. But he continued: 'But we from our side have prevented the killing of innocents, so we are not sorry about it'. Such snipers apparently suffered *less* stress than other soldiers.

The key phrase is 'from our side', the group think, the moral crusade. Tariq Modood (2009) shows how the new anti-Muslim evangelical discourse in the US has three main sources: a) militant pre-millennial Zionism among American evangelicals, couching all Muslim countries as enemies of Israel; b) missionary competition between Muslim and Christian evangelicals throughout sub-Saharan Africa and other parts of the world; and c) the global war on terror with the notion of a 'crusade' between violent Islam and the Christian West.

On the other hand, beliefs that people are essentially good can also foster harm and, ironically, insecurity. Sageman has interesting insights into how the Taliban are still generally misunderstood. They were a religious group formerly composed of Mullah Omar's religious students (Taliban means 'religious students') who wanted to establish the rule of God in Afghanistan. They believed that implementing sharia and creating a Committee to Command Virtue and Prohibit Vice would be enough to accomplish this goal, the government's central focus. The Taliban believed that people were essentially virtuous and would take care of themselves as long as they chose the right path. There was no need for effective central authorities, such as health or social services, as the virtuous did not require the mediation of government. However, the lack of a functioning central government became apparent when Afghanistan suffered the worst drought in its history. 'Ironically, it was the US government's largesse in the form of shipments of flour that kept the Afghan population from starving' (Sageman, 2008: 44).

In Chapter 1, I discussed the complex intermix of central governance (or rules) and local autonomy which allows a society to be creative and progress. There are huge dangers in essentialist assumptions that if people are virtuous, then the state becomes less necessary. There are equally worrying dangers in leaving everything to God instead of the state or to science. Rob Trask has a disturbing account of the role of faith and education in Malawi. He quoted a woman in her late twenties who said:

> 'My reverend told me that he had prayed for me and that I had been healed. So I stopped taking the HIV medication. ... I was told that if I believed in God, then there was no need to take the medicine.'

> (Trask, 2012: 10)

With their emphasis on one's personal experience with God, pastors in Pentecostal churches such as this wield enormous power. The Catholic Church did not drop its ban on condoms until November 2010. However, the more encouraging news is that there is also now MANERELA+, the Malawi Network of Religious Leaders living with, or personally affected by, HIV and AIDS. This progressive group engages leaders from different religions to develop a multifaith response in the fight against HIV.

Politics and religious identity: Using religion as control

A historical analysis also enables us to see the origins of the link between power and religious bands. Jared Diamond in *Guns, Germs and Steel* (1998) discusses how kleptocracies survive, or indeed how any ranked society survives, whether a chiefdom or a state. (A kleptocracy is a system where net wealth is transferred from the commoners to the upper classes.) The key puzzle is why commoners tolerate the transfer of the fruits of their labours to kleptocrats. This question, raised by political theorists from Plato to Marx, is raised anew by voters in every modern election. Kleptocracies with little public support risk being overthrown, either by downtrodden commoners or by upstart would-be replacement kleptocrats seeking public support by promising a higher ratio of services rendered to fruits stolen. Diamond discerns four solutions that an elite resorts to in order to gain popular support while still maintaining a more comfortable lifestyle than commoners:

1. Disarm the populace and arm the elite (easier in these days of high-tech weaponry than in the days of spears or arrows).

2. Make the masses happy by redistributing much of the tribute received, in popular ways.

3. Use the monopoly of force to promote happiness, by maintaining public order and curbing violence. (This is a big and underappreciated advantage of centralized societies.)

But it is the fourth solution which is of particular salience here:

4. To construct an ideology or religion justifying kleptocracy. As Diamond explains:

> ... the supernatural beliefs of bands and tribes did not serve to justify central authority, justify transfer of wealth, or maintain peace between unrelated individuals. When supernatural beliefs gained those functions and became institutionalized, they were thereby transformed into what we now term a religion ... the chief claimed to serve the people by interceding for them with the gods and reciting the ritual formulas required to obtain rain, good harvests, and success in fishing ... The chief may either combine the offices of political leader and priest in a single person, or may support a separate group of kleptocrats (that is, priests) whose function is to provide ideological justification for the chiefs. That is why chiefdoms devote so much collected tribute to constructing temples and other public works, which serve as centers of the official religion and visible signs of the chief's power.
>
> (Diamond, 1998: 278)

This has resonances with what Colin Howson calls 'the proxy-governance of priests', inspiring people to 'God's totalitarianism on earth' (Howson, 2011: 9).

Religion, nationalism, and violence are bound together in many current contexts. To give just one example, Amena Mohsin (2004) discusses religion, politics, and security in Bangladesh and shows how religion was used for nation building. While the new state in 1972 was based on secular principles, the quest began for homogenization and national identity. The leaders of the coup in 1975 obviously wanted to capitalize on the prevailing public mood, which was increasingly enthusiastic about the adoption of Islamic values. They used Islam to secure – and to a certain extent legitimize – their position. President Zia in his new construction chose to emphasize the element of nationalism that would have appealed to the majority community – religion. In the new model of nationhood, termed Bangladeshi nationalism, education and the media acquired an Islamic orientation. The principle of secularism was dropped from the constitution. Ershad then accepted the Bangladeshi model of nationhood but made it more rigid and totalitarian by giving it a totally Islamic orientation. In 1988, Islam was declared the state religion. Madrassas and imam training were encouraged. Discriminatory property laws disadvantaged Hindus. Majoritarian violence during elections, violent attacks on Hindu temples, and women being subject to sexual violence meant even less security for Hindus, and many fled. Mohsin makes an interesting point which fits with complexity analysis: that the out-migration process had a direct fallout on relations between Bangladesh and India. It provided fuel to the anti-Muslim propaganda of the *Bharatiya Janata* Party, which further communalized the political environment in India. Then, the repercussion on Muslims in India has had an adverse impact on the Hindu population in Bangladesh. This is a classic amplification mechanism.

The strong link between totalitarian rulers and the church persists today. A different but equally significant example of where politics lines up with religion was in the imprisonment in 2012 of three female punk musicians (Pussy Riot) in Russian President Putin's regime on charges of 'hooliganism'. The band's song had mocked not only Putin but also Patriarch Kirill, head of the Russian Orthodox Church. The Patriarch complained of the band's blasphemy. The indictment against them thus refers to their denigrating the feelings and beliefs of Orthodox worshippers. Yet the Patriarch was himself involved in political campaigning for the presidential elections in March 2012 by endorsing Mr Putin's candidature. As the *Times* leader column rightly pointed out:

> A society with due process cannot insulate from political criticism someone who ventures political opinions, even a Church leader. Nor can a civilised society legislate and impose criminal sanction for the protection of people's feelings. If it does, there is no limit in principle to the violation of liberty that is permissible to soothe the anguish of those who suffer offence.
>
> (*The Times*, 2012b: 2)

It is the combination of religion and politics which is the most dangerous to freedom of speech – a double whammy. On 17 August 2012, Judge Marina Sylova jailed the women for two years on grounds of 'hooliganism' but stated that 'the girls' actions were sacrilegious, blasphemous and broke the Church's rules' (Halpin, 2012: 1). While musicians as well as world leaders condemned the sentence and the blow against freedom of expression, the call to religion managed to retain some internal support for Putin. The church can complain and the state can enforce, in its own interests, but seemingly with the deity on its side. Even in so-called secular states, the power of the church may be very close to the surface and can be harnessed when necessary. Dissent against a regime is also dissent against God, a far more heinous crime. Even after the 2011 revolution, Egypt's penal code still contains prohibitions on insulting the president and major monotheistic religions, and this is being used to try to prosecute the popular Egyptian satirist Bassem Youssef, who regularly lampoons Egypt's leading Islamists and liberals alike on his Friday night television show.

Victor Sebestyen (2012), the author of *Revolution 1989: The fall of the Soviet empire,* warned Putin to 'remember the Plastics'. These were rock musicians jailed in Czechoslovakia in the 1970s on charges of 'hooliganism' and 'public disorder', and seen as a threat to the state. The Plastic People of the Universe were not a great band musically. They admitted that they did not have much of a message and certainly did not think of bringing down communism. As Sebestyen pointed out, if they had simply been left alone to play, they would probably have got stoned, had artistic differences and split up, like most 1970s rock bands. But they were banned by the leader Gustav Husak, harassed and occasionally beaten up by the secret police, and in 1976 jailed, with a showcase 'trial'. One of their supporters was the playwright Vaclav Havel. He wrote a superb essay along the lines of Kafka's *The Trial,* published in samizdat, which found its way to the West. Their case had a profound impact behind the Iron Curtain. Two months after the trial, Havel and a few other Czech writers, musicians and artists founded Charter 77 which became the most important dissident group in Eastern Europe. For the next decade it influenced a generation of young people to rebel against repressive regimes, and their parents to brave opposition with them. After the fall of the Berlin Wall, Havel became President and among the guests at his inauguration were the Plastic People of the Universe. The Putin case will soon also come to be seen as an overreaction, and now:

> ... previously apolitical and apathetic young people from the iMessage and Twitter generation will see a leader who jails girl pop singers as rather absurd, a man to mock, rather as East Europeans mocked Gustav Husak and his ilk. Pop fantasy perhaps, but Mr Putin may eventually rue the day he messed with a rock band.
>
> (Sebestyen, 2012: 22)

There are many messages for complexity theory here: the small spark that generates massive change; and also the power of satire and humour, the portrayal of a leader as absurd. Yet it also leads to the question of why religion is particularly salient in conflict and can be co-opted and used to manipulate and control. I want now to outline the way that the amplification mechanism of the religion–conflict nexus works, with five links in the chain of effect, five critical junctures.

The chain of amplification in religion and violence

1.Totalitarianism, absolutism and exclusivity

Religion is focused on the absolute and unconditional and as a result can adopt totalitarian characteristics. It is the combination of absolute and exclusive validity claimed by the major monotheistic religions which generates religious fragmentation. Religious exclusiveness may also be hostile to both pluralism and liberal democracy.

Richard Dawkins goes so far as to state: 'I cannot think of any war that has been fought in the name of atheism', for the evil things done by Stalin were in the name of dogmatic and doctrinaire Marxism, not atheism as such (Dawkins, 2006: 278). As Paul Froese points out in *The Plot to Kill God*, atheism in the Soviet Union did have its own culture of symbols, ceremonies and sacred texts, recreating most aspects of religious culture. Yet this was not surprising given that a key characteristic shared by Marxism-Leninism and most religious theologies is ideological exclusivity: 'The exclusivity of a belief system and not its supernatural elements is what leads believers to go to great lengths to defend and fight for a cause' (Froese, 2008: 65). Exclusivity in a faith refers to how prohibitive a religious group is in allowing commitment to other gods or religious doctrines. Religious organizations will understand that exclusive theologies are more powerful than non-exclusive ones. Lester R. Kurtz in his work *Gods in the Global Village* labels these 'exclusive accounts of the nature of reality', that is, followers only accept religious beliefs that they regard as *true* beliefs (Kurtz, 1995: 238). Examples include the 'religions of the book' – Judaism, Christianity, and Islam – because each faith claims authority that emanates principally from sacred texts (albeit similar texts). As Haynes argues, 'Such exclusivist truth claims can be a serious challenge to religious toleration and diversity, essential to our co-existence in a globalized world, and make conflict more likely' (Haynes, 2009: 54).

In contrast to exclusivity, openness to new ideas and tolerance of alternative views can lead to lower levels of commitment to a single ideology:

> As a humorist pointed out, suicide bombers don't tend to leave messages that state 'We are Unitarian Jihad. There is only one God, unless there is more than one God. The vote of our God subcommittee is 10–8 in favour of one God, with two abstentions'.
>
> (Froese, 2008: 66)

Froese does admit that if a religious doctrine's exclusivity can explain its ability to ignite conflict with other religions and to inspire sacrifice, the same might be said for secular doctrines. Yet few secular doctrines are exclusive in a holistic sense. Faith in Keynesian economics does not exclude one from believing in evolution, drinking alcohol or belonging to the Roman Catholic Church. In contrast, exclusive religious doctrines tend to dictate clear conceptions of social justice, norms or social interaction and prohibit a host of political, social and scientific viewpoints. So did Marxism-Leninism, of course, but only when it became a 'doctrine'. This, like religious writing, could be interpreted but never critiqued. Lenin and Stalin legitimated their power and influence through their ability to interpret Marx and Engels 'properly'. Priests do the same thing.

2. Superiority

From exclusivity of a doctrine, the next amplifying step is to superiority: the conviction that one's belief is not just true but *better* than other accounts. Unless one is forced into displaying a religion, or is disbarred from joining one, support for a particular religion is a choice. And like any choice, it is based on preferences and the assumption that this religion outscores others. This notion of the superiority of a set of beliefs almost inexorably, if one is not careful, leads to the superiority of its adherents – that they are superior *as people*. In *Educating Against Extremism* (Davies, 2008), I drew attention to the hypocrisy of those in faith schools claiming that they respected all faiths as of equal value. This is logically impossible. The very reason for a faith school is because educating a child in that faith is seen as a better bet than another faith or than a secular environment. I have requested greater honesty about this. The only way equal value would work is if a believer attempted some sort of pick-and-mix, that this bit of their own religion was better than another's, even if there were some that were not as attractive. But this is not what is said. I talk later of the lack of bargaining potential and exchange among religions.

Hence there is an essential contradiction in the contemporary church position, particularly in and for developing countries. It is instructive doing a discourse analysis on the *All Africa Bishops' Conference Report* 2010. This does admit that:

> The Church's involvement in public affairs has had a mixed role, where church leaders have sometimes been clients or allies in the violation of human rights. Some have also been coopted by the State and their relationship is too close. The Church therefore, in some instances, also has to redeem its image'.
>
> (Council of Anglican Provinces of Africa, 2010: 35)

But is the problem just one of image? It is revealing that this seems to be really about public relations rather than a deeper concern about the vulnerability of the church to violence and corruption. On one level the report affirms diversity – but then the representatives from Nigeria were concerned about the 'surge of Islam' in northern Nigeria and were preparing a response to this. The report ties itself in knots. Diversity is great and divine:

> The Church needs to remind people that God created all human beings to be different, and that this is divine. It also needs to understand and emphasise that cultural and religious diversity is an asset that should be exploited for its positive aspects.

> (*ibid.*: 9)

Yet on the very next page it is stated that 'Evangelising is the primary role of the Church' (10). It admits that evangelization means different things to different people – preaching, winning new converts, expanding ecclesiastical institutions. But the inference is of the promotion of Christianity, presumably as the 'best' religion. It beats any secular direction to life: 'There should not be a large distinction between religious and secular aspects of life because God is in charge of all life … We affirm the Biblical standard of the family as having marriage between a man and a woman as its foundation. One of the purposes of marriage is procreation of children some of whom grow to become leaders of tomorrow' (48).

And in the end, you can blame God for conflict. Rowan Williams says: 'It is the responsibility to show that peace lies with God alone'. He quotes the Bible: 'He will settle disputes among the nations, among the great powers near and far' (46). An outside observer might be forgiven for thinking that He has not done a great job so far.

3. Intolerance

The chain – or path dependence – from exclusivity to superiority and then to intolerance is a heavy-duty one. There emerges among believers a suspicion and fear of 'lesser' religions or of people with no faith at all. As Howson documents, we do have an increasing renewal of religious intolerance, sometimes very violent and always drawing inspiration from holy scriptures. The Quran 'seethes with hatred of unbelievers, expressing God's loathing in language of graphic violence' (Howson, 2011: 10). But Islam is not the only culprit. Every day American television stations spew out bilious condemnation of evolutionary theory, homosexuality, abortion, same-sex marriage and liberalism. There are murders of doctors who performed abortions, in the name of God and his judgement.

Many Americans believe that the United States demands respect not because it is technologically advanced or militarily superior to all other nations but because God has blessed it, making it the best country in the world – as most presidential addresses affirm. The American flag attains its sacredness because it represents 'one nation *under God*'. As Froese (2008) points out, the sacredness of national identity in the US fully depends on a shared religious sensibility.

But this then means a dehumanization of others less sacred. It is significant that Christians are cast as 'slaves of God' – it is no wonder the churches failed to condemn slavery, until enough other people did. God retains ownership of the body – and even the most totalitarian regimes of Nazism or Marxism-Leninism did not do this. Purity and sacredness link to gender, religion, and embodiment and the strictures on female modesty – justifying violence against women if they are seen to contravene these principles. I look more at intolerance towards women below. Homophobia is another aspect. There is a theory that the current hypocrisy from those priests and bishops in the Catholic Church who have made vitriolic attacks on gays but have then been found guilty of sexual abuse of boys is because they are in denial about their own homosexuality. Projection onto others as sinners, the public manifestations of intolerance from those who are supposedly a moral authority, can justify hatred and othering.

4. *Doing God's work: God is on our side*
The next link in the sequence from exclusivity to superiority to intolerance is elimination, the actual attack on others. This derives from the notion that members of a faith are not just believing, but are 'doing God's work'. From the Crusades onwards, and no doubt before, believers have gone into battle in the conviction that 'God is on our side'. The classic example is the Jewish nation as 'the chosen people', with the God-given right to land and hence the duty to defend this. In his discussion of national security in Israel/Palestine, Møller (2003) points up the intricate implications of the national narrative. Israel was originally conceived as a homeland for persecuted Jews. However, not all Israeli citizens are Jews (some are self-defined and recognized as Arabs) and not all Jews are religious Jews, as they may be Jewish through ancestry alone. Interestingly, some orthodox religious Jews refuse to acknowledge the Jewishness of Israel, since it can only be created by the Messiah, and they thus do not see themselves as Israeli citizens even though they reside in Israel. Others have deliberately emphasized the secular nature of the Israeli state, conceived of as a home for the ethnic Jews regardless of their religious observance. But Jewish ethnicity is controversial, as it is not a reflection of

any shared language, nor a matter of race, nor necessarily a common culture. With the national identity of Jews contested, societal security concerns become prominent. Møller asks, what is the 'idea' of the state? Is this just one geographical option or the promised land to which the Jewish nation (as the chosen people) has a divine right? The former allows for land for peace arrangements. If however it is a God-given right, non-Jews are automatically seen as aliens whose presence is tolerated only on a temporary basis. But even for those in favour of a secular but democratic Israel, the Arab population is seen to constitute a threat to the Jewishness of Israel, as they have a higher birth rate. The fear (as in other nations too) is that they will be overtaken.

The heady combination of fear and entitlement feeds the violence. Halleli Pinson *et al.* (2012) talk of the 'existential anxiety' of the Zionist state, positioning the military as an institution higher than any other. There is a contradiction with the dominant Zionist ethos which portrays Israelis as forever 'peace-loving' or 'peace-aspiring'. In this narrative the war is the fault of others, and there is a clear division between 'us' as peace-loving and 'them' the enemy, which are not only to be blamed for the persistence of war but also to be described as 'rejectionists' to the ideal of peace, and hence as amoral and less humane. Casting the enemy as less than human is of course not confined to the Israelis, but has characterized oppression and bloodshed in many contexts – South Africa, Nazi Germany and Rwanda being classic examples.

In the amplifying process, followers are taught not just to look down on the other, but to hate them, and then, by extension, to destroy them. The shift is from forgiveness of violence to positively rewarding it. Atran (2010) documents how in 1073, the future Pope Gregory VII started preaching a doctrine of conquest for Christ that forbade Christians to kill other Christians who agreed with Gregory, but forgave killing all other people, especially 'Saracens' (Muslims) and Jews. The First Crusade, to recapture land from the Muslims, was driven also by divine promise of limitless booty and forgiveness for any cruelty imaginable towards non-Christians. The Spanish Inquisition was equally cruel and divinely inspired. During the Civil War in America, ideology was given a particularly religious cast:

> Civil War armies were, arguably, the most religious in American history. Wars usually intensify religious convictions. ... Many men who were at best nominal Christians before they enlisted experienced conversion to the genuine article by their baptism of fire.
>
> (McPherson, 1997: 62)

Yet this is not just history. Ovadia Yosef, an Israeli rabbi, recently called for prayers for Iran's destruction, that is, that Iran should be included in a traditional New Year blessing in which God is asked to strike down Israel's enemies. 'When we ask God to bring an end to our enemies, we should be thinking about Iran, those evil ones who threaten Israel. May the Lord destroy them' (*The Independent*, 2012).

Violence becomes normalized in the name of God. Most countries will invoke their god before going to war (Dingley, 2009). This is interesting from a complexity point of view, as 'doing God's work' can justify behaviour which is normally not conducive to human survival. Religion can increase aggressiveness and the willingness to use violence. A survey of Palestinian students found 81 per cent believing that Islam allows the actions of the suicide bomber, including nearly 100 per cent of supporters of Hamas and Palestinian Islamic Jihad (Atran, 2010: 342). At a different level, there is the recent case of a mother who beat her 7-year-old son to death because he was unable to learn the Quran by heart.

5. Expansionism for God

The final, most lethal amplification arises when conflict in the name of religion goes global – not just as a conflict between two groups or nations but as an international vendetta. We need to go back in history to examine violence within Islam and how this became expansionist. Atran tells of how for centuries, the reasoning of Islamic jurists (*ulema*) has set down rules of interaction to cover almost any matter of trade, war or peace between *Dar al-Islam* (The House of Islam, Land of Islam) and *Dar al-Kufar* (The House of Unbelief) or *Dar al-Harb* (The House of War). Always clearly grounded in passages from the Quran, these rules have contained lethal sanctions against apostates, idolaters and those who challenge Muslim territorial dominance and the God-given right and duty to expand that dominance across the world.

Yet even more scary is the justification for war against other people that we do not hate or despise but simply have cause for harbouring suspicions about. Kofi Annan (2012) reckons that no leader would carry with him the consequences of the Iraq war more than Tony Blair. George W. Bush had seen the Israel–Hezbollah conflict in 2006 as a simple matter of good versus evil, but Annan knew it was not simple due to its complex regional character, its asymmetry, and its tangle of roots. As he observed:

> For Blair, however, this conflict – no less than Iraq – was refracted through his lens of a meta-conflict between modernity and the medieval, between tolerant secularism and radical Islam.
>
> (Annan with Mousavizadeh, 2012: 5)

Annan saw a change in Blair since the time of his policy on Serbian attacks on Kosovo in 1999. 'Something had changed in Blair and with it, I felt, his ability to act as a credible mediator in this conflict' (Annan with Mousavizadeh, 2012: 5). In my view, what had changed was Blair's increasing religiosity and therefore the increasing tendency to couch conflict in moral rather than political terms. As he repeatedly said, it was 'the right thing to do'. If Blair did have a secularism, it was subservient to his attribution of a religious significance to events in times of crisis – the million-strong march in London to protest against the war was cast as a symbol of our democratic freedom – hence as a *justification* for the war, rather than as something to challenge what Blair increasingly saw as the voice of God. On the other side of the Atlantic, Sarah Palin too claimed that the Iraq war was 'a task that is from God' (Knowles, 2008).

The other form of expansionism is to the duties of *all* members of a religion. Blair required his military to go to war, but not all the people of his country. Atran quotes from the 1998 fatwa from Bin Laden and Zawahiri:

> The ruling to kill the Americans and their allies – civilians and military – is an individual duty *for every Muslim who can do it in any country* in which it is possible to do it, in order to liberate the Al Aqsa Mosque [Jerusalem] and the holy mosque [Mecca] from their grip … [my italics]
>
> (Atran, 2010: 104)

The reasoning is that as there is no pure Islamic state anywhere, then the whole world must be a House of War. Second, because Islam is under global attack by America and the forces of globalization, the whole world is a global battlefield under *fard al-'ayn*. As the social movement spreads, it becomes more global in scope and apocalyptic in its vision. Nor can one leave the faith and its duties. Hadith 260 of Sahih Bukhari is invoked: 'The Prophet said "if somebody (a Muslim) discards his religion, then kill him"'. While the right of freedom of religion is Article 23 of Iran's constitution, sharia law says that the rejection of Islam is punishable by death. However, it has to be remembered that atheism could be punished by death even in eighteenth-century England and Scotland. So is it a matter of time before such extremes dissipate? Can the amplification spiral be reversed? When we look at progressions during conflict, this seems doubtful.

Religion, the state and the end of conflict

Once violent conflict has started, it becomes clear that religion is less than helpful in its resolution. Isak Svensson (2007) explores the growing literature on the relationship between religious dimensions and the escalation, duration and termination of armed conflicts. He argues that if the belligerents' demands are explicitly anchored in a religious tradition, they will perceive the conflicting issues as indivisible, and the conflict as less likely to be settled through negotiation. His thesis, through quantitative research, is that the basic disputed resource in civil war is the state. When the belligerents raise conflicting positions regarding the state, the subjective value will be increased. There can be no substitutes of equivalent value for the disputed state. His study of civil wars has two measures: first, whether the combatants' identities break down along religious lines; and second, the data on explicit demands that include religious dimensions. He uses the concept of 'indivisibility', sometimes used in the discussion of sacred spaces, spaces that cannot possibly be shared out.

The example of Sri Lanka illustrates how religious dimensions in incompatibilities between Sinhalese and Tamils cement perceptions of indivisibility – in this case of the nation-state – and therefore undermine prospects for peaceful solutions. Indivisibility has dimensions of *integrity* – the issue, here the state, cannot be parcelled up or subdivided without diminishing its subjective value. There is only one constitution in a state, which can be either secular or religious but not both at once. In Sri Lanka, the Buddhist nationalists hold the position that the whole of Sri Lanka has a divine mission, given by the Buddha himself, to uphold and maintain the pure form of Buddhist teaching and practice (Harris, 2007). Buddhism has to have 'the foremost place' (in contrast to Tamil demands for a secular state). As I have signalled in my writing on problems of educational policies for pluralism in Sri Lanka, Buddhist ethno-nationalism is portrayed as *the* unified Sri Lankan identity, with little real acceptance of pluralism (Davies, 2012a). Buddhist concepts and discourses of 'inner peace' are held up as solutions to conflict, rather than espousing federal solutions which would give Tamils greater autonomy.

Indivisibility in religion also relates to its lack of bargaining potential. As I illustrated in *Educating Against Extremism,* you cannot say 'I'll give you the loaves and the fishes if you give me the 72 virgins bit' (Davies, 2008). On a much wider scale, the thought of parcelling out Jerusalem is incomprehensible to both (all) sides. Pragmatic arguments do not find favour. Sageman contrasts science and faith thus: 'Science is not a set of beliefs, but a methodology to choose among competing hypotheses. What distinguishes science from faith is that science allows factual evidence to adjudicate competing claims' (Sageman, 2008: 13). Adjudicating between claims founded on religious belief systems is impossible unless factual evidence is brought in.

Factual data may affect adjudication, but may also, if protagonists are willing to compromise, create a new, third possibility. Such working in the possibility space is a central tenet in complexity science.

So the task when engaging in conflict is to try to prevent what starts out as a struggle over land or resources from expanding into the religious realm, as battle lines then become frozen. Monica Toft (2007) has two interesting hypotheses about why religion presents particular problems for resolution. One: there are longer time horizons among people of faith, making it possible to absorb more costs. The present can be discounted in favour of the future, the end time. Two: there can be 'religious outbidding' – political elites who are under threat and in need of external support can reframe the issues of contention in religious terms. Toft, like Svensson, also argues that once religion becomes central, non-violent termination will also be less likely (Toft, 2007). All these factors intermix – indivisibility, longer time frames, religious outbidding – so one cannot say which has the greater explanatory power. Svensson (2007) has three important conclusions:

1) That the religious aspects of armed conflicts are pivotal if we want to be able to gauge the conditions for peace better.

2) That multifaith dialogue may not be the most important priority if we want to seek ways to reduce armed conflicts. It is not religious dissimilarity as such that is the problem.

3) Measures aiming to prevent conflict actors from expanding their demands into the religious realm should be emphasized and developed.

In Israel, once the conflict was seen as an ethno-religious struggle instead of a nationalist conflict, the intractability increased. Non-military ways to handle religious militancy and extremism are indicated. As shown in Central Asia, reacting to militant Islam through increased militarism and political repression has only served to increase the popularity of these movements. Currently we see the impact of drone strikes in cementing support for the Taliban in Pakistan, rather than decreasing it. Even the most simplistic complexity analysis would have enabled discussion of the side effects on civilian attitudes of drones killing their children, however much this is held by the US to be in the wider interests of disarming Al Qaeda.

Gender, patriarchy and honour
Before leaving the bad news section, another amplification spiral needs touching on – that of gender and violence. A lock-in for religion and (in)security is the way that gender relations and family honour come to take

on divine inscription and in turn justify violence. Ayaan Hirsi Ali, the Somali-born social critic, is harsh on Germaine Greer for once writing that female genital mutilation (FGM) must be seen 'within its cultural context'. Ali asks us to remember that Islam is an expansionist religion. FGM was practised in Egypt before Islam came along; Muslims adopted it and it was the Muslims who spread it to Indonesia, which had no history of it. Now Muslim men do not want to marry a girl who has not been 'cleansed'. At the heart of her mission – as 'the Muslim Voltaire' – is to get Islam to acknowledge that the Quran is the work of Man, written in the particular circumstance of seventh-century Arabia, and not the unchallengeable, universal word of God. She cites, in particular, verses that enshrine men's right to beat women – even if with a 'small stick' (interview with Janice Turner, 2011).

It is the reinforcing nature of gender inequality which militates against change. Patriarchy meant female subordination being written into sacred texts, and these texts then being drawn on centuries later to justify subordination as divine. Afghan clerics have produced new guidelines which state that women are subordinate to men, should not mix in work or education, and must always have a male guardian when they travel. This is dangerously reminiscent of the Taliban era, and is actually against the Afghan constitution. The clerics also condone violence against women in certain 'sharia-compliant' circumstances – although they do call for punishment of those who assault women, and they do denounce forced marriage and the practice of exchanging women to settle family disputes over money or honour.

But the whole revived ideology of secondary status for women is alarming. The points agreed by the *Ulema* Council of top clerics are not legally binding, but the statement detailing them was published by the President's office with no further comment, a move that has been taken as a tacit seal of approval (Graham-Harrison, 2012). In Afghanistan, a further complexity – and lock-in – is the tribal code of *Pashtunwali*, which has the sacred tenets of protecting women's purity, the right to personal revenge, the sanctity of the guest and sanctuary. The patrimonial inheritance structure means that there must be no suspicion that the male pedigree (often traceable in lineages spanning centuries) is 'corrupted' by doubtful paternity. Thus, revenge for sexual misbehaviour (rape, adultery, abduction) warrants killing seven members of the offending group and often the 'offending' woman. The Taliban's idiosyncratic version of sharia incorporates *Pashtunwali's* main tenets. In allowing executions for murder or violations of women to be carried out by members of the aggrieved family, for example, state punishment is confounded with personal revenge.

Yet the link between religion and gendered violence is not always that religion or religious law directly sanctions such violence, but that patriarchal relations within religion support male authority, which in turn relegates women to second class citizens who do not therefore deserve respect. Starkey and Tomalin (2013) discuss the complex positioning of women within Thai Buddhism, and the restricted opportunities for women to become monks or take influential positions as spiritual guides. They quote an activist as arguing that such male dominance and lack of affordable educational opportunities for girls has a consequence of different forms of violence against women, such as domestic violence, rape and forced prostitution. In Nicaragua, Lauren Ila Jones (2013) questions the role of Christian Evangelical and Catholic churches in insisting on marital relationships being preserved even if there is mistreatment of the woman – that she has to put up with it 'until death do you part'.

Discriminatory laws in Pakistan similarly have blurred the distinctions between extramarital sex and rape, disallowing a woman's testimony to these crimes and instead requiring the evidence of four Muslim males. It became risky for women to report crimes of rape, and thousands of women who were unable to meet this standard of proof were charged with adultery. Subsequent laws have privatized violent crimes of murder and bodily harm and allowed families to forgive offenders and accept compensation: 'This law creates a loophole whereby women may be killed in the name of honor with impunity because their families are usually complicit' (Critelli, 2013: 332). The normalization and even legalization of rape and killing is a huge security issue for women. However, it is to be hoped that the myriad organizations campaigning against this are having an effect. In complexity terms, the gang rape and killing of a woman on a bus in India in 2012 has generated massive protest and it may be that such attacks can no longer be ignored. It takes a tipping point – sadly, of extreme sadism, but this event could not be normalized.

Yet other forms of personal security can be compromised by a religious interpretation. In the 2004 South Asian tsunami, disproportionate numbers of women in countries such as Indonesia died from drowning because local interpretations of Islam precluded them from learning how to swim (Boudre, 2006). As Chris Williams (2012) points out, access to the global knowledge 'good' – learning how to swim – had been negated through the global 'bad' of a misleading ideology that claimed that women should not learn:

> Taking Islam on its own terms, nothing in the Koran denies
> women the right to have swimming lessons, or even insists on

the wearing of specific forms of clothing. Islamic teachings state 'Teach your children swimming ...' which is gender neutral, but this is sometimes repeated, 'Teach your sons swimming ...'. Yet even if the latter were correct, nothing precludes teaching girls to swim, because a principle of understanding Islamic rules is that anything that is not specifically prohibited is permitted.

(Williams, 2012: 100)

It is to be hoped that these revelations about the impact of the tsunami could lead to another tipping point for girls' survival education, as we argued in a report on education in emergencies in South Asia (Davies *et al.*, 2009).

It is important however not continually to cast Islam as the religion that is particularly bad for women's security. Women's role as defined within a religion is a contested field, and women themselves are not united on the issue. One of the female petitioners *against* women bishops in the UK stated 'We believe that God created men and women equal but different and that difference is seen in the God-given roles that men and women have within the family and within God's household, the church' (Gledhill, 2012a: 6). Others disagree, with campaigners sporting T-shirts saying 'GOD IS AN EQUAL OPPORTUNITIES EMPLOYER. PITY ABOUT THE CHURCH'.

Afghan interpretations of women's place are no more 'backward' than those found in other contexts and among some others of faith. In the UK, Bristol University Christian Union recently tried to institute a ban on women speaking at its main meetings and events, unless accompanied by their husbands. Understandably, there was an uproar. Interestingly, this protest included the Council of Ex-Muslims of Britain (CEMB) which was 'appalled' to learn of this proposed ban. Yet CEMB, while congratulating the campaign on upholding basic principles of equality in the face of religiously inspired misogyny, also remains concerned that the same treatment handed out to women by Islamic societies was routinely ignored, creating a double standard. They were worried that cultural moral relativism meant that reactions to gender segregation and the absence of females from positions of authority, as well as more insidious pressures towards social conformity with regard to dress and behaviour in Islamic societies, were 'ominously muted', while such treatment was being seen as intolerable if found in Christian groups (Council of Ex-Muslims of Britain, 2012). Here we see a complex intermix not just of gendered inequality but of a divided social reaction to it – which is promising. As I explore in Chapter 5, gender can be seen as one of the entry points for change, or, with less reification of the term 'gender', a picture of real women is emerging with the wire cutters snapping the links of the chains all over the place.

Can religion be good for security?

While the preceding accounts have painted a bleak picture of the role of religion in conflict and violence, we should also look at arguments about the positive role of religion in security. This has three main aspects: personal security, group security, and political involvement for security or peace-making – although they do interact and overlap.

1. Personal security

In the psychological sense, personal security can be enhanced by religious belief. Many people – if not most – appear to need a faith, especially in times of crisis. An insight from Atran is that science is not particularly well suited to deal with people's existential anxieties – death, deception, sudden catastrophe, loneliness or longing for love or justice – for which there is no reasonable or no definitive solution. Science cannot tell us what we ought to do; only what we can do. 'Our culture is still trying to come to grips with how to bridge the moral chasm between the two' (Atran, 2010: 76).

As well as showing how religion can be linked to conflict, Jeffery Haynes also wants to demonstrate that religious values can help bring peace. He cites the Christian values of non-violence and 'bringing good news to the poor', for example. In this, he quotes St Paul: 'There is no Jew or Greek, servant or free, male or female: because you are all one in Jesus Christ' (Galatians 3.28). Yet this 'good news' seems to me to fly in the face of reality. It would provide little comfort for someone deeply oppressed because of her gender or servile occupation. It is perhaps only when linked to a political movement (as discussed below) that a notion of unity in the Lord becomes powerful.

In a chapter for a book on *Gender, Religion and Education*, I examined the puzzle of why women persist in fundamentalist religions that appear to oppress them (Davies, 2013c). I identified the appeal as having six components: a strong identity and sense of calling; psychological safety in the familiar, therapeutic space; economic and material safety; cognitive closure in the face of ambiguity and globalization; addiction to being in love with a Jesus figure; and a sense of political purpose – even in violent movements or as suicide bombers. In this sense personal security is not good for national security – they are not nested in each other in a reinforcing way but are, on the contrary, antithetical.

Personal security can therefore be compromised or enhanced through religion. Currently, the practice of bathing in the holy river Ganges is causing illness and death because the river is massively polluted from the toxic effluent from thousands of industrial zones. India's leading environmental engineer, G.D. Agrawal, stood down to become a Hindu holy man, a swami, and in 2012 was on hunger strike to raise awareness of the environmental catastrophe facing the River Ganges and the 480 million people living along its polluted banks. In Varanasi, India's most sacred city, some 60,000 Hindus perform rituals every day along stone steps that lead into the river, before washing in it, praying in it, and often drinking from it. This is also where Hindus come to die. The Hindu scripture says a person whose ashes are placed in the Ganges goes straight to Nirvana. But cremation costs at least $100, so some people illegally dump their dead into the water.

In 2013 as many as 100 million Hindus congregated on the banks of the Ganges close to Allahabad, for the *Kumbh Mela*. They came from across the subcontinent in the belief that the river would wash away sins. Religious devotion to the river is therefore also destroying it (McDougall, 2012). But my question here is whether the swami is also campaigning to *challenge* this religious practice, which is destroying people as much as big business is. It appears not – he himself often takes a 'holy dip' in the river. He is seen as a 'source of inspiration' for youth ('Dr. G.D Agrawal', 2012). This is not to mock his courage and bravery, but rather to underscore the grip that religion has, in sustaining a belief that bathing in a polluted river is cleansing. This is definitely a frozen accident – bathing in the Ganges when it was pure mountain water would have made survival sense; now it does the opposite.

2. Group and local security

At particular points in history, religion can bring security to groups and societies. Diamond (1998) notes that besides justifying the transfer of wealth to kleptocrats, institutionalized religions bring two important benefits to centralized societies. First, a shared ideology or religion helps solve the problem of how unrelated individuals are to live together without killing each other, by providing them with a bond not based on kinship. Second, it gives people a motive, other than genetic self-interest, for sacrificing their lives on behalf of others. At the cost of a few society members who die in battle as soldiers, the whole society becomes much more effective at conquering other societies or resisting attacks.

We start to see the swings and roundabouts of institutionalized religion. It establishes bonds between bigger groups, which is good for social cohesion, but there is a greater propensity for battle with other groups, as catalogued earlier. In its analysis of *Faith Partnership Principles,* the UK Department for International Development (DFID, 2012) acknowledges that while faith often brings people together, it can lead to divisions, and that conflicts can arise or be exacerbated when people from different faiths 'find it hard to live and work together'. Therefore it has drawn up principles for engagement in working with faith groups. The report categorizes different types of faith-based organizations (FBOs), and it is important to note these, as this relates to how intervention and change is conceptualized:

- congregational faith groups focused on worship
- representative faith organizations nationally and internationally
- faith-based development organizations (e.g. World Vision, Islamic Relief)
- faith-based political organizations (e.g. Christian Democratic Union in Germany [there is no mention of Hamas])
- faith-based missionary organizations
- inter-faith groups
- other organizations where faith plays an important role (e.g. Guides, Boys' Brigade).

It would appear that DFID is really interested in the third of these types. The groups addressing poverty are the ones to which people in fragile states turn. DFID cites evidence that FBOs:

- provide services and humanitarian assistance
- empower poor people so their voices are heard
- build resilience and peace
- change beliefs and behaviour
- build support for development and global advocacy.

The often cited figure is that approximately 40 per cent of health services in sub-Saharan Africa (rising to 70 per cent in some countries) are provided by faith groups. Dolan *et al.* also cite faith-based organizations and community-based organizations managing schools and paying salaries: in the Democratic Republic of Congo, for example, just under a fifth of schools are managed by the state, with more than 70 per cent managed by churches and the rest privately run (Dolan *et al.*, 2012). Faith groups often work to longer timescales than official development agencies. Examples of the various sorts of work done by FBOs in areas related to security and development are:

- World Vision: child protection from violence, abuse, exploitation, child marriage

- Episcopal Church of Sudan: trains teachers and heads and constructs schools (with other churches)
- Islamic Relief and CAFOD: humanitarian projects for the vulnerable
- CAFOD: helps poor men and women to understand and demand their rights, for example for health care, safe drinking water and road construction to get to markets
- Tearfund: community work, crop production, livestock, reducing educational dropout rates
- Christian Aid: increased food security, access to water, new agricultural techniques in 500 households (mostly headed by women)
- Progressio: working with religious leaders to build awareness of HIV and challenge stigma.

Only the last one might tackle problems arising from religion itself. What is significant about the partnership angle is DFID's acknowledgement of what we might call uneasy bedfellows. It admits difficult areas. It claims that values have been important in Christian, Islamic and Buddhist groups in contributing to the toppling of authoritarian regimes and promoting human rights in South Africa, Latin America, North Africa and Asia:

> However there are important areas where values and ethical positions are contested by, within and between different faith groups. Contested issues include: contraception; gay rights; abortion; capital punishment; gender equality; freedom of religion; blasphemy; HIV/AIDS; and other cultural and religious practices.
>
> (DFID, 2012: 8)

That's quite a big list.

So DFID's position is that neither faith groups nor DFID should try to agree on everything, and that DFID needs to be clear and transparent about the situations when collaborative work with organizations may not be possible. It also admits the need for more systematic evidence of impact and the distinctive contribution FBOs make.

Islamic Relief is worth a digression. This is a huge operation in humanitarian aid, emergency relief, poverty, and also education and training in the poorest countries. Their magazine *Building a Better Future* (2012) eloquently describes all this work. There is little mention of what is specifically Islamic about all this. There would be a dilemma for all FBOs in terms of any sign of political involvement, or recognition of the roots of conflict, or even the uneven impact of natural disasters. Islamic Relief is brilliant at picking up the pieces and at conducting skilful campaigns for getting people to volunteer and donate. It can draw on Muslim edicts about giving a percentage of one's income to charity. Only on the last page is the distinctive Islamic underpinning highlighted:

> ... to make sure your donations are used in the most effective way possible, because we are accountable to you, to people in need and most importantly We're accountable to Allah.' [*Large print theirs*]
>
> (Islamic Relief, 2012: 32)

This is a powerful message. Secular charities would be very envious of the 'direct line to God' approach rather than having to envisage myriad reasons why people donate ('Press one for guilt, two for compassion, three for duty'). Pressing four to speak to an operator does not have the same appeal as speaking to God.

But FBOs have to be very careful about the dual aims they may have, of welfare and messaging. Amy Stambach's fascinating account of evangelical missionaries working in schools in East Africa found them encouraging girls to 'move beyond' their local community. One female missionary said: 'Tanzanian students have got to use education to see more of life, not just stay here [in Kilimanjaro region]' (Stambach, 2010: 109). This broadening should of course be seen in the context of the missionaries' work to subtly promote Christianity and Christian witness in the lessons they took in schools, and their history of trying to convert people from Islam. The conversion of Muslims was seen as their greatest challenge in the field, linked to promotion of the monogamous family. Witchcraft was another challenge. Yet the 'targets' of the missionary work were often able to use missionary educational work to their own ends, particularly in the 'modern' education that the missionaries provided in computer literacy, technological education and English. Identities could be combined or could coexist. As Stambach points out:

> Religion and education are utopian spaces that define and transcend societal norms, and they are imaginative tropes and institutional forms that reinforce and challenge social and political differences.
>
> (Stambach, 2010: 181)

Stambach's work is important in demonstrating how religion and education are 'structuring categories'. They standardize differences through their own universalizing principles. But they can also challenge difference through what in complexity terms would be a possibility space of the imagination.

3. Political involvement for security

Even more contentious than evangelizing would be the involvement of religion in politics. Hashash (2011) outlines, for example, the complex role of the Muslim Brotherhood in Egypt. This spreads fear to some, but has wide support from the masses and runs welfare projects providing education and health care to Egypt's poorest citizens. The Brotherhood can organize at grassroots level and was able to send messages through the mosques when the internet and telephones were blocked.

In its pro-poor activism, is the Muslim Brotherhood then liberatory more than Islamicizatory? One especially distinctive contribution of religion comes from liberation theology, with its particular tradition in Latin America. Liberation theology or 'progressive Catholicism' has the overall theme that God takes a preferential option for the poor and inspires the liberation of the poor from oppressive and exploitative political and economic systems. Women are particularly prominent in such movements (Hallum, 2003). The educational legacy of Paulo Freire is there, with the emphasis on praxis and learning from the pragmatic knowledge of the poor themselves. Jones (2013) talks of grass-roots participants as 'organic theologians' in the spirit of Gramsci's organic intellectuals, perfectly capable of explaining their religious beliefs and the roles these play in the daily struggle. Their interpretation of the divine will for women in Nicaraguan social movements is that God wants liberation for women, and that they do not have to put up with violence or abuse:

> God didn't put us here so someone could abuse us, we've got to come together to demand our rights. ... This Father, this Father who is so great, didn't send us this type of punishment: I don't believe that God punishes us. God sends us all the spaces that we should take advantage of to move forward.
>
> (Jones, 2013: 48)

Here we see a very active move against violence, using 'the spaces' that God sends. In such movements, skills are learned and rights strengthened – for selves and others. This sometimes represents a shift in focus. Walker quotes Aruna Gnanadason of the World Council of Churches: 'Our concerns have been the sanctity of the family, reconciliation, restoring marriages, when often the first need is for an end to violence, for safety for women and children and for justice for the oppressed' (Walker, 1999: 17).

Similarly, while the Ku Klux Klan was religiously inspired, it was the Southern black churches in the US who kept the sacred hopes of freedom and dignity for all alive in the black counter-culture. As Atran (2010) points out, Ivy League intellectual and liberal youth no doubt helped to rouse national support for the civil rights movement, but the inspiration for sustained struggle and a colour-blind America came from preachers like Martin Luther King and his forebears. They used Christian notions of unity, of all being one in Jesus Christ, to push for and legitimize freedom. Liberation theology is in contrast to fundamentalist religion, which wants to return to some notion of the past. In gender terms, seeing feminism as a 'gift from God' authorizes the challenge to patriarchy and violent machismo, and more broadly legitimizes struggles for rights in the here and now, not in some future end time.

4. Global security and peacemaking

Complexity theory would ask us to look at this role of grass-roots, organic change compared to that of top-down authority. This means interrogating the leadership issue further. A report from the United States Institute of Peace (Smock and Huda, 2009) examines Islamic peacemaking since 9/11. It admits that Muslims in general, and Muslim leaders in particular, have been severely criticized for not condemning the violent acts of Muslim extremists more energetically. The report however shows how Muslim leaders and key Muslim organizations across the globe have spoken out strongly against terror and against religiously related violence. It lists all their various statements, which are indeed couched in strong, unambiguous terms.

Strategically, I am interested though in who the audience is for the statements, and who the targets are. Citing the Quran's prohibitions on killing will be ignored by extremists who find other passages which justify it. The report cites an NGO called Sisters in Islam that seems more direct, advocating against discrimination, and educating women about their legal rights. But in terms of gender analysis it does not acknowledge culpability: 'Emphasising the equality of rights granted through the Islamic tradition, Sisters in Islam has resisted *conservative forces* that want to limit women's participation in the public sphere ...' (Smock and Huda, 2009: 9 [my italics]). Who are these conservative forces? The advocacy does not name names or even specify males. As such, it has no impact, no identifiable target. Similarly, one aim of Muslim peace-building institutions is 'challenging *traditional structures* such as the role of women in society' (10). This is all dehumanized: it is *people* who create and maintain social structures, as Giddens has long been telling us.

This underscores the key question of the impact of 'peacemaking' initiatives. From all the myriad interfaith dialogues and conferences (often bringing together leaders, not followers), is there evidence that the protocols and resolutions actually make a difference? Also, interfaith dialogues rarely include secularists or humanists. Do such dialogues really challenge the complacency that one's religion is the 'right' one? The Organization of the Islamic Conference (OIC) declared in September 2001: 'We condemn these savage and criminal acts which are anathema to all human conventions and values and the monotheist religions, led by Islam' (quoted in Smock and Huda, 2009: 3). The phrase 'led by Islam' means that it is not clear whether there is a genuine feeling of equality between religions. From the mountain of statements, I would like some ethnographic data on whether a) any leaders were changed, and b) whether any followers were, as a result of hearing them. The contact hypothesis would tell us that it might be better when faith groups work together towards a common identifiable target, such as a shared religious perspective against FGM or on violence against women, when they could act in concert to place pressure on governments to enact or enforce legislation.

I look in Chapter 4 at the impact of (re)interpretation of sacred texts and what this means for non-violence. Here my question is whether people and self-organizing groups will always pick what they want. At a huge youth conference in Bahrain I heard the main imam speaker tell the young people that violence was prohibited in the Quran – except in revenge. This could be seized upon in many different ways. And are 'moderate' voices of leadership listened to anyway by those who seek violence and retribution? Boko Haram killed 44 people at a church on Christmas Day in 2011 and there are fears that they want to start a religious war by triggering reprisals from minority Christian groups. Jonathan Clayton (2012) reports analysts as fearing that Nigeria is on the brink of a major religious conflict which will have disastrous consequences for the whole African region. All the elements are there: corrupt leaders, a weak government, and thousands of impoverished and angry youths. Significantly, Boko Haram denounces moderate imams' collaboration with the government. It is fighting to overthrow the government and create an Islamic state. So any words and statements from 'moderate' Islamic leaders will presumably have little effect – particularly if they are seen as collaborating with another enemy, the state.

In challenging violence, there is perhaps more hope from those imams who are specifically telling their younger followers about using democratic means and not violence to convey their frustrations and disagreements. The young Egyptian Muslim televangelist Moez Masoud, who has millions of viewers in North Africa, is said to exemplify a new movement to appeal to younger Muslims, promoting an upbeat and tolerant brand of Islam (Smock and Huda, 2009). The television series addressed poignant and largely taboo issues facing the Muslim world, including drugs, alcohol, gender relations, homosexuality, and the roots of terrorism. The message is that it is possible to combine piety with a modern lifestyle. With our concern about absolutism, it is significant that Masoud encourages doubt, the asking of questions, and asserts that it is normal to wonder, and to be conflicted. At the same time he holds that 'Islam respects the principle of freedom of opinion, as long as the opinion is respectful of Islam'. We seem to be brought back to the idea that the whole of Islam has to be respected, even if there are glaring anomalies and contradictions. This seems a shame, but the idea of critical respect is perhaps a step too far at the moment. It is not dissimilar to the huge board spotted outside the Mount Zion Fellowship Church in the US which proclaimed: 'God's love is unconditional as long as you are obeying Christ'.

It is possible that religious leaders have more impact in a mediation process than simply preaching non-violence. Haynes gives notable examples of religious leaders or representative religious individuals who have been significant in peacemaking. These include mediation in Nigeria in the civil war of 1967–70, undertaken by the Quakers and financed by the Ford Foundation; the All Africa Conference of Churches in mediating a cessation to the Sudan conflict in 1972; efforts made by John Paul Lederach (Professor of International Peace Building at the University of Notre Dame) in Nicaragua in the 1980s; and the more recent work of the Imam of Timbuktu in mediating various African conflicts (Haynes, 2005). It can be presumed though that all were part of a wider reconciliation process rather than single-handedly bringing about peace.

According to Appleby (2008) religious peacemakers are most likely to be successful when they (1) have an international or transnational reach; (2) consistently emphasize peace and avoidance of the use of force in resolving conflict; and (3) have good relations between different religions in a conflict situation, as this will be the key to positive input from them. In his view two problems that limit the impact are, first, that there is often a failure of religious leaders to understand or enact their potential peace-building roles within the local community; and second, that many religious leaders lack the ability to exploit their strategic capacity as transnational actors.

Hence peace-building efforts are mixed. As Haynes (2005) notes, faith-based organizations may sometimes be instrumental in helping to deliver and then sustain peace. More commonly, however, such efforts see partial success – or, put another way, partial failure – and do not unequivocally ameliorate the problem over time. Haynes reckons there is nevertheless evidence that, as a result of increased public recognition and support, and through the development of more effective peacemaking strategies, the conflict resolution and peacemaking skills of faith-based organizations and religious individuals can be encouraged to develop further over time, offering the prospect of greater potential in the future. Peacemaking ability is likely to develop in this way when, acting under the auspices of a religious group, individuals and groups are seen as reflecting a high moral standing, crucially retaining credibility and building stature, to the extent that they can be regarded by all parties as apolitical or neutral in conflict situations.

This raises the perennial tension for faith-based groups and religious leaders in conflict over when to remain neutral. If the conflict does have a religious dimension, then they will not be seen as even-handed, even if they try to distance themselves. Many FBOs therefore simply focus on humanitarian work, using the values of the religion but not proselytizing at all nor evidencing a religious identity. Sant'Egidio worked as a mediator in Mozambique, for instance, because it appeared to have no political or economic agenda. FBOs have to build a reputation for neutrality and compassion, and enlist others with expertise.

Haynes (2005) gives an interesting example of a peace-building workshop in Nigeria, cited in the *Christian Science Monitor* of 2003. When the workshop started, each side was adamant that the other was to blame for religious violence in Nigeria. When it concluded, participants agreed on a 17-point consensual declaration containing various recommendations, including that:

- both Christians and Muslims should love each other unconditionally as brothers and sisters
- both communities should show good will to each other at all times
- it was important to inform members of each religious community better about the beliefs and tenets of the 'other' faith
- it was necessary to cooperate with government in order to hand over for justice those people who continue to use religious violence in contravention of the law.

This sounds like good news. However, my analysis is that only the last is actually achievable and the rest is just unrealistic rhetoric. As with all one-off workshops or even with more extended exchange programmes, participants may at the time be full of love and compassion, but this does not last in the face of the continued reality outside and, moreover, they may not have the power to spread or enforce such messages. There is a disconnect here with the actual sources of conflict and extremism – which are not about lack of love. Questions of exclusivity and superiority are not tackled; and informing people about 'other' faiths only serves to cement otherness and stereotyping.

There is nothing about dealing with rage when a god is insulted; in theory it would not be about telling people to love each other but telling them to stop loving their own god in such a devoted and defensive way. But that of course will not happen.

Rage can very quickly supersede other values. The messages of good will cited earlier are, I would hold, only skin deep, if they are internalized at all. There was a nice description of a football match between two church teams in the West Midlands Christian League. A brawl broke out between Common Ground United and Zion Athletic after a Common Ground player was sent off for a foul. The Birmingham County Football Association's discipline manager said there had never been anything like it. The 'ungodly' brawl was all the more embarrassing because of the strict rules that govern play. Players are expected to behave in a manner that is morally, decently and ethically sound of action and speech, honouring the name of Jesus Christ both on and off the pitch. It ended with five Common Ground players facing violent conduct charges (Bennett, 2012). This may seem a trivial example, but we need such quotidian reminders of the fickleness of so-called deeply held values.

Conclusion

Trying to draw up a balance sheet between religion doing harm and religion doing good with regard to security is bound to fail. These are neither numerical nor additive factors. The influences occur at different points in space and particularly in time. The conclusion from this brief account is that religion may be harmful as a factor in the start of conflict and in its continuation; it may be beneficial in picking up the pieces of conflict in its humanitarian values and efforts, and in using the power of religious leaders to mediate between warring groups. Clearly, all these things can happen simultaneously. Our concern would be educational: if religion is complicit in conflict, then in what ways and how do they interact – divisions, identities, warlike heroes, violent sacred texts, sanctioned violence against women? The educational imperative is to try to minimize these influences and build habits of critique and uncertainty. Where religion is good at patching up conflict, education can capitalize on this, teaching conflict resolution or, if religion is good at charitable work, supporting tenets of volunteering and fundraising. Whether the driving force is being 'accountable to Allah' or is that God has invented feminism becomes less important than that it is a trigger for beneficial change.

How people learn is linked to how religions learn and adapt. Breaking the chain of amplification towards violence is best started at the beginning, at the point of the exclusivity of a religion. From his meta-analysis of countries in conflict, Haynes (2009) confirms that developing countries which apparently have the most serious ethnic and religious divisions are *not necessarily those that experience serious civil conflict*. It seems that it is not the divisions as such that are decisive, but how they can be manipulated or managed. 'Its likelihood may be linked to whether governments manage to deal with effects of widespread, destabilising social and economic changes that affect both local power structures and societal, including religious groups' (Haynes, 2009: 59). In addition to governments needing to manage religious plurality there is the need for the religion itself to adapt to its ever-changing plural context. Casanova for example talks of the future of Islam in America – whether it should be constructed as a segregated defensive sub-culture, protecting itself from corrosive Americanization, or whether it should organize itself as a public, self-assertive cultural option within American competitive multiculturalism. He contends that 'Islam is becoming not just a fast growing religion in America, but an American religion, one of the denominational alternatives of being religiously American' (Casanova, 2009: 163).

But there is a big difference between religion as an option and religion as a takeover. We have seen how faith-based organizations may do their best work in conflict-affected states by *not* evangelizing or attempting to convert through some educative process, but by using the values attached to their religion to increase security for children and teachers. It is when religion thaws out from all its frozen accidents and attitudes that it does its best work.

Chapter 3
Dynamic secularism

I definitely want Brooklyn to be christened, but I don't know into what religion yet.

David Beckham

This chapter is an unashamed plug for secularism, but of a type which I have termed 'dynamic secularism'. Secularism has had a bad press in some contexts, and the task of the chapter is to present it in an affirmatory way and to destroy some of the myths. The scope of discussion is national or cultural, whereas the next chapter deals with the meaning of secularism within education. The chapter cannot hope to cover the whole field of secularism, but isolates particular features which link to concerns about security and to complexity.

The basic definition of 'secular' is the separation of church and state. The principle is that the institutions of government (parliament, civil service, law, the military, the police) should remain separate from religious institutions, their beliefs and their dignitaries. The pluralism of any society requires that there be some kind of neutrality, what Rajeev Bhargava (2009) calls 'principled distance'. Geoffrey Brahm Levey calls the separation between religion and state a 'stunning achievement' for the past few centuries (Levey, 2009: 1). I see this achievement as partial and in need of constant support. It is not to be taken for granted.

One central problem in the debates on secularism is terminology – the confusion between secularism and secularization. The latter, when many analysts use it, does not simply mean a greater *separation* of church and state, but a *decline* in religion. They could be linked but they are two different things. (And I want to show how a greater separation can actually be good for religion.) In 1978 David Martin, for example, in his classic *A General Theory of Secularization,* was arguing that secularization tendencies included:

1) the deterioration of religious institutions

2) the decline of religious practices

3) the erosion of stable religious communities

4) the differentiation of churches from other institutional spheres.

But complexity implies looking at the interaction of these features and needing constantly to update. Does greater differentiation lead to a decline in religion, or does a decline in religion lead to greater acceptance of secularism? Crucially, is there a decline in religion at all? If not, does this mean a challenge to secularism, or can increased religiosity coexist with a secularizing state?

This chapter first outlines the purposes of secularism and then looks at the different types or interpretations and their critiques. This leads to a discussion of contentious issues of inclusion and recognition, and some of the critiques of secularism. What follows is an outline of nine current myths of secularism. Finally I present my version of secularism which can meet the critiques and also support the dynamism needed for social evolution.

What are the purposes of secularism? What is it *for*?

In the UK, the term 'secularism' was first used by the British writer George Jacob Holyoake in 1851 (although the notions of free thought on which it was based had existed throughout history). It is interesting that Holyoake invented the term secularism to describe his views of promoting a social order separate from religion, without actively dismissing or criticizing religious belief – which would cohere to some extent with the stance of this book. He argued that secularism was not an argument against Christianity but was independent of it. It did not question the pretentions of Christianity, *it advanced others*. This advancing of other ideas would be a key attribute of complexity. For Holyoake, the importance was the here and now, that secular knowledge was manifestly that kind of knowledge which was founded in this life, which related to the conduct of this life, was conducive to its welfare and was capable of being tested by the experience of this life.

Holyoake was the last person to be convicted of blasphemy, in 1842, and served six months in prison. It was he who coined the term 'jingoism', derived from the patriotic song 'By Jingo' sung in the music halls. I shall be looking at how secularism is still seen as heretical and unpatriotic in some parts of the world.

The separate social order is not uniform. Bhargava (2009) usefully distinguishes different levels of connection between church and state. In a theocracy, there is no institutional separation between the two – the priestly order is also the direct political ruler. A non-theocratic state is not automatically a secular state, however, as the state may still have a formal alliance with one religion, that is, with an established, official religion. There is a level of disconnection, but it is a question of separate identities, a role differentiation. The function of one is to maintain peace and order, a temporal matter, the other to secure salvation, primarily a spiritual concern. Yet some ends may be the same, and the two share a special relationship. And in some cases, while there is a role differentiation, the laws and policies are justified in terms of the union that exists between state and church. Or multiple religions may be established, each with official recognition and privileges. A secular state, in contrast, has freestanding ends, which are substantially, if not completely, disconnected from the ends of religion. This question of ends is key.

Sayyid (2009) offers an interesting discussion of the contemporary politics of secularism. He groups the proposed benefits into three:

- epistemological arguments about the nature of knowledge needed for a modern scientific state, and who controls the production of knowledge (should this be religious authorities?)
- that secularism is necessary for peace and social harmony, with religious differences becoming a matter of individual taste, not large-scale social organization, with a level playing field and the prevention of contending groups making appeals to supernatural forces
- that secularism presents the preconditions for the exercise of democracy.

This follows Lefort's useful understanding of 'keeping the space of power empty' (Lefort, 1986: 279). Democracy is government based on the sovereignty of the people, which would preclude a sovereign god or a sovereign priesthood. I come back to Sayyid's own critiques of these attributes later.

In the concern for security, the second of these benefits would be the key starting point. The arguments for secularism here revolve around political legitimacy in a plural state. From his erudite historical analysis, Ian Hunter (2009) argues that the entire field of argument and counter-argument – secularism versus anti-secularism, liberal versus multicultural or communitarian – is redundant when we examine questions of political legitimacy. For Hunter, such legitimacy should be understood in terms of the goal of enforcing civil peace between mutually hostile religious or ideological communities, including, on occasion, between communities of secularists and anti-secularists. Should religion and ideologies have access to the state's coercive instrumentalities, as happens in confessional and party states? The argument for a secular state is that communal conflict can be contained only with a unified political authority. Political authority is about coercion, but the 'just cause' is the mutual fear that drives parties to transfer their capacities for political decision and political coercion to the state, in exchange for mutual protection. Hunter shows us how the early political thinkers, unlike today's Kantians, communitarians and critical thinkers, had as a prime concern not a politics based on some independent theory of social justice, but to show how a politics whose prime objective was civil peace could itself be seen as legitimate. 'Their aim was not to show the political authority of morality, but the morality of political authority' (Hunter, 2009: 32). This is my aim in this book too – to show that secular authority can be deeply moral.

In our time it seems wrong or even dangerous to see the state as coercive; but a state must have coercion. Otherwise it lacks the capacity to obligate us as citizens. We exchange obedience for protection. Our question is whether we would all get the same protection from a religiously infused state. This inspires the next set of arguments about how we decide questions of justice. Is there the possibility of reasoned agreement on common norms across all religions and none? Pufendorf (1934) had the premise that rational agreement on fundamental norms is impossible and dangerous to pursue. He was looking at how the fracturing of the Christian churches had precipitated the Thirty Years' War, and argued that the survival of states required that political authority be immune from the private religious aspirations and judgements of its citizens. Pufendorf saw such religious tension as permanent and was never tempted by a 'common ground strategy', a synthetic or syncretistic 'philosophical religion'. I suppose this would be the religious equivalent of Esperanto, which was a wonderful ideal but a fantasy, given our rooted identities in language. The exclusivity of religions as outlined in the previous chapter also militates against a sort of 'Espero-faith'. Hunter (2009) mounts an excellent critique of Rawlsian-type claims for common reason and a higher (natural) law, as well as of Habermas's 'ideal speech community'. Importantly, he critiques Casanova's notions of 'deprivatization' whereby religions lose their own formalistic and repressive aspect, re-entering the public sphere to participate in democratic will-formation on behalf of the 'life world'. As Hunter eloquently points out, 'The metaphysical conception of public is being retrospectively projected onto the actual politico-judicial construction of public as the state-maintained space of compulsory civil tranquillity' (Hunter, 2009: 47). For my concern, the state's jurisdiction is based not on a secularist or metaphysical 'philosophy' but on the imperative to contain conflicting ideological groupings, which can be secular or religious. Secularism is not an ideology but a practical means to try to achieve peace. This does not mean that we should not engage in deliberative democracy, but rather that we should not envisage that there could ever be some sort of end point whereby common autonomous reason has been achieved, and a coercive state was not necessary, but could be replaced by myriad perfectly working associations of civil society. That way madness lies.

Secular governments follow civil laws, as distinct from religious authorities such as Islamic sharia, Catholic canon law or Jewish Halakha, and hence do not favour or disfavour any particular set of beliefs. As Tariq

Ramadan explained, secularism is associated with the rule of law and only law can guarantee the freedom of religious practice (quoted in De Poli, 2010). This is another central point, and represents a benefit *to* religion as well as protection *from* it where necessary.

This leads to the other direction of the relationship, the public–private one. When does the state intervene in what are seen as the expressions of private religious matters? Hunter also has an interesting take on rights. He says that modern liberal states face no fundamental political, juridical or ethical obstacles when banning 'hate speech' from Christian churches or Islamic mosques:

> Once it is seen that the liberal state is not an expression of the rights or beliefs of its citizens, and is only a means of ensuring that they will not harm each other, then it is redundant to claim that such action infringes civil and religious liberties.
>
> (Hunter, 2009: 48)

I take this to mean not that the state has no interest in rights but that the overarching concern is security. The state is not the sum total of all the beliefs of its citizens but a mechanism for ensuring these citizens live together without harm. Rights, as I explore later, are a means to make decisions about competing claims. I acknowledge that there can be disputes about what constitutes 'hate speech', especially in the realm of satire and humour (also discussed later). But in saying that the main end of sovereignty is the security and welfare of its people, we often have to blur the distinction between public and private. Just as feminists will claim that the personal is political, secularists will point out that private ideological commitments can become political when they threaten the security of the state in terms of how people associate with each other. The state also intervenes in the privacy of the family – or the church – when child abuse is suspected. A secular system is not just about managing competing or antagonistic groups but also about the welfare of individuals. Its function is to override practice done in the name of religion or culture if this is harmful to people.

But a secular system is not just about containment – public or private. As in Sayyid's third 'benefit', it has the preconditions for the exercise of democracy and for future change. A complex state needs mechanisms for adaptation, with enough diversity for creativity but not so much that the system is anarchic and dissolving. The law may act in a coercive way, but this is not an imperative from the supernatural, and can be revised. In a multi-party democracy, political parties should not receive funding, as parties, from the state. Similarly, religious groupings should not be privileged as automatically part of governance. Democratic secularism does not exclude religion, nor necessarily privatize it, but merely puts it on a par with any other ideological organization.

Types of secularism

Even if we could agree that the survival of states has been dependent on a secular division, this still means we need to distinguish the type of secularism, as it plays out in everyday decisions about how to regulate communities and their expression.

Barry Kosmin of the Institute for the Study of Secularism in Society and Culture divides modern secularism into two types: hard and soft secularism (Kosmin, 2007). According to Kosmin, the hard secularist considers religious propositions to be epistemologically illegitimate, warranted by neither reason nor experience. However, in the view of soft secularism, the attainment of absolute truth is impossible and therefore scepticism and tolerance should be the principal and overriding values in the discussion of science and religion.

A slightly different categorization is made by Tariq Modood (2009), who distinguishes a 'moderate' secularism from a 'radical' secularism. The French *laïcité*, the radical version, marks the political triumph over clericalism. Islam, with its claim to regulate public as well as private life, is therefore seen as an ideological foe, and the Muslim presence as alien and potentially both culturally and politically unassimilable – hence the ban on the headscarf in state schools. It is possible to be a British Muslim but not a French Arab. The French *etatist* model, with the strict privatization of religion, aims to eliminate religion from any public forum while at the same time pressuring religious groups to organize themselves into a single, centralized church-like institutional structure that can be regulated by and serve as interlocutor to the state, following the traditional model of the concordat with the Catholic Church (Casanova, 2009). This, according to Asad (2006), is an 'illiberal secularism'.

Modood (2009) argues for a moderate, but 'evolutionary' secularism. This stems from his concerns with identity and the politics of recognition. He argues that a positive self-definition of group differences is more liberatory than being treated as equals. Modood calls this form of difference-affirming equality, with its related notions of respect, recognition and identity, 'political multiculturalism'. The demands would be, in rising order of acceptability:

- no religious discrimination
- even-handedness in relation to religion (e.g. in the funding of state schools)
- the positive inclusion of religious groups.

At first sight, Modood's 'evolutionary' model would seem to fit with complexity theory. 'Positive inclusion' sounds progressive. Yet I have grave doubts about the implications. Here, institutions would be judged on inclusiveness of religion, as they are with gender or race. But it is clearly not all religions which are the concern of Modood, but Islam. Muslim positions in the workforce would be monitored, as would representation on the BBC. He acknowledges that political Muslims are ambivalent about this, as a result of previous misrecognitions of identity and distrust of the race relations industry. Wanting a religious identity creates dissonance in a field crowded with minority identities. 'But to infer this is to naively ignore the hegemonic power of secularism in British political culture, especially on the centre-left' (Modood, 2009: 175).

I am not convinced this hegemonic power exists, but I am more puzzled by his reference to sex. Modood claims that secular multiculturalists argue that the sex lives of individuals are a legitimate feature of political identities and public discourse (is he referring to gays?) and that contrary to seeing religion as a private matter, they 'welcome the sexualisation of culture' (Modood, 2009: 174). I am not sure who these secular multiculturalists are, and what the relevance is, but my main concern is Modood's demand to 'include Islam into the institutional framework of the State'. This seems to go back to Bhargava's second level of connectivity and alliances, rather than the current disconnect. It would involve 'some' Muslim schools and, in addition to Anglican bishops, the right would be extended to other Christian and non-Christian faiths. Muslim history would be as important in the curriculum as European history. There would be state-funded religious television, as in the Netherlands.

Modood admits that a 'corporatist' inclusion 'would require Muslims and their representatives to speak in one voice and to create a unified, hierarchical structure when this is out of character in Sunni Islam' (Modood, 2009: 182). Representation means chosen imams and religious leaders. Modood wants an approach which is less corporatist, less statist, less churchy, in brief, less French. This acknowledges a variety of Muslim voices, groups, and representatives. Different institutions, organizations and associations would seek to accommodate Muslims in ways that worked for them best, knowing that these ways might be modified over time and that Muslim and other pressure groups and civic actors might be continually evolving their claims and agendas. Improvisation, flexibility and incrementalism are seen as much better than top-down corporatist inclusion, with its quotas and targets.

I would go along with such flexibility, and this clearly fits with a CAS, but I am still not sure about what is proposed in terms of concrete policy.

Modood says that the accommodation of religious groups 'is as much if not more about recognition and support of communities than about ecclesiastical or spiritual representation in political institutions', but then argues for 'positive action to achieve a full and just political representation of Muslims in various areas of public life'(Modood, 2009: 185). This is something else. It is one thing to argue that communities of interest – be they religious, cultural, or ethnic – might need support from the state in order to overcome discrimination or disadvantage, another to say that such communities should be politically 'represented' in public life. Even the former has problems, in terms of the homogenization of 'the Muslim community' when this community is so diverse and even prone to internal conflicts; translating this into representation of such an 'imagined community' raises immediate issues – whether the representatives are priestly or lay people.

If religion is privileged as an automatic entry into political decision-making, a problem arises. Why not communities of Marxists, or naturists, or eco-warriors? I seem flippant, but I wish to show that singling out a 'prime' identity (a religious identity) and then making demands that this should be represented is always a problem. Atheism is one of my identities, and I occasionally feel discriminated against in that atheists are not allowed to present 'Thought for the Day' on BBC Radio 4, only religious folk. But I do not want someone to represent me *as an atheist* in political life. This would be saying that the ideological position of non-belief has something to contribute to every aspect of governance, or that my atheist representative would speak only when religion came up, or that he/she knows my views on everything. None of these is viable. It is crucial to see people as having hybrid identities and concerns, some of which may be religious, some not. As soon as 'representation' comes up there is no limit to the claims that can be put in on behalf of groups, real or imagined.

This is not to say that religious organizations should not exist and should not lobby or speak or generally make themselves heard – this is actually vital for democratic debate. But they should not occupy positions of power in state decision-making *as of right* just because of a particular world view. I recall a discussion when I was on the board of UNICEF UK, where we were seeking to appoint a new trustee. One member was concerned about the composition of the board, and thought we might look for 'a Muslim', or at least an 'ethnic minority person'. It was quickly established that membership of the board was about particular expertise, not about the apparent representation of a segment of society. We were there because of our expertise in education, or the health sector, or the media, or the work of charities. Our work was not to lobby on behalf of a vested interest but to contribute to a more informed decision-making process, with our professional experience drawn on as appropriate. This made for a better political process than a random collection of sectarian envoys.

Veit Bader also looks for a 'third way' between policies of assimilation of religious minorities and unlimited tolerance of religious practices. He wants an alternative between:

> the strict separation of organised religions from a presumed 'religion-blind' and strictly 'neutral' state defended by standard liberalism and republicanism and, on the other hand, the religious (neo-)corporatism (illiberal and anti-democratic institutional pluralism and rigid 'pillarisation') defended by traditionalist and orthodox religious organisations and leaders.
>
> (Bader, 2007: 19)

For this he argues for Associative Democracy (AD), which supports the legal, administrative and political recognition of organized religions. It balances strong guarantees for individual or 'inner' religious freedoms and strong guarantees for associational or 'outer' freedoms of religion and provides maximum accommodation to religious practices, constrained only by 'minimal morality' and basic rights. This is a departure from the notion of secularism that makes a key distinction between public and private, relegating religion to the private.

But here come the demands. Bader wants, in addition to tax exemptions for organized religions, public funding for faith-based organizations 'in all sorts of care and education' (given public scrutiny and quality standards). This is to provide opportunities for these organizations to be 'even-handedly' involved in standard setting and governance of these services. For him, recognized religions are not only to be explicitly allowed to play a public role:

> ... they should be given specific information rights and corresponding information duties with regard to contested issues on an even-handed basis with other 'weltanschaulichen' organisations (organisations based on 'philosophical ways of life'), they should be given rights and opportunities to participate in public forums and hearings, and they should be included in advisory ethical councils.
>
> (Bader, 2007: 20)

I acknowledge the problems of a strict public/private divide, given the public role that religions do play – it would be foolish to pretend otherwise. But I would not support the notion of tax exemptions just because they were religious organizations. In many countries, tax exemptions are given to charities (with a debate in the UK about independent schools receiving tax exemptions, but that is another story). I accept the argument for even-handedness with other organizations, but contend that state support should be on the basis of the contribution that they make and, in the UK, whether they meet the stringent demands of the Charity Commission, not because they happen to have a religious base. So Tearfund, World Vision, CAFOD and Islamic Relief *as charities* can certainly get tax exemption, but not the overall workings of the churches to which they are attached. I certainly do not support state funding for religious schools. It is not clear either how 'even-handedness' would work, and how one decides between the multitude of claims to funds and participation in governance that would come from such a policy. Bader has clearly never worked in a Ministry of Culture, Science and Sport, let alone, as in Afghanistan, the Ministry of Labour, Social Affairs, Martyrs and the Disabled.

I agree with Bader that supposedly secular states are not so, and that the term is misleading. I agree that the exclusion of religious reasoning ('exclusivist secularism') from public debate is unfair under conditions of reasonable pluralism. But the basic error in Bader's position is that he accords the notion of particular 'rights' to religions for such participation, if this is what he is arguing. There are basic human rights to freedom of information, freedom of participation and freedom of association. But these are individual rights, not accorded in international law to groups or to organizations. People have rights, not religions. I would agree that transparency is needed. If a religious organization wanted to stand for election as a political party, that should not be prevented in an inclusive secular world. But nor should it be given any more recognition or funding than any other party – such as the Monster Raving Loony Party (for non-UK readers, this party actually exists). I agree though that religious competition in what Bader terms 'God's Biggest Supermarket' is important for the chances of religions and for religious diversity. It is not, however, a mode of governance.

There is also the interesting question of whether formal inclusion in the state is actually good for religions, a question raised by work on religious markets. This is the phrase used to describe all the religious activity going on in a society, which is composed mainly of one or more organizations seeking to attract or maintain adherents (Stark and Finke, 2000). There is the push for brand loyalty, as few religious groups want their members to divide their time and commitment among multiple groups, so stress exclusive commitment (I examined the problems of exclusivity in the previous chapter). The theory is that religious monopolies can exist only when a group is favoured by the state. Without religious regulation or in circumstances of complete religious freedom, a religious market will be more pluralistic because it allows for the promotion of multiple religious doctrines.

The interesting part of the theory is that the market model of religion holds that religious pluralism *increases* religiosity because, as in any market, competition is good for business. Demand-side hypotheses of religious growth and decline focus on how individuals seek out religion, perhaps in times of disaster. Supply-side analyses on the other hand focus on the supply of religious goods. Stark and Finke propose that to the degree that religious economies are unregulated and competitive, overall levels of religious commitment will be high. Churches are allowed complete freedom to recruit. But states can also manipulate the supply side by providing direct financial support or by establishing tax, property and civic laws that favour certain religious organizations, or in contrast, they can ban specific religious groups and imprison or execute their members. The collapse of Soviet communism, as Froese (2008) points out, left a religious market with no clear monopoly. Now, the least religiously restrictive regions of the former Soviet Union are also the most pluralistic. Estonia and Latvia do little to regulate their religious markets and both countries have no clear majority religion.

So in our concern for complex adaptability, diversity is needed and in this sense the state should merely allow religious competition and not intervene, as in any market-based economy. Monopoly religions do not occur without state assistance. But rather than a multitude of religions clamouring for state assistance or recognition, it is better for religions to let the market regulate and to do their own advertising and promotional work. Any incorporation of a particular religious group will threaten this diversity, particularly regarding minority religions. A more honest approach to diversity is required. Much is said about 'valuing diversity', when this is actually code for being tolerant towards a multiplicity of ethnic or religious groups and their ideologies and practices. In fact, people do not value all diversity, if this includes paedophiles, terrorists, people who smell, or people who use their mobiles in the quiet zone of the train. In CAS terms, the valuing of diversity has a different meaning. In the natural world, it is a variety of species. In the social world, it is about multiple views of the world and multiple interconnectivity and collisions between those views. But it will be about competition and competing views, and some will go to the wall.

I like the idea of using a market approach. This enables us to see religions on the same level as any business or collective, or any charity come to that. Just as we would look suspiciously at claims for automatic membership or representation in government by Starbucks, or the Ramblers'

Association, or Oxfam, we should not see religious groups as entitled to formal recognition just because they are a religion. Probably fewer people go to church than go to Starbucks, in the UK at least. There would be an outcry if we chose one business interest over another, yet there seems to be blindness to the favouritism that occurs when major religions are somehow called to be represented. If there is a threat of religious discrimination, this can be dealt with by laws and rights. Dynamic secularism in this instance favours the capitalist mode of production. If one religious claim to absolute truth dies out because nobody will buy it, then it probably deserves to. The state in Europe has withdrawn from the enforcement of religious laws such as witchcraft and heresy. Atheism is no longer punishable by death, or this book would be published posthumously. Diversity enables new fitness landscapes, in complexity terms.

Christian Smith, a key sociologist of religion, outlines some of the debates around modernity and secularization and helps us understand that there can be 'multiple modernities', not one standard, linear path (Smith, 2008). Different hypotheses about religious pluralism might be true in different contexts. It is possible for societies to be truly modern and not end up looking like France or Sweden with regard to religion, culture, morality, and views of science. What I like is his assertion that this does not mean having to fall into serious problems of postmodernism and relativism. That is a relief. Ironically, the growing force of terrorism routinely uses all sorts of modern technology, often to promote an 'anti-modern' agenda. So it is essential to understand modernity:

> … not simply as a series of institutional changes which positive
> science can somehow track and predict, but as a cultural project
> of purposive human agents operating from the start with different
> categories and beliefs about humanity, society, morality, purpose
> of life etc.
>
> (Smith, 2008: 1574)

This fits well with the complexity approach – in the notion of 'multiple modernities', in the notion of unpredictability, and in the identification of 'purposive human agents'. What is central too is Smith's demand that we understand religious beliefs sociologically to see how they operate interactively in complex processes of cognitive activity, identity formation, action motivation, collective solidarity, organizational constitution and so on. There is religious treatment of the body – its comportment, treatment, and enactments, and a further agenda of emotions, genetics, ecological contexts, elites and political ideologies. The way religion cuts across so many dimensions of people's lives is another reason *not* to single out faith as requiring special treatment by the state. It is actually superficial.

Critiques of secularism

Writers such as William E. Connolly in *Why I Am Not a Secularist* (1999) argue that modern political secularism is a child of single-religion societies and that while it may be suited to Protestantism and religions that are weakly protestantized, it excludes or is actively inimical to other religions. There is a view that secularism has failed to accommodate community-specific rights and therefore is unable to protect religious minorities from discrimination and exclusion. How can it fight religious hegemony and in the same breath establish itself as the sole basis for adjudication in public life? Connolly says that secularism is a deeply parochial doctrine with universalist pretensions. Bhargava (2009) reports that there are critics who even argue that its peace-talk is mere sham because deep down it is a conflict-generating ideology that threatens pluralist democracies. I agree with Connolly that 'Western' secularism is partial, or dishonest, and often inimical to some religions. We see this in France and Germany where Islam is singled out for privatization compared to other religions. But if community rights are not protected, this is not the general fault of secularism as a political system but a failure of the implementation of rights. If members of a religious or ethnic minority group experience discrimination, the secular law should be there to protect and recompense those individuals. But the law is not there to protect the beliefs underlying their membership.

Sayyid (2009) has an even stronger reason for disputing that the supposed benefits of secularism are global attributes. For him, instead, they are formulated as part of a narrative of Western exceptionality, of modernity, of Western identity. He seems to sense a particular attack on Islam here, with the lack of secularism in Islam contrasted with the presence of secularism in the West, in such a way that the contrast is portrayed as confirming the necessity and importance of secularism if a civilization is to prosper. Yet the articulation of a Muslim identity points to a historical community which has come today to embody a counter-history to the dominant 'Plato to NATO' sequence. Sayyid's contention is that secularism is deployed not to ensure civic peace or epistemological advances, but rather to maintain Western historiographical political hegemony. The current debate is less about separating religion from politics than about the depoliticizing of Muslims. Muslims are portrayed as the permanently transgressive subject, whose 'religious essence' is constantly being undermined by the temptations of the political:

> Secularism, by establishing the boundary between the religious and the political, also becomes another means of policing the boundary between the pre-modern and the modern, and the Western and the non-Western.
>
> (Sayyid, 2009: 199)

Unlike my earlier arguments in this chapter around the need for political legitimacy to contain warring tribes, Sayyid suggests that the opposite of the civil peace argument is true, that the retreat of religion from the public sphere in Islamic history has been most often associated with the breakdown of civic peace. He cites Turkey's coercive secularism, or other de-Islamization colonial projects. In India, Nehru saw secularism as a means of dealing with the religious question in the context of the Pakistan movement. But currently in India, secularism coexists with an institutionalized system of communal violence in which the primary victims tend to be Muslim. Secularism allows Hindu–Muslim violence to be represented as exceptional rather than intrinsic to contemporary India, rendering it almost invisible. 'It could be argued that secularism in India, along with "planned riots" is part of the institutional ensemble by which Muslims in India are disciplined and domesticated' (Sayyid, 2009: 196). This is an interesting and perceptive point. But, again, it is not necessarily a critique of secularism as a concept but of the way that secularism is played out in India, and allowed to become a cover for something else. It is obvious that a passive secularism is not enough to contain violence. Coercive secularism is, I agree, equally dangerous. My arguments for a dynamic secularism will try to address some of these issues, while not pretending this is Utopia – merely necessary but not sufficient.

In summary, the hard, radical versions of secularism which attempt to regulate the supply side of religions by exclusion and by privatization would not meet the CAS requirements for diversity and connectivity. Softer – or partial – versions can be accused of relativism or even hypocrisy. However, neither Modood's (2009) call for official recognition nor Bader's (2007) call for the allocation of rights to religions is capable of permitting the sorts of critical democracy which will mean emergence. It is essential that religions fight for their survival and contribution alongside other ever-changing value systems and organizations. They must not be privileged. The recognition of multiple modernities is antithetical to lock-in.

The critiques of secularism, for example that this is a Western and hegemonic practice, relate not to the concept but to the uses to which a secular approach is put, by whom and why. It is the same as arguing that rights are Western, that democracy is Western, that feminism and gender equity are Western. The elision of a principle and the diverse interpretations of its practice are common in such arguments. But they should be addressed. Dynamic secularism will also need safeguards.

Before I outline my own version, it is necessary to dispel some common misapprehensions about the basic tenets of secularism.

Nine myths of secularism

1. That secularism is oppositional to religion

In a recent article entitled 'We're losing our religion as we become "nones"', on how the number of people with no religious affiliation has increased in both the US and the UK, Ruth Gledhill (2012b: 21) quotes Terry Sanderson of the National Secular Society saying 'the battle between secularism and religion is hotting up'. This is all wrong. Not because the trends about religious affiliation are incorrect, but because it is a gross mistake to present secularism and religion as antagonistic. As seen in exploring the goals of a secular state to avoid negative conflict, secularism is a means by which religions can exist comfortably and equitably in a society. Secularism merely wants to ensure that religions do not do harm to each other or to those who profess no faith. Harm can be violent conflict or it can be domination and exclusion based on membership of a religious group. We have seen how certain versions of hard secularism might be antithetical to religion, as in the great secularization experiment of the Soviet Union; but the basic principle of secularism is that religions – as ethnic groups – are with us but should not be privileged over other groupings and ways of life. Soft secularists in particular do not want to outlaw religion at all, but in fact want to increase tolerance. But look at Tariq Modood's words:

> Anti-immigrant xenophobic nativism, secularist anti-religious prejudice, liberal-feminist critiques of Muslim patriarchal fundamentalism and the fear of Islamist terrorist networks are being fused indiscriminately throughout Europe into a uniform anti-Muslim discourse, which practically precludes the kind of mutual accommodation between immigrant groups and host societies that is necessary for successful immigrant incorporation.
>
> (Modood, 2009: 147)

Why *secularist* anti-religious prejudice? The implication is that secularism is always prejudiced, when the aim is in fact neutrality. I know that Modood is probably thinking of the hard secularity of France, but it is all too easy to slip the word 'secular' into a statement as a generalized negative appellation, instead of being precise about what sort. Elsewhere is the association with the evils of democracy. A few months after the beginning of the uprising in Syria, bloggers on Salafi websites began asking jihadi scholars for fatwas allowing them to join the protest movement. Sheikh Abu al-Mundhir al-Shinqiti advised bloggers to join the protests *as long as they avoided calling for democracy or any other secular slogan* [my italics] (Alami, 2013).

One problem to be admitted is that religious extremism does generate secular extremism. Jihad as a global youth culture will attack the unbounded possibilities that what is cast as a 'secular' society is often seen to tolerate – free love, pornography, hard drugs, making money, and caring just for oneself. This attack then extends to Western 'sacred' values of human rights as equally null and void. From the other perspective, such religious intolerance is portrayed as so dangerous that religion should be wiped from the face of the earth or at least severely restrained. The fellowship that Christopher Hitchens called the 'Four Horsemen of the Apocalypse' (himself, Richard Dawkins, Daniel Dennett and Sam Harris) invokes a constant struggle against religion, with the vision to diminish its influence. Yet, as I repeat constantly, secularism does not *have* to be antagonistic to religion. It has been counterproductive for the secular fundamentalists, much as I love reading them, to demand abolition. It is about as useful as prohibitions on liquor. Religion will remain with us; it serves certain purposes.

Paul Froese begins his fascinating account of the failed Soviet secularization project with the words 'It is easier to invoke God than to get rid of him' (Froese, 2008: 1). He demonstrates how faith survives and thrives, and argues that 'the idea of the supernatural, and, more specifically, the idea of God is a fundamental cultural element common to all modern societies, so common as to make it a core belief' (Froese, 2008: 2). Empirical evidence shows that humans universally are drawn to religious explanations of the world. They need a transcendent horizon or framework of understanding derived from above and beyond themselves to be given significance. Froese speculates that historically established world religions provide this framework better than any existing secular ideology, at least for the vast majority of humanity. 'Organised religions are sustainable only to the extent that humans are attracted to the transcendent explanations and meanings they offer. Otherwise they would simply fold for lack of interest' (Froese, 2008: 20). This also fits the market analogy discussed earlier.

It is important to accept this. However suspicious one might be of the negative sides to belief in the supernatural, one cannot abolish religion; nor can one wait for religions to become unfashionable. One would wait a long time. Secularism must not be portrayed nor understood as the enemy of religion. Coexistence is the only proper – and possible – aim, not suppression. There have been fears that, for example, the 2010 Mexican legislation to make the government formally *'laico'* (lay or secular) was actually in order to suppress the Catholic Church's ability to engage in public policy debates. But secularism, while not privileging religion, does not need to relegate it to some unpardonable place.

2. That one cannot be religious and support secularism

Following on from the previous myth of automatic opposition is the notion that if you are religious you will not support secularism. In fact many religious people and organizations are only too aware that secularism is the best protection for their faith. There are secular Jews, secular Christians and secular Hindus. There is a thriving organization, British Muslims for a Secular Democracy (BMSD), which has as its first objective to:

> Raise awareness within British Muslims and the wider public, of democracy particularly 'secular democracy' helping to contribute to a shared vision of citizenship (the separation of faith and state, so faiths exert no undue influence on policies and there is a shared public space).
>
> (British Muslims for a Secular Democracy, n.d.)

BMSD wants to tackle Islamophobia, but also has an aim of 'raising awareness of religious influence on UK domestic and foreign policies, particularly those which may lead to undue effect on civil liberties'. Religious supporters of secularism are very aware of how undue religious influence in public policy can curtail freedoms for themselves and others. I would defer absolutely to their take on freedom of religious expression in a secular state, particularly as it relates to security:

> BMSD supports the right of men and women to dress how they choose on civil libertarian grounds. However, freedom of expression is a qualified right, subject to limitations in the interests of (including but not restricted to): national security, public safety, the protection of health or morals, or for the protection of the reputation or rights of others. ... We believe that people who interact with public-facing workers in all sectors have the right to do so on the basis of equality. These transactions cannot be considered equal if the employee in question has deliberately concealed their face – whether the mode of concealment is a niqab, a hood or a mask – because the concealed person can recognise the person he/she is dealing with, yet the other person cannot

see what is behind the face-covering. In terms of public security, we are aware that the full Afghan burka – pulled down over the face – has been used on several occasions by men to conceal their identities. We therefore support restrictions on the face-veil in particular settings such as banks, airports and any place where child protection issues are invoked.

(British Muslims for a Secular Democracy, n.d.)

This is a good example of the 'principled pragmatism' which characterizes a secular approach, with the understanding of 'qualified rights' in freedom of expression. BMSD has been shortlisted for the Secularist of the Year prize.

3. That secularism is a belief system and therefore a rival to religion

As explained earlier, secularism is not a metaphysical philosophy grounded in a set of beliefs about the nature or origin of the world. It is a political order, designed as a practice, and equivalent to other political orders of law or jurisprudence. The nature of the English language means that one can talk of 'believing' in a secular approach, but this is not parallel to a belief in a deity. There are no sacred texts of secularism, no leaders to worship unconditionally, no weekly or daily rituals to observe. The Soviets recognized people's needs for ritual and attempted to replace religious ones with atheist ceremonies. They had Soviet alternatives to baptism, confirmations, marriages, funerals and many other celebrations. The government declared that 16 and 25 December would be Days of Industrialization, with obligatory presence at work. On the other hand there were lots of public holidays, such as the Day of the Land Reclamation Worker. But the difference to current humanist weddings and naming ceremonies was the attempt to turn the profane *into* the sacred. Historical materialism was sacred scripture. Soviet leaders were hailed as saint-like and deserving of holy reverence. Earthly paradise could be achieved only with the eradication of religion. Because religion was officially illusory, believers could be deemed insane. On one level the Soviets understood and tried to parallel the attractions of supernatural belief, but they were always on a hiding to nothing in casting the *absence* of religion as offering something.

The psychological aspect of religion also means that parallels cannot be drawn. Dawkins (2006) advocates evolutionary theory to explain this, maintaining that religious belief initially served some survival value and consequently got instilled in human psychology. But now one cannot theoretically detach the biological or genetic foundations of religious preferences from the social and cultural location of the individual, which explains why religion takes so many different shapes. Yet apparently belief in a 'caring God' is more predictive of religious participation than whether an individual had attended church as a child, was married to a religious person, or had a religious experience. Individuals are drawn to religion because of the desire for a personal relationship with a supernatural being. As Froese points out, 'this key aspect of religion cannot be replicated in secular terms' (Froese, 2008: 186). So, sadly for some perhaps, secularism cannot hope to offer comfort or salvation or someone to talk to. But that is not its purpose. As a political stratagem or system or order it should not be judged in these terms, any more than should an ecological movement.

4. That secularism is the same as atheism
This is one of the biggest confusions of all. Atheism simply means not believing in the divine, the supernatural, in deities who control the world. In this sense of belief/no belief, atheism would be seen as a rival to religion and has been the subject of conflict over the centuries. As already stated, I would have been burned at the stake not too long ago. Yet atheism is not the same as anti-theism; it can remain at the level of personal ontology. It is definitely not the same as secularism. Atheists would probably support a secular approach to government and education, but this does not mean that atheism and secularism are coterminous. One relates to belief, one to governance. If, as some Islamists do, one thinks that belief and governance are the same thing, then it is understandable that secularists and atheists would all be tarred with the same brush, and labelled as heretics. But secularism is not there to reject notions of divinity, but to contain them as an umbrella protection. The communists were not trying to promote a secular society, they were trying to promote an atheist society. This is one reason why the experiment failed.

Atheists might object to the notion of an 'absence' of belief – it is a bit like being labelled 'non-white'. Yet they would claim that the burden of proof does not lie on the atheist to disprove the existence of a deity but on believers to demonstrate empirically its existence. It is interesting that there can be 'Christian atheism' – this is an ideology in which the belief in the god of Christianity is rejected or absent, but the moral teachings of Jesus are followed. This is conceptually similar to humanistic Judaism.

It is not clear why people appear so terrified of atheism. Froese (2008) claims that only 1 per cent of the world is actually atheist (excluding the Chinese, which seems to me a big exclusion). It is not that the rest are devoutly religious, but very few are willing to actively deny the existence of a deity. There are only 5,300 members of the American Humanist Association and 16 million members of the Southern Baptist Convention. Is this because atheists do not 'join' things as much? There would be few outlets for atheist proselytizing – and not all atheists are proselytizers. Even the Soviets were hard pressed to find atheist crusaders. One satirical Soviet cartoon depicts rural Communist party officials praying to God for an atheist lecturer to visit their region (Froese, 2008: 130).

But this does not prevent fear. In Caraballo-Resto's study of secularism among Scottish Muslims, all informants perceived secularism to be opposed to Islam: 'In other words, if the former exists, the latter is corrupt' (Caraballo-Resto, 2010: 156). This is because respondents consider secularism to be an attitude which either denies that there is a god, prophethood and revelation or declares that the role of these is limited to the personal lives of Muslims. In this light, some informants compared secularism to the Arabic term of *kufr* – a wilful and conscious decision to refuse God's message. Or they approached the concept by referring to the Arabic words *al-Ilhād* (the belief in no god). There would clearly be huge educational work to do here about the difference between secularism and atheism.

The language issue is not confined to Arabic. In Belgium, '*laïcité*' has a double meaning. It refers either to the separation between church and state or the community of citizens that reject religion and follow a secular way of life, such as free-thinkers. To distinguish between the two concepts, this community is also called *georganiseerde vrijzinnigheid* (Dutch) or *laïcité organisée* (French). The distinction between rejecting religion for oneself and rejecting it for all others is difficult to keep clear, but remains essential work.

5. That secularism has no morality

Secularism is sometimes presented as a moral vacuum. 'Secularists see believers as believing in what's crazy; believers see secularists as mired in what's meaningless' (Atran, 2010: 476). Yet, as argued earlier, secular authority has at root the ideals of peace and of social justice. No one set of beliefs is to be automatically privileged over another, nor adherents of one faith privileged over others. Secular law will have a basis in the moral framework of human rights. While the origins of conventions on rights may well stem from religious commandments, the difference is that rights now have a transversal, international mandate and have a contemporary application, not gaining legitimacy from divine sacred jurisdiction as spoken in previous centuries and times. Significantly, Charles Taylor (2009) draws his three requirements for secularism from the ideals of the French Revolution. This means liberty (no one must be forced in the domain of religious belief, and it includes the freedom not to believe); equality (between people of different faiths, with none having privileged status); and fraternity (all spiritual families must be heard). He adds a fourth, of relations of harmony between groups. This strikes me as a deeply moral position.

Yet it is amazing that there can be such misunderstanding in some quarters. The lead of a research team funded by the Templeton Foundation, which produced a report in 2009 on the so-called 'crisis of character' among England's underclass teenagers, claimed 'No government or other secular tradition has been able so far to replace the Judeo-Christian moral tradition' (Templeton Foundation, 2011: 1). This is breathtaking in its partiality and confusion, especially as the report earlier talked about Muslim teenagers being faithful to civil society's values. It is worrying that academics are apparently unable to bracket their own religious beliefs, and, worse, that secularism is somehow seen as to blame for summer riots.

6. That secularism has no spirituality

Related to the above is the vision of the proponent of secularism as some sort of cold naysayer who finds no spiritual joy in the world. This is linked to the mistaken idea that spirituality is confined to religion. Yet it can be a unifying feature: a political secularist, a hard-line atheist and a devout believer can all enjoy and experience the spiritual – in music, art, love of the countryside or whatever. It can be religious governance that bans spirituality, as in some hard versions of Islam that forbid music or dance. Tony Wilkinson (2007) makes a case for a form of secular spirituality in which the motivation is to live happily and to help others. Qualities such as love, compassion, patience, forgiveness and responsibility are seen as humanistic qualities, not confined to religion. They would be aspects of the world which go beyond a purely materialist view. Spiritual practices such as mindfulness and meditation can be experienced as beneficial without any supernatural interpretation or explanation. There is even postmodern spirituality. In 'Four ways to be absolutely right', Anderson (1995) describes how postmodern spirituality refers to new forms of spirituality in the contexts of postmodern societies in a globalized world. Former universalistic world views of modernity become contested, old explanations and certainties questioned.

One 'certainty' to be questioned is that of beauty being evidence of God. Both our sense of beauty and the creator of it are held by some to be divine. We can look at a scene of beauty and see God. Yet as Howson (2011) points out, there is some reason to believe that evolution has endowed us with a positive emotional response to various types of beauty. Fresh air, fast-flowing water, unpolluted landscapes are good to appreciate and seek out. Then there is the appreciation of human beauty which is plausibly linked to considerations of reproductive fitness, such as symmetry in human physiology, and our concepts of masculine and feminine beauty. We now know more too about the neurological components of appreciating music, that these are the same as those involved in language processing. There is a grammatical structure in music, in the rules of harmony as there are familiar rules of grammar in language: as humans we seek regularity and predictability, and these have survival value. Rhythm is found to be deep in the brain, in a very old centre of the brain, the basal ganglia, which control motor activity.

Making music and listening to it are essentially social activities, fostering cohesion and belonging. I still think that we do not fully understand the particular thrill that music provides, and why it is so linked to emotion – neurological processing does not fully explain it for me. Complexity theorists say that music is an intellectual scandal – we just do not understand the connectivities in the brain which lead to our making and enjoyment of it. But that is no reason to say that it is a proof of God. I can enjoy belting out hymns and revel in my passion for sacred music without feeling at all hypocritical. But knowing that Bach drew inspiration from his reverence for God does not mean that this is proven to be the source. The fact that I am deeply grateful for his belief does not make me a believer too. This is another principled pragmatism perhaps – a dynamic secularism happily capitalizes on all sorts of motivations as long as they contribute to a greater sum of human happiness.

7. That Islam is incompatible with secularism

It would be foolish to pretend that a key issue of our time in talking about secularism and security is not Islam. As Carl Brown reminds us, Islam, unlike Christianity, has no tradition of a separation of church and state. 'One simple reason for this difference … is that Islam knows of no 'church' in the sense of a corporate body whose leadership is clearly defined, hierarchical and distinct from the state' (Brown, 2000: 46). The political aspect of Islam stems from the tribal origins of the religion and the talents of its founder, Muhammad, who excelled as prophet, military general and civic leader. Combining his political and religious genius, Muhammad was able to establish a vast Muslim empire governed by religious law – 'an ideal that would forever intertwine politics and religion within the doctrine of Islam' (Froese, 2008: 91). It would seem that being soldiers of Christ does not even approach this. No theocratic ideal exists in the history of Christianity. Christian institutions were independent of state governments. Religious and political domains were autonomous even if mutually dependent. There were working compromises between doctrinal purity and logical consistency, a 'nebulous but manageable middle way between the two extremes' (Brown, 2000: 46). I like the idea of a nebulous but manageable middle way.

One problem for Islam is language. As Larsson (2010) points out, there is no direct equivalent of 'secularization' in Arabic. The words *dahriyya,* which means 'materialist' or 'atheist', or *ilmaniyya,* used of whatever deals with the world or worldly matters, may be used when referring to processes that resemble secularization in the Arabic-speaking world. It would not be surprising if there was resistance to secularism if it only meant worldly or, worse, non-godly.

But one should not paint a picture of Islam as implacably opposed to secularism in the sense of a separation of church and state. Sharia provided the blueprint for governance and divided the world into *dar al-Islam* (the land of Islam) and *dar al-harb* (the land of warfare). After Muhammad, the complexity of governing expanding Islamic communities demanded a division of labour between *ulema* and sultan. Yet while the sharia provides a basic political theory for governance of an Islamic community, it does not outline the specifics of how to legislate and govern rapidly expanding states. In the modern era, as Antony Black (2001) shows, Islamic theorists are split on how to deal with the political import of sharia: either 'syncretism' – justified by seeing certain Western ideas as expressions of true Islam, or 'revivalism' – going back to the sources of the revelation. With regard to syncretism, Brown (2000) reveals how those Muslims who seek democracy argue that Muhammad was the first democrat, and that the early Muslim community was the first democracy; those advancing socialism depict Muhammad as the first socialist and the early community as the first socialist state and so on, as political styles change. Some Islamic thinkers even saw communism as a means to settle centuries-long conflicts within the Muslim community.

The point is that Islam is not the enemy of secularism, or of democracy, or any other political system. Islamic fundamentalists might claim that in 'true' Islam there is no distinction between religious belief and political action and that the creation of a pure and global *ummah* is their absolute duty, but they ignore the fact that there is little or nothing in the Quran about the politics of building an Islamic state. The Quran does not specifically discuss power, not its possible connotations, and Muhammad died without indicating a successor and without leaving instructions on the nature of the government of the *ummah* (De Poli, 2010). As Hassan, the would-be extremist in Sebastian Faulks's wonderful novel *A Week in December* ruminates, 'there was of course plenty of other practical advice – be kind to orphans, pay the alms levy, go to Mecca if you can, sleep only with the servant girls of your own house, not with other men's and so on' (Faulks, 2009: 106). But, interestingly, as he found out, the prophet seemed not directly concerned with the logistics of empire building. And, as seen above, many Muslims are deeply committed to political secularism.

8. That secularism is to blame for everything

Tristram Hunt, the historian, broadcaster, and Labour MP for Stoke-on-Trent Central, said that he was a 'critical friend' of the new history proposals in the UK, adding:

> Having an appreciation of British history up to the age of 14 is a worthwhile endeavour. In the old days a lot of British children understood history through church, chapel and family. But the passing down of historical knowledge has fallen away with secularism.
>
> (Buchanan and Hurst, 2013: 8)

This is bizarre. I don't know what Sunday school Hunt went to but it was not like mine. All we did was Bible stories and cards for Mothering Sunday. We certainly did not do the Tudors or Magna Carta.

9. That secularism has meant a decline in religion

This is one of the biggest myths – or fears – of all. Modernization is held to be the culprit – the causal engine 'dragging the Gods into retirement' (Svensson and Rangdrol, 2009). Yet the separation of church and state by itself does not logically lead to non-belief, as Froese (2008) points out. Modernization does not affect belief on its own, unless modern political and scientific world views are inherently anti-religious. It is not clear that modernization has indeed promoted secularization globally, and there is an argument that globalization and modernity act to increase the search for unique identity in the face of globalizing forces which appear to render us indistinguishable. These identities include religious identities.

In our concern about security, the secularization thesis would imply that as the role of religion diminishes, so would its influence on conflict. Yet as the previous chapter has shown, religion's influence on conflict is alive and well. Bhargava (2009) argues that it is secularism that is 'under siege', with an increasing number of theocracies or states with theocratic or Islamist tendencies. Movements that challenge the 'undisputed' reign of secularism have, however, not been restricted to Muslim societies: there are ever stronger Sinhalese Buddhists in Sri Lanka, Hindu nationalists in India, religious ultra-orthodox Jews in Israel and Sikh nationalists claiming that Sikhism does not recognize a separation of religion and state. Christian movements are emerging more strongly in countries as far apart as Kenya, Guatemala and the Philippines. Christian fundamentalism is an increasingly visible force in American politics.

Even if not overtly, there are few signs that states are shedding previous religious trappings. In the UK, the Queen is leader of the Anglican Church, and the coronation is a religious act. The Upper House of the UK legislature, the House of Lords, still has 26 seats reserved for Church of England bishops. The Church of England has vigorously opposed relaxing the UK law on assisted suicide, despite 70 per cent of the British population being in favour of it. This is also despite the fact that regular Church of England attendees currently make up fewer than 3 per cent of the population, with an average age of over 50. The bishops have worked indefatigably in defeating every Private Member's Bill on this – yet they are supposed to be an independent voice. In Germany, it has been shown that the banning of the headscarf is less a sign of secularization or of the maintenance of neutrality and more to do with the reassertion of a national German identity, of Germanness. The *Leitkultur* (guiding culture) into which immigrants should assimilate has deep Christian roots (Sandford-Gaebel, 2013). This has had huge implications for citizenship and exclusion.

A major problem is that what are held to be secular states are pseudo-secular ones in terms of a less than transparent participation of religions in governance, so that religion is actually alive and well. Nepal declared itself a secular nation, but the official religion is Hinduism. Burma is now supposedly secular, but the Buddhist government is persecuting the Muslim minority, using violence and destroying villages. Froese (2008) shows how Orthodoxy in Russia currently acts as a 'pseudo-state' church. This threatens religious freedom for other religions. In Central Asia, all the 'Stans' returned to strict religious laws that favour Islamic groups with current links to power. Froese notes how many Communist mainliners have claimed a faith in Islam to legitimize their grip on power. One Uzbek official imprisoned Jehovah's Witnesses for nothing more than proselytizing. In general, the major religious groups, Islam and Eastern Orthodoxy, suffer fewer problems as long as they do not criticize the government.

On the other side of the world, Modood (2009) analyses how the US is a deeply religious society. Churches, mainly white and mainly in the south and mid-west, campaign openly for candidates and parties, raise large sums of money for politicians, and introduce religion-based issues into politics, such as abortion, HIV/AIDs, homosexuality, stem-cell research, prayer at school and so on. It has been said that no openly avowed atheist has ever been a candidate for the White House. The US contains over 21,000 distinct religious groups from myriad world religious traditions. Yet whatever the religion, many Americans reference what they believe God wants as the rationale for their specific political attitudes (Froese, 2008). Froese reveals how the 'Republicanization' of American Protestantism is a fairly recent phenomenon, marking the successful courting of dominant Evangelical religious groups by the Republican Party. It is interesting that nearly all individuals who believe that God favours their political party are Republicans. In education too, Michael Apple has catalogued the increasing and disturbing influence of the conservative evangelical right (Apple, 2006: 2013). Thus, although the US is a country that forbids institutional collaboration between its church and state, religious sentiments play a powerful role in setting the political agenda and determining election outcomes. And as we know, Bush had God on his side.

The UK presents a different picture. A recent government report *Future Identities* (2013*)* found that since the 1980s religious identities have shown a long-term trend towards increasing secularization. Church attendance has been declining and the Christian religion has become less important for many people's identities. In the 2011 Census, the number of people identifying themselves as having no religion was 25.1 per cent of the population, compared to 14.8 per cent in 2001. Younger people tend to be less religious than older people. Yet the overall UK trend of rising secularization is less pronounced in Northern Ireland, and among both the Muslim and the Roman Catholic populations in the rest of the UK. Muslims are more likely to state that their religious identity is important to them. A range of reasons are analysed for this, including a reaction to Islamophobia, and wanting to assert a 'pure' version of the faith (Foresight Future Identities, 2013). But the reason would not be secularism as such – if anything, it would be a reaction to the pseudo-secularism and continued Christian influence of the British state. So, as discussed in the introduction to this chapter, there is no automatic causal link between secularism and secularization. On the contrary, it may be that in some contexts secularism *increases* religiosity.

Dynamic secularism

Having hopefully cleared up some of the myths around what secularism is and is not, I turn to my own version of secularism as reaching the maximum 'fitness landscape' for a plural world. This is not a middle way between hard and soft, but a different recombinant, to align with the workings of a complex, adaptive society.

In complexity terms, dynamic systems are constantly evolving, not just in terms of individual species but in these species fine-tuning their interactions with other species, honing their ability to survive and evolve. This is not everyone working to the same end, but rather the phenomenon that 'collective adaptations to selfish ends produces the maximum average fitness' in Roger Lewin's terms (1993: 59). If we replace species by belief systems or religious classes, we can see how ideologies need to break down their exclusivity and isolation and co-evolve for their own fitness to the overall landscape. This in turn enhances overall system fitness. This is more than just interfaith dialogue and finding common ground, rather the possibility of change *within* a belief system. It is my contention that dynamic secularism best enables such co-evolution.

The term 'dynamic' refers primarily to secularism itself, how in governance terms this is not static but under constant scrutiny and challenge as new configurations and demographics emerge. In complexity terms, it is highly adaptable. Secular laws are constantly under revision. The dynamism of a secular society comes in fact from allowing – even encouraging – a diversity of religious and other belief systems, as these populate a rich landscape of possibility. This is equivalent to the diversity in the natural world which enables adaptation and survival. As I have argued, any locked-in feature of society represents a threat to that adaptation. Dynamic secularism (DS) does not close down religious or other debate; neither does it quarantine religious groups from participation in public life.

DS has certain requirements. Bhargava (2009) has ten features of a (value-based) secular state that at first sight map well onto my dynamic one. These include principles of being non-theocratic, of non-establishment of religion, and of promoting peace between communities. There should be no discrimination by the state on grounds of religion to entitlements provided by the state. Nor should there be discrimination in admission to educational institutions on grounds of religion. (I come back to this in the next chapter.) Religious liberty includes the freedom to embrace a religion other than the one into which a person is born, and to reject all religions. It also includes 'religious liberty to any one religious group' by which Bhargava means the liberty or indeed right of members of a religious group to criticize, revise, or challenge dominant interpretations of their religion. This perhaps starts to move into a more contentious realm, appearing to be state interference in religion. The final feature relates to active citizenship: no discrimination on grounds of religion in the right to vote, to deliberate on public matters or to stand for public office. Bhargava makes an interesting point on general freedom of speech: that it is entirely possible that a state permits *religious* liberty and equality but forbids other forms of freedom and equality:

> For instance, a person may challenge the authority of the religious
> head of his own denomination but not be free to challenge the

authority of the state. This is impossible in a secular state that is committed to a more general freedom and equality. Thus another critical value to which a secular state is constitutively linked is the quality of free citizenship.

(Bhargava, 2009: 92)

I like the idea that the notion of a secular state is not confined to dealing with religion but has positive and more general values of active citizenship. Secularism is necessary but not sufficient: the principles underlying state neutrality with regard to religion have of course to be applied to other possibilities of sectarianism and inequality.

Bhargava's feature of 'toleration' however might need more discussion. His definition is that the state does not persecute or allow the persecution of anyone on grounds of religion. As he admits, this may be seen by some to be superseded by the discourse of rights, but in certain contexts it has relevance. He gives the example that there are areas of society that remain beyond the reach of the legal regime of rights. Courts are ineffective when overburdened with claims (here his Indian context becomes apparent). Hence out-of-court settlements are encouraged. 'In the same way, it is sometimes better to waive one's rights and rely instead on a policy of live-and-let live. A secular state must have room for this' (Bhargava, 2009: 90). This would fit with a complex adaptive society where rights form both the judicial and the moral basis, but where adaptability and creativity sit on top of this framework. Yet a CAS might want to prescribe the limits of 'tolerance'. With secular goals of peace and doing no harm, then intolerance of harmful practices such as FGM or honour killings would be a precondition. I have concerns about the power questions of who decides that there should be a policy of live-and-let-live and when.

This leads to discussion of tolerance of religious symbols, currently a recurring question with regard to the headscarf, burka and niqab, but also to wearing the Christian cross. In the hard secularism of France and Turkey, religious symbols are to be banned. Yet in DS, everything can be permitted unless it does harm. Here ensues the debate that people may be 'offended' by a display of religion, or that women may be forced into bodily covering and that this therefore does them harm. The first does not stand up to scrutiny. The people who say they are offended by the sight of a burka do not always report being offended by the sight of a nun or a priest or of anyone in odd clothes that demarcate difference. Being offended is code for 'othering' – the underlying offence is that these people are not attempting to assimilate into 'our' society. It is right to have a debate about whether Sikhs can wear a turban instead of a crash helmet when riding a motorcycle, as that is a question of safety and public expense if they are hospitalized. Earlier the question of the inadvisability of full face coverings in teaching or at airport security was raised. But normally what people wear or display should be of no concern to a dynamic secular state. Making an issue of it simply leads to more tension and less integration. Whether Islamic dress is a sign of female oppression has to be a debate within Muslim communities, and not something to be legislated for by the state.

Other debates relate to individual freedoms. The National Secular Society in the UK campaigns for 'challenging religious privilege'. This includes the withdrawal of state subsidies to religious schools, the end of tax exemption for churches and to the public funding of chaplains in prisons, hospitals, and the armed services, as well as keeping religious influence out of health care, legislation, human rights and equality issues. It has been highly involved in the abolition of blasphemy laws and thus does good work in ensuring principles of freedom of expression. Perhaps a more contentious issue it campaigns about relates to the conscientious objections by doctors and pharmacists to administer certain procedures or treatments and their refusal to treat certain patients. Here we get to the core of what it might mean to 'respect' religious beliefs. A DS would accommodate all sorts of expressions, but ones in which patients are potentially harmed would not merit this accommodation.

It bears repeating that dynamic secularism is not just the soft version of tolerating absolutely everything, but a pragmatically principled one of minimizing harm. This relates to the mistakes made, or the misuse of the notion of respect. First, in the Conventions on Human Rights, religions do not have rights, people do. Therefore, one can criticize a religion without it being contrary to such conventions. Second, there is no right not to be offended. What is happening is the pressure by some religious groups to make it against the law to offend a religion. In his book *Objecting to God* (2011) Colin Howson reveals how in March 2009 the UN passed resolution 62/154 'Combating the Defamation of Religion', urging member states to limit by law any expression of opinion which is not respectful to religion(s). The resolution specifically seeks to protect Islam from criticism, but officially all religions are within its scope. What is happening is the elevation of religion above other sorts of opinion. It would still be legal to defame a political opinion or an economic opinion. Why should religion be elevated above these? As Howson points out, publication of his book would be illegal in any country which incorporated that resolution into its law. This is deeply disturbing. Religious adherents claim that they are personally offended or disrespected if a religion is criticized. But equally I could claim that I am offended if not just humanism but socialism or environmentalism or indeed anything that I 'believe' in is critiqued.

One task of education is to make people more resilient to offence; but also to express critiques in ways that do not personalize. The three levels must be distinguished: Marxism is rubbish; you are stupid because you are a Marxist; and a placard in a public place or a tweet on Twitter which urges death to all Marxists. The first is acceptable although it would need explaining; the second is not illegal but is hardly the way to go about things; and it is the third which might (rightly) come under a law of hate crime. What is happening is the conflation between the last type of statement or action and the other two. A CAS must allow the first two, albeit perhaps providing a learning environment for greater sophistication in expression.

Critics of secularism are correct when they focus on hard versions. Secularist interpretations can be as fundamentalist as religious ones – frozen, exclusionary, rigid. They are also utopian, in the vision of a sort of end time of a religion-free, or at least publicly religion-free, society. There seems to be the problem of constant vigilance in hard, radical versions. Froese asks, why did decades of re-education, propaganda, forced migration, industrialization and urbanization do so little to dispel the nineteenth-century identities of the Soviet public? His answer was 'perhaps the Communist party simply tried too hard' (Froese, 2008: 162). The forced promotion of scientific atheism kept religious ideas and symbols at the forefront of Soviet society. Similarly, banning the headscarf is, ironically, to say that this attire has huge meaning for *non-Muslims* outside its function as a head covering. As always, the motto should be a bit more of 'whateverism'. DS then does not try too hard. It does not keep religion in the forefront of its concerns. It acts only when religion bumps up against other ways of working, such as human rights.

DS has to address the question of belonging. In the context of talking about citizenship tests, Geoffrey Brahm Levey asks how liberal states might respond to the cultural diversity of their population. He asks 'do we need a new settlement or pact?' He then answers his own question, but points out how the notion of a 'settlement' is misleading: 'Our so-called religious settlements mostly are and always have been dynamic and evolving arrangements' (Levey, 2009: 20). This leads to the question of accommodation of religious practices. In one direction, in a CAS, it does no harm to accommodate things like prayer rooms in schools, halal meat, even the wearing of ceremonial swords. The number of national holidays is a little trickier – too many and business suffers. In the UK the current mix of official and unofficial holidays seems to work. Taxi firms in Birmingham are almost exclusively Muslim and

I just to have to accept that I will not get a taxi on Eid al-Fitr. But Levey points out how this accommodation now goes both ways. Some Australian Muslims have even begun to refer to themselves as 'Aussie Mossies'. He says that this is a good example of what Parekh means by 'neglected identities' being brought 'into creative interplay with the religious identity' and individuals being encouraged to freely define and relate them (Levey, 2009: 23). Australia has a specially designed hijab for Muslim policewomen, and the burka has been modified to meet Australian lifestyles, with a burkini now available to Muslim women training to become lifesavers. Levey refers to all this as 'interpretive diversity' – which is a great fit for complexity.

The other useful phrase to return to is 'principled pragmatism'. It is pragmatic insofar as it is responsive to contingency and changing needs; it is principled because exponents typically seek to show how new thinking respects what are taken to be foundational values. 'This flexibility is doubtless one of the reasons why liberalism has proved so resilient' (Levey, 2009: 24). But are there limits to accommodation? Should places such as France, Germany, and the UK adjust their legal codes to accommodate a religious tradition that was not a party to the original peace compacts, and that may not accept some of the limiting terms of modern liberalism? The complexity answer would be that it could change if that change was seen to have universal benefit. The issue would be that this aspect of a religious law was held to be better or more just than the existing one, not because it was divine but because it was practical. It would be in the interests of improvement and co-evolution, not in the interests of religious accommodation. As always, religious practice must not be elevated above other sorts of ethical or value systems, and has to argue its way alongside those.

Conclusion

To summarize briefly, the principles of a DS are, if not of keeping the space of power empty, then of not foreclosing it. In the optimum fitness landscape:

- a diversity of religious and other beliefs and lifestyle choices is seen as productive
- religious belief, religious membership and religious identity are not elevated or privileged above any other ethical system, cultural grouping, political movement or personal identity; religious organizations and members are subject to the same laws as everyone else
- there is freedom to hold a belief and to leave it, and to reject all religions
- there is freedom of religious expression (as long as this does not harm others)

- there is freedom to challenge religion: critiquing or satirizing a religion is seen as the same as critiquing or satirizing a political, economic, social or any other way of seeing the world, and is subject to the same, *but not more* constraints on doing harm
- there is no discrimination on the grounds of religion in citizenship rights, duties and activism
- religious schooling is permitted, but is not funded by the state; there are no tax exemptions for religious organizations as such
- religious associations are accepted, can lobby, and can be consulted, but there is no official recognition or representation in the machinery of governance; religions compete in the marketplace for influence with other vested interests
- accommodation to religious belief can occur if it does no harm to others, makes no difference, or is within the framework of existing legislation; tolerance of religious practice has to be within the framework of rights
- it is accepted that we have multiple, hybrid and recombinant identities, and the system supports connectivity across these in the overall landscape.

Chapter 4

Secular education: Control, values and learning

To most Christians, the Bible is like a software licence. Nobody actually reads it. They just scroll to the bottom and click 'I agree'.

Waleed Al-Husseini

This chapter moves on from the general discussion of secularism to explore how a dynamic secularism translates into the educational sphere. The exploration has three components: the relationship of state and school in terms of funding and control; the question of order in a non-religion-based school, that is, the underlying temporal value system; and the types of learning required for a complex, adaptive society. Dilemmas are acknowledged throughout: between the need for diversity yet not segregation; between rules or order and flexibility; the need for provisionality and yet not relativism. The chapter does not promote an ideal system – that would be an irony – but rather a set of workable compromises and adaptations.

State and school: Funding and control

As explained in the last chapter, in a dynamic secular state, religious organizations can and will play a part in public life – it is just that the state does not bankroll them to do so. The logic is that the state does not fund what in the West are termed 'faith schools'. Historically the UK, a supposedly secular country, has got itself into a mire because the history of state funding of Church of England and Catholic schools has led the state to have to start funding Muslim or even creationist schools as a sign of equity. No government would have the courage to withdraw funding from church schools, to nationalize them. So in the UK it is a question of damage limitation, rather than calls for sweeping change in state–church relationships.

Turkey, with its renowned secular governance, also has historical complexities. In the 1920s all madrassas were closed down and all courses concerning religion removed from the school curriculum, in the interests of national unity. After the military coup in 1980 mandatory religious education was introduced into secondary schools, albeit with the aim to strengthen Ataturkism, national unity, and human love from a religious and ethical perspective. But religious education in Turkey continues to be open to two opposing forms of criticism – it is seen either to undermine the secular principle in state education or, insofar as it is taught for non-religious reasons, it is not religious enough (Huddleston, 2012). The religious–secular fault line runs through other areas of educational policy, such as the funding of *imam hatip* (vocational religious schools) and introducing optional Islamic classes in other schools. The underpinning idea of a dominant religion remains: civic education is still defined in terms of a single 'culture'. Muhammad is described as 'our prophet' and there are no references in civics textbooks to non-Turkish and non-Muslim groups living in Turkey. Discussion of the Kurdish question is forbidden for teachers as well as journalists.

The two examples of the UK and Turkey are given to show how so-called secular education systems are only partially so, but also how the funding of Muslim education might be introduced for different reasons – one in the interests of multiculturalism and one to promote national unity and the idea of a monoculture. This chapter argues that both are dangerous for security, but it takes almost the opposite line when it discusses religious schools in countries such as Afghanistan and Pakistan. Here, religious education is deeply rooted in security and one might argue for *more* government involvement, not less.

In *Educating Against Extremism* (Davies, 2008) I outlined 12 arguments against faith schools in a plural society. This was particularly in the context of extremism, but has equal relevance for general security. Without repeating all the detail of the arguments, and collapsing some, the six main types of objection were (and remain for these contexts):

1. *The danger of isolation*: that students of one faith rarely meet or interact with other faith groups, and rely on interpretations of them from the media or parents. Even some faith leaders are worried about the increase in racism and religious bigotry that is evidenced in segregated systems. A key problem is the lack of opportunity for face-to-face dialogue with others with whom one might disagree.

2. *Amplified segregation*: that other forms of segregation (such as social class or ethnicity) were compounded in the choice and allocation to schools; the challenge to gender inequality and to the socialization of young people into fixed gender roles was less in evidence in some faith schools.

3. *Promoting superiority*: that religious schools provide students with the disposition to favour those who share their faith. Both the faith and the people who believe in it are implicitly seen as better than others – otherwise there would be no need for division. Parents were encouraged to choose separation and the elevation of their religion over others.

4. *Locking in cultural identity*: that there was the early labelling of children with the religious ascription of their parents (in a way we would not dream of doing for, say, a parental orientation to atheism or Marxism or fascism). This relates to 'imagining community', when a religion is seen as the most important, or sole, aspect of a community, when it may be hybrid and changing, as are people's identities. This also means problems of exit – do faith schools give the opportunity to leave the faith? This may be a particular issue for fundamentalist religious sects.

5. *Compromising autonomy in thinking*: that there are problems of critical reflection when told of absolute truths and when mistakes made in the name of religion are not addressed.

6. *The misuse of taxpayers' money*: that it is tyrannical to take tax funds from one believer in order to advance the beliefs of another. If the government decided to fund all religious schools, this would have to include intelligent design, Mormon schools and Wicca groups. If not, it would have to take the intolerable step of nominating state-approved religions.

Five years on, the same issues are there. Many faith schools in the UK are granted exemptions from the equality legislation which stipulates that schools cannot discriminate against pupils because of their religion or belief. When voluntary-aided faith schools and religious academies are oversubscribed, they are permitted to use religious criteria to give priority in admissions to children, or children of parents, who practise a particular religion. Recent research supports the National Secular Society claims of discrimination in faith schools based on selection of pupils from wealthier families. Religious schools in the UK take in 10 per cent fewer poor pupils than are representative of the local area (National Secular Society, 2010). In the Netherlands, the plurality of educational options both facilitates and maintains high levels of segregation. The proportion of school segregation, even in mixed neighbourhoods, is the highest in the industrialized world (Merry and Karsten, 2011). These are not insuperable problems, but they certainly lead us to question whether, in a plural society which hopes for adaptation and survival, we can afford to take these risks.

These arguments were made in the context of a religiously and ethnically diverse society. Do they hold in an almost monotheistic society where the vast majority are of one religion? Do they hold in a country where the state cannot afford to educate all its citizens? The stance from DS is that there would be differences in the survival issues across countries and that one cannot make global assertions. In Afghanistan, state schooling *is* religious schooling. In fact, in order to persuade the Taliban to permit schools, they have to appear even more religious than they are. The Ministry of Education approach is pragmatic and flexible. It chooses an adaptive strategy in cooperating with the Taliban and other insurgents who *de facto* control large parts of the country. A Ministry of Education spokesman reported that if it is necessary to call a teacher a 'mullah' or a school a 'madrassa' then the MoE will do so, as long as education provision is maintained (Sigsgaard, 2011). Here, the aims are modest – not an education that is necessarily transformative, but one that is conflict-sensitive and resilient and that at least does not exacerbate conflict, nor trigger attacks on schools. These are also the conclusions from a report for the International Network for Education in Emergencies (INEE) Working Group on Education and Fragility (Davies, 2011).

The question of madrassas is very complex. This book cannot go into the many spellings and distinctions between types of madrassa. The actual translation is 'school', but madrassas are generally dedicated to teaching an Islamic curriculum, sometimes for the purpose of preparing religious scholars or *ulama*, and preserving Muslim culture and traditional forms of knowledge. Madrassas in countries such as Pakistan, Afghanistan and Indonesia are frequently cited as being incubators of terrorism where students are directly trained to hate the West and to use weapons in holy, militant war – and they are also portrayed as the predominant type of education in the region. The truth is very different. Closer and more evidence-based research on numbers attending and the types of activity paints a different picture. For most in Pakistan, secular subjects have been integrated, and the 'jihad' (literally 'struggle') is to work out an acceptable and indigenous form of Muslim modernity (Berkey, 2007: 55). This is not to say that madrassas are all successfully educating Pakistani children, but that other institutions may be equally unsuccessful in the move towards global co-existence. The issue may be more that most schools in Pakistan – madrassa, state or private – are authoritarian and do not engage in the critical thinking needed to challenge violent radicalization or misinterpretations of the Quran.

In looking at state–madrassa relationships, then, the first question is whether they are really terrorist havens and need to be controlled. Media hype and over-generalization about madrassas is problematic, and may add to problems of hostility to the West. There is much literature showing that Osama Bin Laden and other terrorists did not attend madrassas, with their ideology coming from elsewhere (see Bergen and Pandey, 2006). Only in Bali did madrassas play a role, yet even here the madrassa graduates teamed up with better-educated counterparts to execute the attacks. An interesting point is that 'Masterminding a large-scale attack thus requires technical skills beyond those provided by a madrassa education' (Bergen and Pandey, 2006: 123). In looking at Jemaah Islamiyah (JI) (from which a militant minority were responsible for the attacks in Southeast Asia in 2000–2005), Magouirk, Atran and Sageman (2008) state that there is no evidence that madrassas in general produce terrorists although a small segment in Indonesia and Malaysia are linked with participation in JI terrorist attacks. The key is translation of attitudes to actions.

For Pakistan, Rahman (2008) shows that pupils in madrassas have a significantly greater propensity to militant attitudes than their colleagues in state and private schools. However, his study does not prove unequivocally that madrassas produce intolerant young people or identify whether parents choose madrassas for their children because madrassas convey a world view that is similar to their own. Both are possible. Winthrop and Graff (2010) say that madrassas in Pakistan are not the principal reason for a rise in militancy. Their popularity is more a question of the government being unable to meet the high demand for education – filled both by private schools and madrassas. Jeffrey *et al.* (2008) similarly say that the reasons for parents choosing madrassa education for their children, and for students valuing this form of schooling, do not in general relate to preparation for jihad. Sometimes it is that madrassas offer food and board for poor families. Muslim men in Uttar Pradesh found that even if it did not give them access to work, it offered access to a meaningful masculine religious life. It is not clear whether this would work for females too: while this education did not prepare them for employment, they did expect to marry a man with at least as high a level of education as themselves.

Consequently the secularism/security question in such contexts does not relate so much to pluralism or even extremism, but to employability as a source of stability. The link between frustration about being unemployed and being susceptible to ethnic mobilizers has often been proposed (Collier, 2009), with arguments that economic growth and youth employment should be the target for policy. An interesting initiative in Bangladesh has been the way Islamic banks specifically recruit employees from madrassas, looking to integrate their graduates into the mainstream. They are provided with on-the-job training to fill gaps in their education. The idea is to build up the lure of more moderate madrassas whose graduates go on to get jobs. The banks also benefit, as the graduates are studious and have a good understanding of Islam (Singer, 2001).

Analysing Muslim 'educational backwardness' in India, Ahmad (2012) makes a strong case for trying to overcome the 'chasm' between secular education and religious instruction. He is doubtful about a full education in madrassas, not because they are a site of extremism, nor because he does not believe in their value base, but because they do not prepare for jobs in the modern economy and so foster the advancement of Muslims. He makes an interesting comparison:

> Islamic education is based on a myth of unity and strength derivable from the notion of brotherhood or Islam as well as a belief in cultural superiority, and Islamic schools are a symbol of this myth. On the other hand, secular education is based on the myth of modernity, nationalism, change, progress and 'success' for the meritorious individual. Islamic schools seek as cultural symbols to buttress Muslims' sense of unity and superiority but put them at a distinctive economic disadvantage by foreclosing the children's options for social mobility. Secular schools equip them for greater participation in a competitive society but erode the myths upon which Islamic education is founded.

> (Ahmad, 2012: 142)

Ahmad points out that he is using the term 'myth' in an anthropological sense, not as being necessarily false. Yet the clash of 'myths' is the key issue, regardless of their foundation. Interestingly, Ahmad argues for a solution based in the community, with the community organizing its own secular institutions where secular education is carried out side by side with religious education. I return to the role of community in later chapters.

As with madrassas, one should not see all faith-based schools as successfully indoctrinatory. We saw in Chapter 2 that Amy Stambach's *Faith in Schools* (2010) showed the evangelicals in Africa trying to convert Muslims and declare Jesus to be their saviour but finding Muslims 'especially resistant to Christian penetration'. Much of the evangelicals' language was confrontational and aggressive: they were 'preparing the students for Christian battle'. When converting one Muslim boy they appeared less bothered about how he might be beaten by his family than exultant that they had scored another victory for Jesus. Financial support for missionary work from the US had increased to more than $3.8 billion. Religion is a major American export to the world, just as it had been in the British Empire. Yet what Stambach found was not brainwashing but creative accommodation by the recipients. Africans objected to their beliefs being seen as superstitious. National leaders would appropriate the successes of non-state organizations in providing social and educational services. People fled to churches in Kenya not because of shifts of belief but because they provided scholarships and paid salaries. Bible colleges survived by becoming vocational training schools, and internet programmes were added in Uganda. (Similarly I have a photograph of a building in Botswana with the sign 'Assemblies of God Commercial School'.) What emerges is an ambiguous domain of merging ideas of social and spiritual salvation, of rescuing people from welfare and teaching them marketable skills.

Afghanistan provides a classic example of how one cannot make sweeping generalizations about religious or secular education, or about education reform. Rüdiger Blumör (2012) has provided a highly nuanced analysis of this, and of the Taliban position on education. There is a long tradition of religious education in Afghanistan, and it would be a mistake to describe madrassas as 'medieval outposts'. Afghan madrassas are part of a transnational network, with connections in countries like Iran and Pakistan, and much travel in between, even if this is not politicized. Any attempt on the part of the Afghan government to reform religious education often encounters difficulties on account of these personal relationships and informal links. Religious education at state schools fulfils various functions – teaching children the basic laws and doctrines of Islam, training *mullahs* (clerics with no higher religious education), the religious scholars (*ulema*) and legal scholars. While Islamic educational institutions provide free education and in some cases free board and lodging, contrary to common perception poverty and a lack of alternative opportunities are not the only reasons for families to send their children there. Many prosperous families also opt for a madrassa because they seek a religious education and madrassas represent a value in themselves (Borchgrevink, 2010). Religious education generally is held in high esteem, reflecting a desire for morality in public life and a just and fair government. People are suspicious if they think that education reform is just about curbing radical and militant extremism. Blumör discusses how this creates a problem for development cooperation, which is hesitant (as I would have been) about the idea that religion should play such a dominant role in education:

> For from our own historic experience the dominance of religious education belongs to a stage of social development now considered obsolete. Presumably for these reasons, religious education – if observed at all – has been marginalised by organisations involved in promoting education. Such organisations, both in Afghanistan and elsewhere, will have to grapple more intensively with religious education if they are to achieve sustainable outcomes. So will education promotion perhaps be forced to depart from the familiar model of secularisation? The new model of reformed Islamism

could embrace secular education and at the same time offer an alternative to the radical fundamentalist theology of the Taliban.

(Blumör, 2012: 13)

This is a key point, and the notion of a reformed Islamism 'embracing' secular education and challenging fundamentalism is indeed a way forward.

The position of Al-Azhar in Egypt is another example of the extreme complexity of state–religion relations. The thousand-year-old Al-Azhar is the foremost religious institution in Egypt – part mosque, part university, part centre of religious research and knowledge (Brown, 2011). It is now a state entity which runs large and dispersed parts of the religious and educational apparatus of the country. In addition to higher education, a national network of schools is overseen by the institution. With something like two million students, it teaches students a combination of a secular and religious curriculum. It is selective and gender-segregated. It plays a key role in cultural censorship, depicting publications as offensive to the teachings of Islam. But there is currently debate about the role of Al-Azhar in politics and whether it should be more independent of the state. Morsy (2013) argues that Al-Azhar should fight for its autonomy – but stay out of politics.

As Brown discloses, defining the relationship between religion and state has become central to the struggle over Egypt's political transformation. This is not just about greater freedom and democracy. Religion is a part of the educational curriculum and broadcasting. Many mosques in the country are state-owned and managed through the Ministry of Religious Affairs. Nobody in Egypt is arguing for a separation of religion and state. The dispute is over the terms and ways in which they will interact. For commentators such as Brown, the most likely outcome of this post-revolutionary struggle is a religiously influenced state, but not an Iranian-style theocracy. The current situation embraces the electoral strength of Islamists, a growing public presence of Salafis, and the legalization of the Muslim Brotherhood's political party. Al-Azhar's prestige makes for a complex and ambivalent relationship with the Islamist movements in the country – there are links with the Brotherhood but also a competitive element. So should Al-Azhar confine itself to a theological role, take a more political role against Islamist tendencies, or take on an administrative role over other religious institutions?

The real issues are who controls the institution and what the institution controls. Two extremes – a secularist divorce between religion and state and an Iranian system of clerical rule – are not really on the table. But that leaves a vast variety of alternatives in

> between … If al-Azhar is indeed more autonomous, it might be
> able to play a stronger and more demanding role in national life.
>
> (Brown, 2011: 16)

The Al-Azhar example is classic in terms of how religion is seen in politics and the mechanisms by which it has influence. In the previous chapter we saw Modood (2009) arguing for greater recognition and representation. But it may be a question of 'be careful what you wish for'. Morsy (2013) comments on how Al-Azhar has received praise for convening and consulting with diverse groups of Egyptians in ways that the government failed to do, but this praise effectively places unwarranted approval on Al-Azhar playing a political role it should avoid. Funding seems to be a double-edged sword. The government maintains control over the institution's finances by way of the Ministry of Religious Endowments. The state also reserves the right to provide 'sufficient funds for al-Azhar to achieve its goals' – leaving the door open for continued state influence and even coercion.

This section cannot tour round the world identifying each state's degree of distance between it and religion in terms of schooling but it uses the above examples to show the complexity of the situation. One key is conflict-sensitivity: where provision of a religious education on balance amplifies segregation, mistrust and lock-in, or where religious education is used deliberately for indoctrination into violence or subordination, there are arguments for state intervention in terms of regulation and scrutiny, whether the schools were private or state funded. If schools funded by religious organizations did no harm and rather provided services and security that the state could not, there is little reason to challenge them. If there were to be any state support or partnership it would be not because schools were religious and had some sort of inbuilt right, but because they were valuable for both personal and national security and did not promote values at odds with principles of inclusion or equity or freedom of expression.

So a combined secular and complexity approach to the relationship between the state and religious schools looks closely at context. Put baldly, in a multifaith, developed context, separated faith schools are an anachronism and likely to lead to greater segregation and division. In a context of poverty and inadequate government resources, schools funded by local or international religious organizations might give opportunities for learning otherwise denied to children. It might well be that having a religious orientation is the only way that such schools will survive. They might actually provide a bulwark against extremism, especially when religion is deeply embedded in the community. The point is that their work should be evaluated as would that of secular organizations: were they non-discriminatory and gender equitable, did they not foment hatred or violence, and did they provide economic or personal security for their students and thence their communities?

Rules and order

As explained in Chapter 1, a complex adaptive system has two levels of operation: a basic organization and then the enabling conditions for change, and creativity, and new connectivities. The basic organization is a set of rules by which a system operates. Religions do have their own rules – that is one of their main functions; our question is about the rules in a secular institution. In educational terms, this means some sort of ethical code, whereby a reasoned and relatively consistent set of rules enables participants to connect and act. As Steven Pinker (2002) points out, even the most atheistic scientists do not advocate callous amorality. The brain may be a physical system made of ordinary matter, but that matter is organized in such a way as to give rise to sentient organisms with a capacity to feel pleasure and pain. And that in turn sets the stage for the emergence of morality and for establishing a moral code, even if the price is having to adhere to it oneself (e.g. paying taxes). Belief in any afterlife goes both ways. Would life lose its purpose if we ceased to exist when our brains died?

> On the contrary, nothing invests life with more meaning than the realization that every moment of sentience is a precious gift. How many fights have been averted, how many friendships renewed, how many hours not squandered, how many gestures of affection offered, because we sometimes remind ourselves that 'life is short'?
>
> (Pinker, 2002: 190)

For a secular education in a plural society, clearly one particular set of religious precepts cannot be chosen or privileged. Instead a cross-cutting, more universal system is needed for our short lives, and the winning system is that of rights. As with secularism, there are misunderstandings over the implications of this, and admittedly some challenges. An education based in rights is distinctive in many ways. The first relates to the inherent nature of rights. All have rights, just by virtue of being human. These are not earned; they are not a gift from someone; and they cannot be taken away, except in extreme circumstances, or when the exercise of a particular right would harm the rights of others. This has two key implications for education:

- Vertical equity: all members of the school community have the same or at least parallel rights in a large number of relevant areas. Both adults and children have rights. Children are not the possessions of their parents or of the state, neither are they people in the making.

- Horizontal inclusiveness: a rights-based approach can incorporate all faiths and value systems. While the ethics attached to rights may have their roots in different religions, they were identified in the conventions as a universal, religiously neutral system which all countries of the world have accepted in theory, if not in practice. They are a supra-national code.

The codification of rights as represented in all the different conventions that have been written since then go back much further, to Thomas Paine's *The Rights of Man* in 1791 and the Declaration of the Rights of Man and of the Citizen by the National Assembly of France which preceded his book. There are African and Islamic statements on rights. As said, the ethical base to rights has its roots in, or parallels with, many religious precepts or cultural traditions. The argument that rights are a recent Western invention does not hold up.

The implications of both equity and inclusiveness can be contentious for education. Do children have the same rights as teachers? The formulation of the Universal Convention on the Rights of the Child (UNCRC) was an important and necessary breakthrough in extending rights to children and hence school students, but can imply that there are different sets of rights for adults and children. In fact, the UNCRC has the same base, but provides additional safeguards. The key binding principle is the recognition of individual human dignity whereby both teachers and students have equal rights to dignity and should treat each other accordingly (Osler and Starkey, 1996).

Further, dignity is arguably more than just reciprocity of treatment; it tackles self-worth, self-respect and 'face' as well as living conditions. It would translate differently in different languages (which is one of the issues in universality of rights), but it is probable that all cultures have a related concept. Children's right to dignity and respect is, I maintain, preferable to some religious notions of unquestioning obedience to parents and authority. While there are differences between the Universal Declaration of Human Rights (UDHR) and the UNCRC with regard to responsibilities and also differences linked to age categorizations regarding voting or marriage, there are nonetheless many key equivalences. They include the right to life, right to a nationality, right to liberty and the right to education. They also include a prohibition on torture, and cruel or degrading treatment; non-discrimination;

freedom of opinion and expression; freedom of thought, conscience and religion; freedom of association; and an adequate standard of living.

Additional rights for children include the well-known Article 12: the child's right to express an opinion and to have that opinion taken into account in any matter or procedure affecting that child. Others relate to rights to protection, for example with regard to adoption, and to children in special categories: refugee children, children with disabilities, and children without families. One interesting right which appears only in the UNCRC is Article 17: 'Access to appropriate information' (the role of the media in disseminating information to children that is consistent with moral well-being and knowledge and understanding among peoples and which respects the child's cultural background). The state has to protect children from harmful materials. Yet there is also an important implication about access to information in order for children to make informed choices. These questions of expressing an opinion and access to information are pivotal in a complex adaptive system, as developed below.

The differences between the UDHR and UNCRC lead to interesting questions of responsibility. Some of the articles of the UNCRC talk of 'the State's responsibility' to ensure a right. Are teachers and schools agents of the state in this regard? Or are they themselves subject to the state, as in Article 19, 'the State's obligation to protect children from all forms of maltreatment perpetrated by parents and others responsible for their care'? Other articles do not mention the state, and it is in fact these where the school will be part of the enactment of that right – such as freedom of expression or association, and of course the right to education. Religions tend to talk more of their adherents' duties – to God, and to others – and can complement rights. But it is clear that religions on their own cannot ensure rights, and that this is the task of the state and of its institutions.

There is an important distinction between a rights-based approach and a needs-based approach. By identifying what children are seen to lack the latter can act as a deficit model which casts children as victims in need of some treatment or intervention. A rights-based approach in contrast sets out the rights which all children have and places a permanent duty on those in power to ensure those rights are the norm, not specially provided only when a need is identified or resources are available. As has been pointed out with regard to minority groups such as the Roma, a rights-based approach is *not* a charity (Davies, 2012b).

Cultural rights are a trickier matter. There are huge debates about cultural or minority priorities as against national legislation or school rules. Concerning issues of dress, for example, as discussed in the last chapter, the relevant right is freedom of religious expression. The question for schools is whether the right to education supersedes this, that is, whether cultural or religious dress codes for teachers or students can be held to hinder learning and are therefore a lower priority.

This leads to the final area of distinction between rights and religious codes. Rights do not provide a blueprint for all actions, and are not a list of commandments. There can be absolute rights (such as freedom from torture) but there are also qualified or limited rights, such as freedom of expression, or the right to privacy in the home, where other rights (for example, to freedom from abuse) might be seen to take precedence. Rights provide a solid framework for debate, but not always definitive answers to every question. This is both their beauty and their challenge. Rights can be subject to critique in ways that are less easy or comfortable than a critique of religious precepts from within a religion, as the origin of rights, as enshrined in conventions, is secular or man-made rather than divine.

Rights provide a dynamic and participatory way of considering social justice, behaviour and actions. Just as rights apply to all, everyone can take part in considering their relevance to contemporary, immediate contexts. This does not have to be left to scholars. Rights constitute an ethical system as much as religions do. But they are not a belief system, and that is the crucial difference. They are based on entitlements, not on commandments. While they have a historical base, they can be put into context more easily than sacred texts written in a particular location for that time, which then have to be reinterpreted – or efforts made to maintain them. Rights occupy ground that neither religion nor science can, since science (as argued earlier) does not have a particular morality. Rights circumvent the problem of 'tolerance'. They provide a framework on what *not* to tolerate. This is particularly important in questions of human security – for example FGM.

Various aspects of security emerge here. First is personal security. The almost mind-blowing realization that one has rights regardless of ability or background or previous record is immensely powerful for a child. The right to learn and the right to respect and dignity promote a feeling of self-respect and confidence, crucial to being an active learner. In a study of the qualities that children value in a teacher, Hopkins (2010) found that 'a teacher that respects you' was top of the list, followed by positive praise, and knowing how to improve. Targets were much more valued than prizes. The implication is the need to identify what every child in the school can experience and benefit from. Rights are not competitive; there are no losers in rights.

For school security, rights promote greater mutuality and discipline. Research on schools that have adopted a rights-based approach finds that the 'contagion' effect (Covell and Howe, 2005) of learning about one's own rights results in support for the rights of others – regardless of age, ethnicity, disability and so on. The 'power distance' between teachers and taught decreases, and politeness evinces politeness in both directions (Sebba and Robinson, 2010). 'There used to be a lot of screaming and shouting when I first came to the school, but now people talk to each other.' The recognition that teachers have rights improves the quality of their own experience. It is not just children who have rights, and the forging of a rights-respecting school or rights-based culture should not be an additional burden for teachers. Adults may have some additional responsibilities, for example in safeguarding, but these would be part of a teacher's duty of care anyway. It has to be stressed that teachers have no more rights than children. The right to education may imply a 'right to learn' but there is no 'right to teach' in the conventions. Yet teachers do have the right to dignity, and to freedom of thought and expression, which impacts both on the way that students should treat them and also on how they, as teachers, participate in a school democracy. This includes the way they are treated by management, by colleagues, and by parents. Covell and Howe (2005) also report teachers feeling 'empowered', feeling that teaching rights and respect was a 'morale-boosting' experience. It reminded them of why they went into teaching. One aspect of security, then, is that they are more likely to stay.

The right to a voice links closely to a complex adaptive system. Avenues for voice can be formal structures, such as school councils, class councils, or school parliaments or they can be mechanisms whereby students routinely give feedback to teachers on their teaching, participate in decisions on teaching styles or future curriculum developments, engage in self-assessment of learning, or take part in audits of the school on their adherence to rights. Attention at the same time to the right to information means the need for both *informed* choice or informed participation and for feedback on what happens to opinions, views and suggestions which are expressed at various levels and in various contexts. Feedback *down* a chain of representative democracy is equally important to the initial expression of opinion. Lundy (2007) writes from a legal perspective to draw attention to the need to consider space, voice, audience and influence in facilitating Article 12, with the final question of influence, i.e. that the voice is acted upon, being equally important to the first three. The right to express a view is often enshrined in activities such as being involved in the appointment of teachers or head teachers, or in participating in induction days for new teachers. Teachers report being impressed by the 'professionality' of students in undertaking this task (Yamashita and Davies, 2010). Another study found that students giving feedback on teaching learned to talk in 'observation mode', finding the appropriate register (Davies *et al.,* 2011).

Security from harm derives from the mix of Article 12 on voice and Article 27 on cruel treatment, implying a collaborative drawing up of codes of conduct based on rights. These are more life-long and more reflective of the adult world than those confined to school rules, which can seem arbitrary and juvenile, and they include everyone – students, teachers, support staff and parents. A key benchmark is whether someone's behaviour disrupts another's right to learn. The counterpart to this, difficult for some schools, is that if something is irrelevant to learning (such as hair length or a headscarf) is a rule about this required? Instead, the discussion is around rights-based sanctions: for example, if someone's rights have been violated, how they can be restored in a rights-related way? A restorative programme might directly work with the designated victim; or it can mean the offender doing something to enhance the rights of others (for instance building a community playground so that children have the right to play, or working with old people to help maintain their right to dignity). But in a rights-based school, each day is a fresh day, in that behaviour is dealt with as it relates to rights, on that day, ideally without reference to previous infringements. Children are not ascribed permanent behavioural identities, and thus avoid labelling. A rights base means a positive slant on rules and powers: a 'no running' rule is seen to derive from the right to safety, not from some desire to inhibit childish energy. The school's legal powers to search pupils for weapons or drugs can be seen as in the child's best interests, as, again, being about safety. Knowledge of rights by all parties enables discussion about the equal right to be treated with dignity or about the right to privacy, and how to enact the powers that teachers have legally in ways that minimize harm to other rights.

Rights also give a safe space for discussion, a language and vocabulary to talk about difficult things. Teachers will comment on how they have a set of concepts they can articulate. They can talk about diversity with less embarrassment for minority children in the classroom because of the focus on rights. A Catholic school reported that the rights respecting work had given them the opportunity to be open to different perspectives, not just that of the church. One teacher said that rights were a 'peg to hang things on', that the school could discuss difficult issues such as abortion under this framework, which they could not do before (Sebba and Robinson, 2010).

A fully rights-based education is not just about learning the international texts and the legal basis to rights, but also about experiencing critical pedagogy and 'the law in action' (Reynaert *et al.,* 2010b). A right to learn also covers content and the entitlement to particular aspects of the curriculum, again with important implications for security. The right to health and safety sometimes means placing the child first rather than parents or religious leaders. In the UK, the Children, Schools and Families Bill rescinds the 'right' of parents to remove children from sex education once they have reached 15, although this is still being challenged. Similarly, the right to safety can be used to press for Muslim girls to learn to swim, as mentioned in Chapter 2 in the context of tsunami-affected countries.

Articles 12 and 13 also imply the right to investigate one's situation, and therefore the need to develop research skills. Lolichen (2010) gives a useful account of children researching the local community in India – including how they worked through concerns about the rights of that community and the ethics of research, including the impact of dissemination. More broadly, global citizenship education includes the realization that rights are universal – and this immediately implies a geo-political education about countries where rights might not be upheld because of poverty, conflict or an inhumane government. A relatively critical approach is required, however, so that it is not just transferring Western ideas to other contexts. Play, and what is required for this play, might be seen as a very Western concept. Are toys the priority post-conflict or disaster, or are food, shelter and education? An important part of citizenship and global citizenship is developing the skills of advocacy, and orientations to try to do something, however small, about the rights of others. Global citizenship is not just about fundraising and empathy for the poor, but about the challenge to social injustice. This entails developing knowledge of international law, and the skills of running campaigns.

At the local level there is the concern about community cohesion. The respect for the right of religious belief and thought is relevant here, together with the realization that freedom of expression is not an absolute right and needs to be treated with care. Yet, as has been found in Northern Ireland, the rights base provides a safe platform to start discussions and help children overcome prejudices and sectarianism (NAHT, 2010). It is held that there can be parental resistance to rights, but that this is not insuperable: an interesting project in Afghanistan by Save the Children developed booklets for parents in Farsi and Pashtun which showed that the concept of rights could be found in various passages in the Quran; parents could then understand the right of girls to education. The booklets were enthusiastically received and made an impact on the attitudes of families (Interview, Save the Children Kabul, November 2012).

Snags with a rights base

It would be foolish and not in the spirit of this book to present rights as a utopian vision of a perfect secular state. A number of problems emerge with the language and concepts around rights in education, sometimes because of a misconstruing of what they imply.

First is the juxtaposition of rights and responsibility. It is often said that there are no rights without responsibility, or that rights imply duties. Yet children's rights are not contingent or conditional on the exercise of responsibility. Children do not have to earn the right to education. We are not directly or even indirectly responsible for the *enactment* of others' rights. What we can do is *respect* others' rights. This does not guarantee their enactment, but at least does no further harm. The notion of responsibility can nonetheless be useful in denoting mutuality in rights (addressing the fear by parents or authorities that it is just about according rights), and in establishing boundaries. One Year 6 class contract in a UK secondary school stipulated that: 'we have a right to have a laugh but a responsibility to know when enough is enough' (NAHT, 2010). I doubt whether the right to have a laugh is codified in the UNCRC, but the message is clear: behaviour is usefully seen as a mutual responsibility, not emanating from the fear of punishment or from adult-generated rules.

The bracketing of rights with responsibility can also have its pitfalls: the teacher might state that they have the responsibility to punish children, which can then be seen as the *right* to punish them – which is not in the conventions. A teacher might claim that because children have not exercised their responsibility sufficiently, they can lose their right to play or to keep hold of their mobile phones.

The notion of respect itself has considerable risks and dangers, and this is where knowledge of rights wording is useful. People have a right to their religious convictions. We should respect that right. But we do not need to respect *actions* that infringe others' rights which are done in the name of religious belief. It is often said therefore that we should respect people, not their actions. This is difficult and sometimes impossible: I cannot bring myself to respect a murderer, or a rapist, or an inciter of racial hatred, or a member of a government who commits human rights violations. The actions of people *become* those people. It is disingenuous to say that we can somehow differentiate between them. All we can do is respect certain rights they have – so that regardless of what they have done, they have a right to life, or to freedom from torture, or to a fair trial. 'Respect' is often used in a woolly or unhelpful fashion. One cannot 'respect diversity' – this would imply we should respect all diverse forms of human behaviour – including criminality, torture and discrimination itself. Respecting diversity is a shorthand, but it is a dangerous one, implying cultural relativism and making little distinction between what we do and do not respect.

We should be warned that the language of rights can be twisted in the interests of control. The Alan Steer report on raising standards of behaviour and discipline in schools refers to the fact that poor behaviour cannot be tolerated, because it is a 'denial of the right of pupils to learn and teachers to teach'. It also states that 'respect has to be given in order to be received' (DCSF, 2005: 2). This official line can in some ways be used to support a rights-based approach, but equally it shows a misunderstanding of rights. Teachers do not have a right to teach. And the according of respect is not a precondition for receiving it. The report suggests: 'In secondary schools this [classroom management] could include: all pupils being greeted by the door, brought into the classroom, stood behind their chairs, formally welcomed, asked to sit and the teacher explaining the purpose of the lesson' (DCSF, 2005: 18). This could be seen perhaps as the teacher being respectful; but it could equally be seen as authoritarian, and not based on children's own understandings of the need for mature and sensible ways to enter a room and facilitate a lesson to begin. Rights enable children to manage their own behaviour. This is not fully understood by the Steer Commission.

A further problem is that rights and empowerment can get confused. The work of Michael Gallagher demonstrates that power is not something that children possess or do not possess, or which can be 'transferred' from teachers to students, but is something that is messy, fluid, dynamic, negotiated and contextual (Gallagher, 2008). Adults need to recognize the inherent, sometimes spontaneous power in the popular, networked and viral everyday settings that children are currently constructing and reconstructing. It could be that the ways we currently conceive of giving children power (school councils etc.) do not match the way they currently network and use social media to influence others. Rights do give children confidence to speak out, to be empowered to disclose how they are treated. In theory the school has to follow this information up. Yet pupils can feel disempowered if they realize their rights are not met outside school and that they cannot change the situation. While an awareness of rights may, for example, enable children to challenge corporal punishment in the home, this may not be effective and may act to alienate parents from school rather than support it (Reyneart *et al.*, 2010a).

Participation rights can present another conundrum – do children have the right *not* to participate, not to enthusiastically join in the discussion and all the things we think so crucial in learner-centred education? The agenda for children's citizenship involves more than just participation. Neither is it just a few high-profile one-off events, such as appearing at the G20. Instead, the exercise of civil rights might mean taking part in auditing government services and review of policies. Here the community level is better than the national level; public decision-making routinely informed by children's views is better than high-profile events (Theis, 2010). Decisions also need to be made in schools about rights to demonstrate: when children and young people engage in anti-war protests they can be labelled as truants or deviants and punished, rather than seen as active citizens (Davies, Harber, and Yamashita, 2004).

Rights may challenge vested power interests. Bhatterai (2010) raises the question of the children's clubs in Nepal which are promoting among other things the issue of child rights, particularly in the area of corporal punishment and violence against children. This is very successful – teachers are referring behaviour to the clubs or, when teachers are involved in actions that are against the rights of children, the club holds a dialogue with them. Members of the clubs have counselled children who were afraid to come to school for fear of punishment after they made a childish mistake. This peer-to-peer communication is very effective. Yet there is a debate about the merit of the clubs. First, they are seen to be functioning like trade unions and the moral authority of the teacher is seen to have no meaning. Second, it is thought that it is too much to expect of children; they should be studying. And time spent on advocacy work is arguably especially inappropriate for poor children who have to contribute to the family's livelihood. Third, there are concerns that teachers are only going along with the initiative because it comes from aid agencies; when these withdraw, teachers will be as oblivious to children's rights as before. While the UK research reveals no school that has abandoned a rights-respecting approach once begun, this may not be true of other contexts, or where rights are less embedded.

This relates to the difference between a rights-based schooling which infuses the whole institution and what can be a separate subject of human rights education (HRE). Spajic-Vrkas (2012) gives a detailed account of the experience of trying to promote human rights education in Croatia over a period of 15 years, and it provides a salutary case study. Progress was linked to the changing political climate, to the passivity and submissiveness of citizens and their survival skills. There was conceptual confusion over what sorts of rights were being promoted – social, economic, civil or political? There were controversies over individual versus collective rights. A particular problem was the recognition and implementation of pluralism in education, especially ethnic and religious pluralism. This was not only because of

Croat-centred and Catholicism-centred educational policy, but also due to fear that pluralism would lead to instability in a time of war. Teachers were divided as to whether HRE was about national and cultural identity or about strengthening democratic decision-making and intercultural understanding. A key contextual question was 'How can teachers who think of human rights in terms of the rights of nation states over the individual be trained or persuaded to change their opinion in a political climate in which such opinion is legitimate?' As Spajic-Vrkas points out, 'the HRE literature is silent on this' (Spajic-Vrkas, 2012: 326). In spite of massive endeavours at all levels, including university and teacher training, together with the production of materials, the position of HRE is still blurred in the Croatian education system, and also in the majority of national documents, including laws on education and national programmes for gender equality and children's rights. Spajic-Vrkas indicates the need for integration at all levels, and the development of a database on HRE practices. I would add that doing HRE only as a curriculum subject has serious limitations, and that it is preferable to embed a rights-based approach in the school as a total way of life.

The final issue concerns universalism. In arguing for a rights base to values, this chapter does not shy away from the problem of whether there can be a set of global ethics, supra-national standards, what Sen (1999) calls 'grand universalism'. Certainly, religions have espoused sets of ethics as global, or have influenced ideas in global directions. In Europe, some of the first commercial, now international, banks were based on the honesty and integrity of religious groups such as the Quakers (Williams, 2012) – even if these values seem to have been almost totally eroded in the banking scandals. Global *ummah,* the global nation, was seen as linking all Muslims through common notions of ethics and justice. The Roman Catholic Church claims to be 'universal'. Buddhist teachers roamed the world establishing a globalized view of ethics and fairness. The question is how all these so-called universal ethics can be reconciled, and how competing world views can ever be said to be universal.

One solution is the argument that all these codes of ethics were actually formulated as human rights and have a common base. The Cyrus Cylinder from Persia (539 BC) has been described as 'the world's first declaration of human rights' and in the 1970s Iranian Shah Mohammed Reza Pahlavi even linked his regime with Cyrus to enhance its legitimacy. 'The Code appears to bestow religious freedoms and abolish slavery, which could be interpreted to mean that the Iranians abolished slavery 2,293 years before the Americans discovered it' (Williams, 2012: 98). But Chris Williams makes a point central to complex adaptive systems. In terms of global public goods, the centrality of knowledge and ideas are the global resource. 'From this global perspective, the 'ethic' is the access to *diverse* ideas rather than a set of universals' (Williams, 2012: 99). Yet does this still beg the question of how to make judgements on all these ideas without a set of universals? Is everything provisional or circular? I am reminded of Ambrose Bierce's definition of mind in *The Devil's Dictionary*:

> Mind, *n*. A mysterious form of matter secreted by the brain. Its chief activity consists in the endeavour to ascertain its own nature, the futility of the attempt being due to the fact that it has nothing but itself to know itself with.
>
> (Bierce, 2002: 164)

But it is the mind's access to diverse ideas together with the mind's propensity to structure and to categorize that form its complex adaptability. I am not sure whether potential universals such as rights constitute a safety net or a springboard, but I do think their secular nature gives the mind a good platform for action.

Workings of a dynamic secular school

Having achieved this relatively secure base, the third section of this chapter proposes how a dynamic secular and complex adaptive school then productively generates turbulence. These are enabling conditions, not pathways. The counter-intuitive picture is of an organization without end-goals. I was intrigued by a discussion by Firth and Wheeler (2009) on complexity and teacher education, and what it means to be 'human'. Rather than taking a linear approach to education, they take from the work of Gert Biesta (e.g. 2007, 2008) that what it means to be human is an open question, one that can be answered only by engaging in education, rather than as a question to be answered *before* we engage in education. Forms of education may differ from each other, but all are founded on the idea that for education to be *educational* it has to be *for* something – and that has to be defined before education can take place. But an approach that looks for emergence is different. The point of the critique of humanism is that we cannot know in advance what it is to be human, and that there might be greater danger in foreclosing opportunities than in keeping our options open (Firth and Wheeler, 2009: 138). This does not mean that no judgement is involved, but it has to come *after* the manifestation and experience of different ways of being human. This does raise the question in my mind about the basis of judgements, which might have to be to an extent 'pre-thought'. Biesta (2007) would claim that rights are a firm delineation of what it means to be human, implying a lack of openness to new formulations, and on this I have to agree. Yet I would still argue that complexity and emergence require some form of order, and some sort of basis for judgements to be made, however provisional. These surround three sorts of encounters that characterize the dynamic secular school (DSS): encounters with people, encounters with text and encounters with doubt.

1. Encounters with people

Keeping one's options open in terms of what it means to be human has the first prerequisite of exposure to others and to other ideas. The key is the encounter with difference, and the ideas of Lingis are interesting and relevant here. As well as a community where we rely on things we have in common (the 'rational' community) there is also a community of those who have nothing in common and which interrupts the rational one, when you respond to the responsibility to the other whom you see. 'It is not realised in having or producing something in common but in exposing oneself to the one with whom one has nothing in common: the Aztec, the nomad, the guerrilla, the enemy' (Lingis, 1994:10). This idea resonates clearly with Atran's *Talking to the Enemy* (2010).

In terms of education and religion, there would be exposure and, importantly, response to those with different belief systems or ethical systems – or apparent lack of them. There is a dilemma here, in that some critiques of multiculturalism (mine included) point to how the 'exoticization' of cultures, the constant emphasis on diversity, and that we should understand and tolerate different ethnic groups doing things differently, leads to stereotyping and to othering – which is not good for community cohesion. Yet the counter emphasis on 'what we have in common' can be superficial (that we all have rituals of marriage, birth, death, feast days) and does not begin to tackle what can be quite distinct ways of seeing the world and positioning oneself and others. Nor does it provide an understanding of how discrimination occurs, and the histories of tension and mistrust.

Megan Boler (1997) reveals how, in a teacher education context, the well-intended use of multicultural narratives can lead the student reader to develop 'passive empathy' – essentially the illusion that they understand – while leaving them uninformed about the actual contexts and causes of injustice, and the ways they are implicated in the persistence of such injustices. Role play, when students are insufficiently prepared to actually make sense of unfamiliar misconceptions, carries a similar risk of reinforcing misconceptions rather than provoking careful thought or inquiry (Bickmore, 2005).

As Kathy Bickmore reveals in the Canadian context, service learning is seen as better than such passive empathy, when notions of community involvement are broadened to include social action and political advocacy with and on behalf of marginalized groups. But this is not to be cast as charity towards those less fortunate lest it reinforce a sense of superiority. History textbooks sometimes give the false impression that historical events were inevitable and universally agreed upon (the causes of the whatsit war) – instead of portraying the vagaries of culpability. Robert Nash cites US Supreme Court decisions ensuring schools' right and responsibility to teach about multiple world religions in a balanced fashion, yet laments that such topics are typically avoided or presented in woefully misleading ways (reported in Bickmore, 2005: 163).

Similarly, as I have argued in the Sri Lankan context (Davies, 2012a), encounters are more productive when they bring young people together to *do* something, not just to be 'exposed' to each other. When working in a common cause, what is common is easily established – as well as whether differences really matter in that context. Sri Lanka's policy on education for peace and social cohesion did have some misguided attempts at multicultural/multifaith education. In co-curricular activities, there was a constant emphasis on learning about 'difference' and about 'others', which actually cements stereotypes and generates confusions between culture and religion. The language was of learning about 'their' dances, 'their' music, 'their' prayers, instead of about finding bonds. There was an obsession with 'parallelism', which caused great problems when teachers tried to put on 'Muslim dancing' to match the displays of Sinhalese and Tamil dancing. Now, Sinhalese and Tamil children coming together to work on community problems (such as human–elephant conflict, which is currently a nightmare for villages as elephants break in and destroy crops) enables greater recognition and acceptance than simply doing exchange visits (although these can be valuable too). Up-to-date creativity is needed: it was discovered that all students seemed to be on Facebook and could use such social networking to continue their links and ties, as well as to spread them more widely. Teachers we spoke to did not seem to think of this. In the end, it will be the students who have to grasp the nettle of social cohesion and make the processes of social integration their own.

2. Critical thinking and encounters with 'the Word'
The second type of encounter is that related to our old friend 'critical thinking'. Like 'child-centred', this now appears in education manifestos across the world. In terms of religion, however, this has an additional edge. It involves critical examination of sacred texts and the religious practices

that they propound and defend. It is well established that many sacred texts have exhortations to violence, slaying and smiting. There is a wonderful website Skeptic's Annotated Bible where, in the 'Dwindling in Unbelief' section, contributors were asked to rate God's Top Fifty Killings. The winner was 'All flesh died that moved upon the earth'. So, the site concludes, 'God drowns everything that breathes air. From newborn babies to koala bears – all creatures great and small, the Lord God drowned them all' (Skeptic's Annotated Bible, n.d.). They did a nice alternative to Cliff Richard's 50 top Bible stories for kids, including lots of killings and drownings. The site also drew attention to the racist elements in religious texts. According to the Book of Mormon, God apparently cursed the Lamanites, causing 'a skin of blackness to come upon them', in order to make them appear repulsive to the 'white, and exceedingly fair and delightsome Nephites'. Jacob 3.8 stipulates 'Unless ye repent of your sins that their skins will be whiter than yours'. Most people would see this is a prime example of a cultural perception of the time being written into sacred text, yet, as always, racism is given divine sanction.

As Dawkins points out, the Bible prescribes the death penalty for adultery, for gathering sticks on the Sabbath and for cheeking your parents. He asks, if we reject all this, as enlightened moderns do, then which bits do we accept? 'And if we have independent criteria for choosing among our religious moralities, why not cut out the middle man and go straight for the moral choice without the religion?' (Dawkins, 2006: 57) For me the moral choice, the independent criteria, are as I have argued best situated in human rights. Yet this is not as easy as it might sound. Critiquing from within a religion has personal and social consequences.

This is nowhere more clear than when looking at gender and religion. The recent collection *Gender, Religion and Education* (Gross *et al.*, 2013) shows great diversity across countries and contexts in terms of whether religious schooling appears to subordinate women or at least reproduce gendered family roles, or whether learning within a religious framework enables emancipation. The link between gender and security is twofold. At the national level, research by the RAND Corporation in Afghanistan (Bernard *et al.*, 2008) sets out strong arguments that gender parity plays a critical role in state stability. They use the analogy of the 'canary in the mine' test: if a particular decision or compromise is bad for women, it will be bad for human security, bad for development and detrimental to genuine peace. Logics of male privilege have been found to link to the assumption of entitlement and hence to corruption, to the acceptance that power gives the right to bypass rules. The RAND study found no evidence that taking an early and bold approach to gender equality in peace-building and state-building is destabilizing. It must be acknowledged however that in attempting to shift gender cultures, working with male gatekeepers is needed. Again, this is 'talking to the enemy'.

The link to personal security for women is discussed in Chapter 2, specifically in terms of the attractions of religion for women. The present chapter on education is not however relativistic about the potential for gender inequality in a religiously framed education – or admittedly in any education. Flexibility does not mean acceptance of locked-in injustices or dead ends. Howson asks whether women's rights would be better protected under a secular system and he would have, on balance, to say yes. 'Christianity and Judaism contain more than a strain of misogyny' (Howson, 2011: 13). The persistence of such misogyny in current times needs explaining. The case of Bristol University Christian Union banning women speakers (mentioned in Chapter 2) evoked this response from a 'True Christian':

> Women shouldn't have the opportunity to speak at meetings due to their inferior relationship with God. Eve was the first sinner and so all women are born with original sin. Therefore they should not try and tarnish the men with this sin and should not be able to teach at meetings.
>
> (de Bruxelles, 2012: 14)

This seems extraordinary in any setting, but in a university, which presumably has highly educated students, it is even more bizarre.

The explanation for such views lies in the easy return to the ancient myths and their certainties. Religious narratives are the most powerful way of communicating patriarchy. It is interesting how, across nearly all religions, when narratives become gendered, the ideal of woman is of loyal and obedient wife and of chief homemaker. The Bible and the Quran's views of women are strikingly similar, with women worth about half to two-thirds the value of men. Tamar Rapaport (2013) shows how for Zionism, secularism is bracketed with permissiveness and feminism and all are a threat to family, the building block of the Jewish collective. In the end, as Tamar Ross (2013) admits, we cannot see reality in any other way. Ross gives an eloquent account of her personal and academic struggles with orthodox Jewish texts that appear to subordinate women. A postmodern approach would posit alternative interpretations and see religious texts as a series of social constructs. But, as Ross reveals, once one accepts the human filtering of the divine, this appears to weaken the religious commitment mandated by that (divine) message. Does feminist critique of religion leave believers with a watered-down version? Ross draws attention to political barriers, distinguishing the orthodox 'pure' religion from other denominations more willing to take social and cultural context into consideration. But, she asks, is this replacing God with sociology?

One key debate therefore is over the source of texts – is the negative portrayal of women in the Buddhist Pali Canon a later insertion into the texts or directly attributable to the Buddha, as Starkey and Tomalin (2013) query? Earlier permissions to ordain women do appear to have been either suppressed or ignored. The linked debate is about definitions of terms in divine texts. In Islam, for example, much revolves around notions of modesty. Islam does argue for equality in fields such as learning; yet notions of modesty become interpreted differently for males and females. In their work on physical education in Middle Eastern countries, Tansin Benn *et al.* (2013) point out that there is nothing in the Quran or the Hadith that explicitly precludes men's or women's participation in physical activities, provided it does not take precedence over faith. So there is no simple way in which Muslim people embody the idea of modesty as part of their faith. For some it is internalized, for others it is 'embodied faith', externalized as the practice of covering hair, arms and legs in public. There is also nothing in the Quran or the Hadith that explicitly stresses that a strict segregation of the sexes is required. Here we see classic examples of religious and cultural conflation.

The underlying question for education is *who* is allowed to question divine texts. In Islam, is it only Islamic scholars who can exercise *ijtihad* (the rigorous examination of sacred texts)? In Jewish orthodoxy, only the erudite? In Japan, only men, as found and experienced by Kawahashi *et al.* (2013)? In contrast, Lauren Ila Jones (2013) talks of grass-roots participants in Nicaragua who are 'organic theologians', perfectly capable of explaining their religious beliefs.

The collection on *Gender, Religion and Education* (Gross *et al.*, 2013) does provide inspiring accounts of the challenge to the defensiveness of 'established' interpreters of divine will. But do even believers have to accept that religion is a social construction? There seem to be only three choices. For the atheist, these are only stories anyway, dreamed up and retold to maintain power and hierarchy for nations, leaders or for men – often in some combination. For the believer, the narratives can either be seen as absolute unquestionable expressions of objective truth or as divine will filtered through contemporary social mores and thus open to discussion, debate and updating. Feminism in this last perspective can be seen as a gift from God – albeit a bit late arriving.

I am slightly ambivalent about all the revisionist attempts that say that the Quran has been mistranslated and misunderstood, and replacing some words with others – for example in the Oxford Muslim Students Empowerment Programme (Hussain, 2008). Apparently the verse stating that believers should not take Jews and Christians as friends is problematic because the translation of '*awliya*' should have been something like 'protectors' or 'allies'. Historically, these people could have been apparently the 'enemy within', and therefore to be distrusted. But the resultant message is still to accept the right way to behave as coming from an authority – not thinking about the principles behind behaviour. Changing the word of the authority does not necessarily mean greater critical thinking.

3. Encounters with doubt and certainty: Religious education in a dynamic secular school

For maximum encounter with ideas, a dynamic secular education would definitely include learning about religion. But it would be in comparative terms, with religion examined within social or political science, clearly not as instructional. It would examine differences and similarities in religious commandments – which are not guidelines or suggestions, which people can take or leave. Not by accident are the Abrahamic religions called 'command religions'. Study would include awareness of religious law – as in sharia. It would examine the positioning of women. It would include economic aspects, for example Islamic financing and banking. It would compare what religions actually say about the body. It might well examine things regarded as good that are done in the name of religion – for example liberation theology which foregrounds social justice and works on behalf of the poor. Crucially it would at the same time expose mistakes and harm done in the name of religion – from the crusades, to slavery, to the Pope's position on contraception. The recently resigned pope declared in December 2009 that saving humanity from homosexual or transsexual acts was as important as saving the rainforests (Howson, 2011: 6). This would make a nice exam question. Such religious analysis would merely parallel the same interrogation in political history. It is not singling religion out for particular praise or censure, just using the same critical lens that one would expect in history, politics and social science. Religion is not to be seen as precious in the sense of being unassailable.

Of some importance is the analysis of the role attributed to divine will and how we are supposed to respond to it, as explored in Chapter 3 in terms of the justification for conflict. Another recent improbable instance (matching the idea of women as original sinners) is the furore in the United States over culpability for rape. In the run-up to the presidential election, the Republican Senate candidate Richard Mourdock said: 'even when life begins in that horrible situation of rape, that is something God intended to happen'. And

Todd Akin claimed: 'If it is a legitimate rape, the female body has ways to try and shut the whole thing down' – i.e. that if pregnancy did occur, it would be the woman's fault (Blakemore, 2012). The nonsensical oxymoron of a 'legitimate rape,' justified by God's will, did not go down well with female voters, and may have made some contribution to the Republicans losing the election. But presumably there are others who believe this sort of thing – which is the more worrying.

One entertaining activity which students enjoy is discourse analysis – discussing the violent or misogynist or racist elements of sacred texts as well as the more loving ones; but also looking at how language is used. Mark Twain is brilliant here in his description of the writer of the Book of Mormon:

> The author labored to give his words and phrases the quaint, old-fashioned sound and structure of our King James's translation of the Scriptures; ... Whenever he found his speech growing too modern – which was about every sentence or two – he ladled in a few such Scriptural phrases as 'exceeding sore', 'and it came to pass,' etc., and made things satisfactory again. 'And it came to pass' was his pet. If he had left that out, his Bible would have been only a pamphlet.
>
> (Twain, 1984: 617)

Students also engage enthusiastically with paradoxes such as those of omnipotence: 'Can God create a stone he cannot lift?' Was God, as Woody Allen suggested, simply an underachiever? The conflation in religion of omnipotence and worship is a good debating point. It would in theory be possible to conceive of a deity who was all-powerful, but this does not automatically mean that one has to worship him/her. Howson asks 'should we worship because the universe is a beautifully designed machine?' His reply is that we do not worship Dr Guillotin because he designed a highly efficient means of execution (Howson, 2011: 50).

Students might debate ancient exhortations about cleanliness: 'When ye rise up for prayer ... if ye ... cometh from the closet, or ye have had contact with women, and ye find not water, then go to clean, high ground and rub your faces and your hands with some of it' (Quran 5:6). Obviously this predated wet wipes.

Students should also have fun with extremist secularism. Froese recounts how an anti-religious pamphlet in the first Five Year Plan period in the Soviet Union was entitled 'Prayers or Tractors' and a widespread poster elaborated on the alleged contradiction between 'cross and tractor':

The illusions about 'atheist tractor' were however soon shattered, especially when peasants affixed crosses to them and priests celebrated thanksgiving services at their arrival in the villages. While for scientific atheists the tractor proved that God was not in control of agricultural production, the peasants knew otherwise.

(Froese, 2008: 57)

The mention of scientific atheism leads to the subject of the interactions between science and religion, particularly over questions of evolution. Definitions of creationism vary but about 40 per cent of adults in the US and perhaps over 10 per cent in the UK believe that the Earth is only some ten thousand years old, that it came into existence as described in the early parts of the Bible or the Quran, and that the most that evolution has done is to change species into closely related species (Jones and Reiss, 2007). In 2008, almost half of Americans rejected evolutionary theory because they believed it to be in conflict with the Bible (Howson, 2011). This is not just with regard to evolution: the Islamic theocracy in Iran has proscribed the teaching of philosophy, together with other humanities subjects in Iranian universities. Ayatollah Ali Khamenei is reported as saying 'Such teachings will lead to the dissemination of doubt in the foundations of religious teachings' (*Daily Telegraph*, 2010).

But it is exactly the dissemination of doubt which is crucial in critical thinking and equally crucial in tackling extremism. (This is discussed further in Chapter 6.) Howson acknowledges that many passages in sacred texts have been rejected even by believers as the production of primitive, pre-scientific societies – 'but these jurisdictions like Iran have deliberately regressed to a primitive state' (Howson, 2011: 17). Evolution can of course be misused, as we saw with Hitler's notion of the extinction of inferior races, with superior races deriving their vitality and virtue by their genetic purity. Interestingly, although Hitler disliked Christianity, he was not an atheist, and was emboldened by the idea that he was carrying out a divinely ordained plan (Pinker, 2002: 154).

As with questioning gender roles discussed above, questioning creationist myths also has wider implications. As Pinker says, if the Bible got it wrong on biology, can you trust it for anything else? There is an extensive literature on issues of teaching science and religion with regard to evolution, particularly with regard to Muslim or other science teachers who promote a creationist perspective. Some find congruence, others find the 'border crossings' difficult or even insurmountable. In our concern with security, one interesting piece of research used 'terror-management theory' to explore whether fear of death was linked to the propensity to favour intelligent design over evolution. Existential anxiety may be assuaged by world views that find life purposeful, orderly, and likely to lead to an afterlife (Tracy *et al.*, 2011).

The problem for a secular education, and secular science, is that it appears unable to give comfort to those who fear dying. Ironically, the evolutionary processes in the brain actually gear us into wanting survival – as well as wanting revenge – and militate against enjoying a secular approach to the meaning of life. The opposition to evolution is also fuelled by moral fears, a dislike of the idea that we were not put here for a purpose (to live a moral life according to God's commandments). But our concepts of justice also have a learned social utility. Daly and Wilson (1988) say that the almost mystical moral imperative is the output of a straightforward adaptive function to ensure that violators reap no advantage from their misdeeds:

> The enormous volume of mystic-religious bafflegab about atonement and penance and divine justice and the like is the attribution to a higher, detached authority of what is actually a mundane, pragmatic matter: discouraging self-interested competitive acts by reducing their profitability to nil.
>
> (Daly and Wilson, 1988: 256)

Religion will however enable people to skirt around justice. I like the story of the boy who said 'I wanted to pray to God for a bike but I know that God doesn't work that way. So I stole a bike and asked for forgiveness'.

I think religious education in a DSS should engage with creationism and intelligent design in order to blow them apart and match what is being taught in science. Here, there would be no accommodation. Whether in science or religion, the basic issue would be about the evidence base on which we claim to 'know' something. The problem is that faith is elevated above evidence, and the possession of a faith seen as a prime virtue. Doubt, and the search for evidence, becomes a sin. 'Once it is taught that there are knowledge claims for which evidence can be dispensed with in favour of personal conviction and the word of authority then the dark night of unreason is upon us' (Howson, 2011: 36).

Satire is a useful tool against unreason. After the decision in the UK that the state would fund free schools, *NewsThump* carried an article with the headline 'Creationist school syllabus only takes 7 days':

> Michael Gove [Education Minister] has defended his decision to allow some state funded free schools to be run by creationist groups, insisting their ability to cut out billions of years of facts

highlights their overall efficiency. Grindon Hall Christian school in Sunderland, a private school due to reopen in September with state funding, says on its website that it will present creationism as science and perform exorcisms on any child absent as a result of sickness. The Grindon Hall principal, Chris Gray, insisted that pupils would be free to ask questions, and denied that they would adopt a 'teach the controversy' approach to get around free schools not being allowed to teach 'creationism' or 'intelligent design' in science lessons. "We will actively encourage children to ask questions because the answers are all right here in the Bible," he said. "However, any further questions based on these answers will result in pupils being sent to the heresy room." With dinosaur denying and rib counting expected to form part of the curriculum, Mr Gove said that the schools would provide a unique opportunity for pupils to experience education from a completely different perspective. ..."Sometimes it's important to form a child's understanding of the world on stories that are so far-fetched they make Lord of the Rings look like a fly-on-the-wall documentary... It's all about choice."

(*NewsThump*, 2012)

Creative doubt is the hallmark of the DSS. Encounters with others or with other narratives have a central function to foment doubt and question authority – whether human, or of the Secretary of State for Education, or of the supposedly divine. Holloway (2012) catalogues the history of the way that authority has schooled men not to reason why before driving them into the valley of death, be it the charge of the Light Brigade or in Vietnam, Iraq or Afghanistan. The rhetoric is always the same, and 'TINA' (there is no alternative) is always invoked, with our welfare at stake if the charge is not ordered. As he points out, this is not confined to military folly: mutually exclusive economic policies are promoted by their disciples with 'apostolic fervour'. Nietzsche pointed out that stupidity followed every stable institution like a shadow. It is those who love tradition most who most imperil its survival because of their reluctance to question and challenge its follies. 'The paradox is that it is the doubters and the disloyal who inoculate institutions against decay by bringing in new ideas into the bloodstream' (Holloway, 2012: 21). Artists (and I would add satirists) seem to understand this better than politicians and theologians. Holloway quotes Graham Greene in 1948:

I would emphasise once again the importance and the virtue of disloyalty. If only writers could maintain that one virtue ...

unspotted from the world. Honours, State patronage, success, the praise of their fellows all tend to sap their disloyalty ... Loyalty confines us to accepted opinions: loyalty forbids us to comprehend sympathetically our dissident fellows; but disloyalty encourages us to roam experimentally through any human mind; it gives the novelist the extra dimension of sympathy.

(Holloway, 2012: 21)

Is the spirit of creative disloyalty missing from our great institutions today? I might hold that Nietzsche and Graham Greene would be early complexity theorists, foreseeing the scientific arguments for dissonance, protest, and challenges to orthodoxy.

In this light, religious education would include an examination of secularism and of secularization itself. Excessive, hard secularism can be just as authoritarian as command religions. Yurchak pointed to a key paradox:

The Soviet citizen was called upon to submit completely to the party leadership, to cultivate a collectivist ethic, and repress individualism, while at the same time becoming an enlightened and independently minded individual who pursues knowledge and is inquisitive and creative.

(Yurchak, 2006: 11)

You cannot have it both ways. The Soviets were not prepared to take the risks of autonomy, and many educational institutions probably think likewise. On the other side of the coin, not all religious writings are uniformly authoritarian. Joachim Fest, in his fascinating book *Not Me: A German childhood*, describes how his father, a Catholic, conservative figure and head teacher, did not move seamlessly into support for the Nazi regime in 1933, but instead was dismissed from his job for 'disparaging the Führer'. He later instructed his sons in his philosophy. He put a piece of paper in front of them and dictated 'Etiam si omnes, ego non', explaining that they were Peter's words to Jesus on the Mount of Olives, from St Matthew's Gospel: 'Even if all others do, not me'. Fest recalls this to have been his guide to a 'truly free life'. He relates an anguishing family debate about pragmatism. Fest's mother, struggling to cope without an income, tried to persuade her husband to join the Nazi party to regain his job. It was a formality, she suggested, and would not change anything. 'After all, we remain who we are!' 'Precisely not', he replied, 'it would change everything!' (Fest, 2012)

Conclusion

This chapter has drilled down from the overall control of schools to the broad ethos within them and then to the pedagogical elements which make for adaptive learning. First, dynamic secularism in terms of the state funding of schools means taking keen and constant account of context. In a religiously plural, multicultural society, schools deliberately segregated by religion do not help social cohesion, and the state should avoid perpetuating division in its funding strategies. In other contexts, the state may wish to make religious schools more moderate or more modern, and therefore financing them acts as a control mechanism. There should not be proscription on religious groups setting up their own schools privately; and in contexts of poverty, there may well be partnerships between government and faith-based organizations to ensure that there is access to school for all. The aim is to minimize the tensions that come from one religion avowing superiority over another, and to avoid the links to class inequality.

Second, a secular school will need a value base which cuts across all religions and none in order to secure a platform from which decisions can be made, learning relationships forged, and creative and flexible learning can occur. A rights base is the best fit that we have.

Third, a secular pedagogy is there to foment uncertainty. This means three sorts of encounters – with people, with texts and with doubt. Religious education is an important component, but a critical one which does not elevate religion over other ways of seeing the world and where there would be critical challenges to religious orthodoxy, including critical discourse analysis of sacred texts, particularly where these foster injustice, inequity and violence. The aim is the search for evidence and proof but also the autonomy which comes from challenging groupthink.

Chapter 5

Secure schools and schools for security

> *A gentle Quaker, hearing a strange noise in his house one night, got up and discovered a burglar busily at work. He went and got his gun, came back and stood quietly in the doorway. 'Friend', he said, 'I would do thee no harm for the world, but thou standest where I am about to shoot.'*
>
> James Hines

The question of 'safe schools' is a huge international concern, ranging from campaigns to end corporal punishment, to school shootings, to attacks on educational institutions. This chapter cannot tackle all aspects (anti-bullying, cyberbullying, disaster risk reduction, child abuse and child protection) but, in line with the remit of the book, focuses on those aspects of school security that relate to religion. The chapter aims to see whether this means specific strategies or whether general initiatives to ensure or improve school safety can also encompass the religious dimension. Three aspects are considered: schools that are safe from outside attack; schools that provide security for their religious minority students; and schools that try to prevent or disrupt religious extremism.

Schools that are safe from outside attack

The Global Coalition to Protect Education from Attack (GCPEA) tackles the situations of worldwide armed conflict where combatants are targeting schools, students and their teachers. This includes closure because of threats and intimidation, the military use of schools and the use of schools as recruiting grounds. Targeted killings, abductions, sexual violence or even just threats of these can be as effective in shutting down schools as direct attacks. There can also be attacks on pro-education activists, including teacher unions or any teacher group because of their political activism. There can be damage and destruction of learning materials, student files, and administrative records. I recall interviewing a head teacher in Kosovo who was trying to restart a school which had been occupied by the Serb military. As well as physical degradation, the school suffered the loss of registers, which meant not knowing how many children should be there nor what educational needs they had. Not as dramatic as a school having been bombed, but an attack on learning nonetheless.

In its definition of an attack on education, GCPEA states that 'Attacks may be carried out for political, military, ideological, sectarian, ethnic, religious or criminal reasons' (GCPEA, 2011: 2). Clearly this book would be interested in the religious and ideological reasons, although the overall strategy of casting attacks as violations of international law and therefore as war crimes is a powerful one across all types and motivations. It is sometimes difficult to isolate religion or ideology as a cause, as this is so intertwined with politics. Brendan O'Malley's significant and well-known work authoring the UNESCO publications *Education under Attack* (2007, 2010) reveals the complexities. In the 2010 version he documents 17 categories of motives, of which the first two are particularly relevant: 'Attacks on schools or teachers as vehicles for imposing an alien culture, philosophy, religion or ethnic identity'; and 'Attacks on schools, teachers and students to prevent the education of girls' (O'Malley, 2010: 65).

But attacks on academics for researching sensitive topics, and attacks on students and academics to silence human rights campaigns, may also have an ideological slant. The 'real' purpose and the underlying one are often hotly contested. Attacks in Thailand, for example, are now mostly agreed to be rooted in the government's assimilation policies. The conflict-affected area was once known for its Islamic teaching and attracted scholars from around the world. Successive governments sought to ban Islamic schools and attire and to outlaw the Malay dialect, Muslim names, and the teaching of local history. Such bans were later lifted, but the government has tended to concentrate on security operations rather than acknowledging the socio-cultural roots of the conflict. 'Schools are thus perceived with some historical justification as being a vehicle for suppressing both the local Islamic Malay identity and hopes of rekindling autonomy, and have been on the front line of attack since the first day of the five-year insurgency' (O'Malley, 2010: 69). A leaflet found near a burned-down government school gives the flavour:

> Now Patani Muslims are at war with the occupying forces of Siamese infidels. You must be aware that our attack on the symbols of their occupying forces – such as burning of schools – are carried out to completely destroy the Siamese infidels' rule. You are warned not to send your children to their schools. They will convert your children, and take away their awareness as Patani Muslims ...You are warned not to ... help ... [them] rebuild their schools. Any assistance to the occupying forces of Siamese infidels is a sin and will be severely punished.
>
> (O'Malley, 2010: 70)

In Afghanistan, similarly, people are warned by the Taliban that it is 'the Islamic duty' not to continue the girls' schools. The threats are ideological and physical. For the Taliban, girls' schools were run under a system imposed by the British and are seen to promote 'obscenity and vulgarity in society'. Here is the clue – the Taliban may be against not girls' education as such, but the forms it has taken. The religious-based justifications for attack merge with political ones. Human Rights Watch (2006) was able to show how education and personnel were being attacked in Afghanistan for three overlapping reasons: opposition to the government and its international supporters; ideological opposition to education other than that offered in madrassas, with particular opposition to girls' education; and opposition to the authority of the central government and the rule of law by criminal groups.

In Pakistan, the Taliban appeared to soften their stance in January 2009, allowing girls to go to school up to fourth grade but maintaining their threat beyond it. Giustozzi and Franco's (2011) detailed study of the Taliban reveals differentiated educational thinking – albeit shaped by a primarily religious self-image – which shifts between fundamentally rejecting Western-oriented education and at the same time recruiting pupils from such secondary schools, together with the promotion of various sorts of religious education. There are concessions in relation to teaching and learning objectives and syllabuses. Whether winning 'hearts and minds' is just tactical or represents a fundamental change is not yet clear, but as Kate Clark (2011) points out, the revised version of the code of conduct of the Taliban movement (*layha*) of 2010 contains no justification for violence towards schools.

As said, isolating religion as a sole cause of attacks on schools becomes difficult. Al-Shabaab in Somalia is religiously inspired and funded, but their attacks on schools are about targeting students for recruitment and for use in armed conflict. One cannot really cast Israeli attacks on schools and higher education in Gaza as having religious motives, even if Hamas is an Islamic movement. It is part of Israel's own war on terror and its attempts to destroy all operations of the Hamas government. UNRWA schools for refugees have also been hit, as well as the American International School. Such attacks will not be solved by appeals to human rights nor to ideology.

However, Iraqi academics have been murdered simply because they were Shia or Sunni and their campuses were controlled by the opposing sect. But is this about theology or about power? Sri Lanka is another complicated example. The Tamil Tigers (LTTE) in Sri Lanka had a policy of Muslim ethnic cleansing, but this was part of their own separatist claims and a cultural/territorial drive, not one of theological prejudice. The difference in political views and the emergence of an exclusive political party for Muslims triggered a sudden forced eviction by the LTTE, driving a total of 75,000 men, women, and children from the area. The impact on education was felt in terms of their resettlement in other Muslim areas, and the consequent pressure on schools and households there, as well as different cultural interpretations of Islam between the displaced people and 'host' communities (Davies, 2013a). Schools were also occupied or destroyed by government forces in Tamil areas.

International responses to attacks

GCPEA say that the UN Security Council's overall attention to attacks against schools has been weak, although the Security Council has now identified the category of 'attacks on schools or hospitals' as one of the six grave violations that are to be monitored by the UN's Monitoring and Reporting Mechanism (MRM). Attacks are seen to violate international humanitarian and criminal law, and to be war crimes or crimes against humanity as set out in in a number of international regulations, protocols and statutes. The MRM is triggered into action when the UN Secretary General names those parties to armed conflict who commit grave violations of children's rights. States are then obliged to allow the UN to set up the MRM and monitor all six grave violations. In 2009, the Security Council expanded the 'trigger' of the MRM to include killing or maiming of children as well as rape and other grave forms of sexual violence against children. After monitoring, key GCPEA recommendations are: using data to inform responses; finding preventive measures; criminalizing attacks on education; restricting the use of educational institutions by state armed forces and other armed groups; and investigating and prosecuting through domestic, regional and international tribunals.

But law-making about school protection can be convoluted. A fascinating article by Gregory Raymond Bart (2010) on 'The ambiguous protection of schools under the law of war' details how states tend to treat school buildings less respectfully than they treat hospitals and religious buildings, with one important cause being the privileged status accorded under the law of war. This law forbids targeting hospitals, religious buildings and other civilian buildings unless they become justifiable military objectives. There are tortuous twists in the law. Religious buildings are to be protected because of their 'inherently humanitarian, cultural or spiritual value'. I would ask, so why not museums or libraries as well? In Sarajevo, there was deliberate targeting of the library and administrative buildings by the Serbs because of their symbolic cultural value to the inhabitants of the city, a matter of history and civic pride. Bart explains how the 1977 Protocol then expanded the scope of protection to *most* religious buildings, independent of their historic or cultural value, with spiritual heritage specifically applying to places of worship. (I contested this narrow definition of spiritual in Chapter 3.) But it still did not extend to all places of worship, only those that express the religious nature, the 'conscience' of the people. And not to all places, as such buildings are 'extremely numerous' and 'often have only a local renown of sanctity which does not extend to the whole nation'. This seems to privilege majority faiths, those that claim to represent the people – with 'people' seemingly a synonym for nation or country.

Overall it does seem wrong that religion is privileged over education in terms of protection, and that even if for some reason spirituality could be privileged over learning, this applies only to certain sorts of spirituality. Clearly the makers of the protocol tied themselves up in knots as to whether you can recognize any tinpot little religion. All this seems to sidestep the key issue that armies should not be targeting public or civil buildings at all – to imply it is acceptable to target small chapels or houses designated as mosques but not the grand cathedral-like buildings misses the point. Worse, the current protocol contains no clear prohibition against armed forces using school buildings for military purposes, 'as long as civilians and non-combatants are not present'.

The situation is now complicated by the securitization of aid. The 2010 edition of *Protecting Education from Attack* (UNESCO, 2010) has a disturbing chapter by Mario Novelli on 'Political violence against education sector aid workers in conflict zones'. He draws attention to the idea of 'development as counterinsurgency', where activities are seen as having potential 'security benefits'. As part of the US military's counter-insurgency strategy in places such as Iraq and Afghanistan, 'humanitarian and civic assistance' included non-emergency services such as constructing schools, performing dental procedures, and even vaccinating the livestock of farmers:

> Educational provision (particularly for girls) became a key discursive justification for the military intervention in Afghanistan. Educational progress was seen as demonstrating the success of the occupation, while attacking education was and is a key strategy of the Taliban.
>
> (Novelli, 2010: 90)

As Novelli points out, education has become a central battleground in the war, intensifying the dangers that all education personnel and students face there:

> Most problematically, education provision is increasingly becoming interpreted in this polarized context as a battle between Western

secular education and Islamic madrasa education, heightening the potential dangers. This also appears to be happening in Somalia ... and Iraq.

(Novelli, 2010: 90–1)

All this poses a huge dilemma – and risk – for education aid workers. Novelli quotes the United States Agency for International Development (USAID) policy on education in 'Muslim countries' as having a special emphasis on 'developing civic-mindedness in young people'. Yet civilian modes of counter-insurgency aimed at winning the hearts and minds and producing certain types of behaviour and outcomes may increase the danger for all involved.

This is not just the securitization of aid but also what I might call the 'religionization' of aid. The UNESCO *World Education Report* of 2011 also warns of the increasing risk of the close dovetailing of educational measures with counter-insurgency, blurring the distinction between civilians and combatants. Locals are no longer making a distinction between those organizations that are working for the military and those that are not. The attack on 13 August 2008 on a marked International Rescue Committee (IRC) vehicle, which killed education sector aid workers Shirley Case, Nicole Dial and Jackie Kirk, together with their driver Mohammed Aimal, was a shock which was felt internationally. All Western-based international humanitarian organizations were judged by the Taliban as partisan and therefore as combatants, together with private security and service providers.

The current issue in the religionization of aid, and in the response to it, is the conflation of Western, secular and anti-Muslim in the minds of those usually termed 'insurgents'. Malala Yousafzai was targeted by the Pakistani Taliban because she was promoting not just girls' education but Western education. As with Boko Haram in Nigeria, this is seen as a double threat to radical Islamism. The dilemma is that the more Western aid is seen to support girls' education, the greater the threat and the greater the violent response. I use the case of Malala Yousafzai in a discussion of dynamic change in my final chapter.

If international intervention is hazardous, is localized work safer for all? And can this be done by religious groups or organizations? At the Lambeth Conference in 2012, 'Education for Children Affected by Armed Conflict', chaired by the then Archbishop of Canterbury Rowan Williams, recommendations from individual speakers included:

- faith-based groups at the field level should connect with their congregations and governing structures at the national and global levels to advocate for adherence to and implementation of international humanitarian law prohibiting attacks on schools, as well as promulgation and implementation of domestic law prohibiting military use of schools

- religious leaders should prioritize the examination and resolution of child protection and education related violations, exercising caution and judgement, and taking into consideration the best interests of the children involved.

As is always the case with broad-brush recommendations, it is not clear how influential the 'connecting' and 'advocacy' at all these levels would be, nor what 'exercising caution and judgement' would really imply. However, their view is that the neutrality of faith-based groups and the respect accorded to them may have particular influence in negotiating or facilitating dialogues with armed groups and in encouraging them to stop attacking schools or using them for military purposes. It becomes interesting when there is a proposal that 'faith-based groups can educate religious leaders in communities about progressive interpretations of their own religious texts that are consistent with human rights principles and promote the value of education for all' (Lambeth Palace, 2012: 3). This is seen to add legitimacy to EFA campaigns. Of relevance to complexity and adaptation is the critique that donors who 'don't get out of bed to disburse less than a million' miss the value of smaller projects to develop relationships and working norms with local partners (Lambeth Palace, 2012: 4). I return to the power of small interventions in Chapter 7.

Community initiatives

Questions arise of how NGOs – faith-based or otherwise – work with local partners, and how grass-roots people and partners then shape their own community to become more secure. The classic and well-known example is the Schools as Zones of Peace (SZOP) campaign in Nepal. Briefly, this is the declaration of a school as a safe zone, having no political interference from either side of a conflict. The early advocacy was based on a fervent appeal to all parties to respect children's rights. 'This approach was based on the premise that the manner in which opposing groups treat children needs to be used as an important indicator in their credibility' (Smith, 2010: 264). Advocacy alone was however seen to be not enough, and a Schools as Zones of Peace module was developed as part of the Quality Education Resource package prepared by UNICEF and partner organizations. This had several crucial components: developing school codes of conduct in which local community facilitators convened negotiations with the Maoists, army, civil society and other stakeholder groups to cease targeting schools; mobilizing the media to monitor threats to schools; providing psycho-social care for those affected by conflict; support and coping skills for teachers; and teaching landmine awareness. There were also practical strategies such as painting signs on roofs to discourage the army from bombing them, and posting the codes of conduct in public places.

Later there were national children's consultations and an extension of the codes of conduct to cover violence within the school as well as 'social, cultural and religious activities that disturbed school operations' (such as agricultural activities, animal slaughter, and weddings), and disturbance by district-level strikes. SZOP criteria became widened to include localized issues such as banning alcohol, smoking and cattle grazing on school premises – thus promoting SZOP as a politically neutral process (Save the Children and Davies, 2012). The whole SZOP campaign has had significant successes, as well as spin-offs such as the improved school governance due to the community process required in negotiations. Schools without functioning school management committees were apparently more vulnerable to political interference. SZOP schools reported improved transparency about finances and decision-making, as well as resolution of internal conflicts (Smith, 2010).

There is a debate about whether the SZOP formulation could be applied elsewhere. Extracting the principles of community negotiation and agreed codes of conduct suggest that this seems possible. O'Malley (2012) reported on the work of the Global Education Cluster which is developing training materials to prevent the targeting of schools. At a pilot session in Pakistan, education and development officials simulated negotiations between leaders of a village, teachers, religious leaders and the local Taliban commander. Their mission was to reach agreement that local schools should not be blown up or attacked in any way. The role-play exercise was drawn from the real experience of communities in Nepal who negotiated for the conflict between Maoists and Royalists to be left outside the school gates. In Pakistan the heated discussion centred on parents' fears for their children's lives versus the concerns of religious leaders and Taliban commanders that schools were not teaching or working by Islamic principles. The head teacher sought to steer all parties to agreeing to respect schools as a zone of peace in return for reassurances that certain Islamic principles would be met. For instance, although both girls and boys could attend the school they would only do so in separate shifts.

Whether this would work or has worked in reality has yet to be reported, but the interesting parts are the underscoring of the need to approach the military commanders, and the need for compromises and bargaining around any sticking points of Islamic principles. As in Afghanistan, it does not cost much to make the schools more Islamic. This is not the time to propose a secular, modern approach to learning. The aim is to keep schools open so that there are greater chances of communities being able to rebuild when the conflict ends.

The UNESCO report (2010) details various ways in which physical protection can be enhanced for schools. Not using schools as polling stations and for voter registration might be an obvious start. Transporting children, particularly girls, as well as their teachers to school is another tactic, sometimes using armed escorts, bulletproof vehicles or armoured buses. Another strategy is assigning security guards to schools, arming teachers and reinforcing school infrastructure and architecture. This might be seen as making schools into prisons, but UNESCO also suggest 'organising the community defence of schools', which would fit the SZOP model.

Dana Burde (2010) however cautions on the role of community-based schools (CBS) in terms of preventing violent attacks. In her detailed studies of Afghanistan, the CBS, which were schools set up in people's homes with volunteer teachers, primarily relied on teachers with limited training and education who were often the local village mullahs. Many mullahs do not share the extreme views of the Taliban, and Islamic education has a rich history. Mosque schools offer a form of early childhood education that is underappreciated by many Westerners. 'Nonetheless, relying extensively on undereducated religious leaders as teachers of the Afghan national curriculum could bring unforeseen costs as well as benefits' (Burde, 2010: 258). For Burde, the potential of community-based schools to mitigate violence in Afghanistan appears to be most promising in response to criminal and ideological attacks. Distance to school is critical, as criminal violence that targets children and teachers en route to school would likely be curtailed if the distance were reduced. However, 'among ideological actors, since the Taliban pursue persuasion and domination not annihilation, attacking a community-based school, particularly in a Pashtun region, could undermine the Taliban's social base' (Burde, 2010: 258). Elsewhere, communitarian rivalries are more significant than Taliban attacks in spurring violence that affects education. In this case the type of school – whether government or community based – becomes irrelevant if the intention is to eliminate the community and if the whole population is under attack. But overall, Burde concludes, community-based schools do have characteristics that should serve to deter violence.

What is important about studies such as Burde's is mapping the type of violence (criminal, ideological, communitarian) against motivations for attack – or for desisting from an attack. How exactly community-based schools can be protective in an arena such as Afghanistan is complex and shifting. The community defence initiative established school protection *shura* (councils) where there were no school management committees, and instituted child protection officers. Marit Glad's (2009) study *Knowledge on Fire* found a mixed impact of the scheme, but that clear community involvement in the running of schools and the defence of schools seems to be correlated with a reduced likelihood of attack and a greater chance of negotiated prevention. CBSs do receive threats, forcing suspension of operations, but suffer very few physical attacks.

Save the Children have helped support the setting up of community-based child-protection committees in Kandahar province. With the support of NGOs, the committees encouraged imams to give Friday sermons about the importance of education and decided to place night guards at schools. The NGOs also trained the committees on the Convention on the Rights of the Child and issues surrounding corporal punishment, psycho-social support and school protection. District School Protection Committees negotiated with locally based attackers to allow attendance at schools and agreed to rename their schools as madrassas for the afternoon shifts of the school day (UNESC0, 2010: 29). As well as such renaming, communities have been permitted to nominate a local trained teacher of their choice to join the school's staff and ensure that nothing anti-Islamic is taking place. The school *shuras* are involved in going through the curriculum or textbooks for such monitoring. Schools have been told to build prayer breaks into the timetable.

However, school *shuras* are still seen to need much development and support. I facilitated a somewhat edgy workshop in June 2012 intended to bring together Provincial Education Departments (PEDs) and school *shura* representatives. I was glad that, as in the instruction posted on the door, weapons had been left outside, as the discussions were heated in the extreme and at times appeared near violence. Some pilot research for the workshop had established that *shura* elected representatives were almost exclusively male. A local woman speaker talking of education for females was shouted down with cries translated roughly as 'what about the men?' One PED representative refused to fill in this speaker's activity sheet on the grounds that some words were in English. Yet the *shura* representatives themselves were happy and able to do SWOT analysis, admitting nepotism, conservatism and unequal gender balance, as well as being able to identify many successes in school material improvement, observation of teachers and relations with the community. While *shura* positioning and power with regard to local administration is variable, it seems that they are established as a force within the community, and can be drawn upon further.

In a very different setting, community action has also been seen as efficacious in Northern Ireland. Sectarian attacks in Belfast in 2001, where Catholic school children had to pass through a Protestant neighbourhood to get to school, led to a violent dispute lasting three months. Parents and children had to be guaranteed access to school on a daily basis and were subject to verbal abuse and threatening behaviour, including a pipe bomb attack, from protesters. It is interesting that legal routes to resolve the dispute were explored but proved too slow. International observers commented and acted as witnesses but this instrumentalized children and families in abstract debates about issues outside the community. High-profile media coverage locally and internationally was both praised for drawing attention to the situation and yet criticized for making it more difficult for the parties involved to end the confrontation. The incident ended when parents, community members, and clergy negotiated that the protest be 'suspended'. 'Once the children's right to education was re-established', government was able to negotiate to resolve grievances (UNESCO, 2010: 30). Rights appear to have played a role here.

Cutting across these examples of successful resolution of school attacks in Northern Ireland, Nepal, and Afghanistan is the importance less of the creation of legal frameworks and more of agency at local level, particularly in negotiation. The role of community in the security of schools is critical, even if, as Burde (2010) suggests, it is not to be taken for granted or thought to provide a simple mechanism. When attacks have a primarily religious basis, is the aim to shift the ideology of attackers or to retain the ideology and change its expression or impact? This arises again in the next chapter when discussing the mentoring of extremists.

The legal framework
However, it is important to emphasize the state's role in protection too. The useful British Institute of International and Comparative Law Handbook *Protecting Education in Insecurity and Armed Conflict* (Hausler *et al.*, 2012) details all the rights that states have the duty to protect against infringement: the right to education, the protection against discrimination and the right to freedom of expression. Expressions of hate or intolerance, for example offensive graffiti, are prohibited under International Human Rights Law. Legal prohibitions on discrimination use the principle of 'reasonable accommodation' for those with disabilities, 'whereby modifications or adjustments that do not impose disproportionate or undue burden must be taken if necessary to ensure equality of enjoyments or the exercise of other human rights' (Hausler *et al.*, 2012: 126). This principle could also be used

for religious accommodation, although the handbook does not specify this. The Convention on Discrimination in Education (CDE) does allow for separate religious systems in some instances, such as gender separation or for religious or linguistic reasons 'as long as the opportunities are equal in all systems' (126). However, the handbook acknowledges that the matter of separate schools is a debated issue as it may reinforce stereotyping.

International law is very clear on freedom of thought, conscience, and religion, which is helpful in decisions within dynamic secularism:

> This means that anyone can manifest his religion or belief in teaching. It also means that the content of education itself must be neutral and objective. Neutrality in education does not necessarily mean that schools have to be entirely free of religious signs. The ECtHR [European Convention on Human Rights] decided that the presence of crucifixes in classrooms is not against religious freedom even though it highlights the dominant religion of a territory. However, if a religious symbol is part of a process of indoctrination, if a school curriculum contains compulsory religious teaching against the beliefs of the students, then there is a violation of freedom of religion through education. A school may also offer teaching of a particular religion but it must then offer an exemption (or an acceptable alternative) to this religious instruction if it goes against a child's beliefs.
>
> (Hausler *et al.*, 2012: 127)

The handbook is also helpful on parental rights. Parents have the right to choose freely the religious and moral education of their children, and send them to private schools to facilitate religious upbringing. However, and this is important:

> The need to respect the parents' convictions are limited by the primary right of a child to receive education. Thus, for example, a parent cannot decide to take a child out of school on a particular day because of religious beliefs. While parents can object to a particular religious education, they cannot oppose other educational matters or demand that a State school provide a specific school to cater for their religion, as long as knowledge is provided in a neutral and objective manner.
>
> (Hausler *et al.*, 2012: 127–8)

Two crucial aspects that support a secular approach appear here: a) that education constitutes the primary right, superseding parental convictions;

and b) that parents cannot demand a specific school to cater for their religion. This underscores the arguments that in a DSS, religion is not privileged.

On the other hand the law does protect religious freedom. An interesting case is that of *Jehovah's Witnesses v. Argentina* in which the President of Argentina had decreed the closing of all the Kingdom Halls of the Jehovah's Witnesses and the outlawing of their literature and the practice of their religion. As well as religious freedom, the Inter-American Commission on Human Rights (IACommHR) considered whether the decree also violated the right to education, as more than three hundred children of primary age had been dismissed from a school or prevented from enrolling into school because of their religious convictions. Those who continued their education at home were then denied the opportunity to sit exams to obtain a qualification, again on the basis of their religious affiliation. The IACommHR concluded that the decree and its implementation violated the right to equal opportunity in education and more generally the right to education, and recommended its repeal.

Protection of religious minorities in school

This leads to the second main theme of this chapter, the security of religious minorities in a school, and whether this security is compromised by various forms of discrimination. As with the discussion on school security, the question is whether general strategies on inclusion and protection sufficiently relate to religion and religious minorities, or whether specific action needs to be taken. I use the example of Islamophobia here, as this is something I have been working on – and struggling with. I was part of a small team (with Jasmin Zine and Sarah Soyei) that was commissioned to produce a set of guidelines for the Organization for Security and Co-operation in Europe/ Office for Democratic Institutions and Human Rights (OSCE/ODIHR), which came to be called *Guidelines for Educators on Countering Intolerance and Discrimination against Muslims: Addressing Islamophobia through education.* The somewhat unwieldy title gives a clue to the sorts of discussions that went on in our team and then in a larger group of scrutineers of our work: Was the problem one of 'intolerance'?; Was it about religious discrimination or anti-Muslim racism?; Should we use the word Islamophobia, as the phenomenon was more than simple 'fear' of Muslims?; Who was the audience for this? The OSCE (together with the Council of Europe and UNESCO) wanted something to parallel the guidelines for educators that had been produced on anti-Semitism, to be able to publicize and disseminate the recommendations around different parts of Europe. The end result was quite a bland document, with many controversial parts redacted. It was interesting how an in-depth discussion of Islamophobia was somewhat compromised by what I might call *bureaucraphobia*, the fear of anything beyond an official line. Nonetheless, the experience of writing and researching the field for this document and for other work gives many insights relevant to the discussion of security.

There would probably be agreement that while most strategies around discrimination, racism and xenophobia could apply to all vulnerable groups, stereotypes about Islam and Muslims in recent years have taken unique forms. This has been fuelled by the War on Terror, as well as by the actions of radical political Islamists. The complication is that 'Muslim' does not just apply to the holding of particular beliefs but relates to cultural heritages and community membership – real or imagined. In *Islamophobia* (2010) Chris Allen shows that the phenomenon is neither consistent nor uniform, and that while it may have a historical legacy, the nature and products of the phenomenon are shaped by the contemporary national, cultural, geographical and socio-economic conditions. Our *Guidelines* made the obvious point about the huge variation among those self-designating as Muslims – and also that intolerance and discrimination were often extended to those who were thought to look like Muslims. It was not difficult to collect myriad examples of intolerance and discrimination in schools in different countries where Muslims were a minority – name-calling, excluding, verbal abuse, derogatory comments about being jihadis, joking about identity and faith, spreading lies and rumours, and physical bullying.

Schools themselves had practices that were discriminatory, relating to dress codes, food, holiday schedules and sports. Some reports suggested that female students wearing a veil were more likely to be placed in lower academic streams or encouraged to avoid academic subjects. Omission of the culture and history of Islam was also cited as a problem.

While I would not automatically privilege religion in terms of recognition and participation in governance, it is clear that the matter of religion needs to be recognized if it relates to discrimination. Certain principles of decision emerge, of which one is freedom of speech. There can be an obvious tension between freedom of expression and respect for others. I was pleased that we were allowed to include the statement 'Freedom of expression does include the right to be critical or even disparaging of religions or religious practices' (ODIHR, 2011: 21). However, as we saw earlier, international instruments draw a clear line on this dichotomy, prohibiting any advocacy of national, racial or religious hatred that constitutes incitement to discrimination, hostility or violence. And while name-calling and other disparaging comments may be legally protected forms of free speech, this does not mean they are appropriate or acceptable in a school.

Avoiding victimhood and exceptionalism

In a thought-provoking article on Islamophobia in South Africa, Ebrahim Rasool (2010) discusses among other things two contentious debates – the type of relationship South Africa should have with religion, and avoiding Muslim exceptionalism. Muslims had discounted the two extremes – the theocratic and atheistic models of relationships – and discussed the two versions of secularism, namely the Chinese Wall or the Porous Wall approaches. They preferred the Porous Wall to the absolute separation of church and state, for a number of reasons – as a tribute to the active role of religious communities in the struggle for freedom; the need to keep infusing social and political life with a religious dimension of ethics and values; and the desire to utilize the full infrastructure of religion in the reconstruction and development of South African society. But it is significant that Rasool talks of the negotiating process between the apartheid government and the liberation movement:

> Muslims could recall from the Qur'anic and Prophetic precedents at Sulh al-Hudaibiya, that negotiation, compromises and not winning all that you desire was sanctioned, if it was at the hand of higher purposes and more sustainable outcomes.
>
> (Rasool, 2010: 150)

Rasool also talks of the problem of avoiding Muslim exceptionalism, which we struggled with in the *Guidelines*:

> It requires sufficient caution when elevating one form of hatred as the defining feature of what is being done to people, at the expense of other forms of suffering. Islamophobia, racism, sexism, anti-Semitism, xenophobia, homophobia, and all related prejudice and discrimination are all the offspring of that moment when coveting another's power, freedom or resources meets up with an intolerance of difference.
>
> (Rasool, 2010: 151)

He explains how South African Muslims, had they been hooked on the idea that they were suffering only because they were Muslims, and that their situation of oppression was unique, would have been unable to recognize the suffering in others, make common cause with them, enter with them into life and death struggles for survival and adopt a set of common objectives towards freedom from oppression and a state of equality. It was instructive that the one moment in post-apartheid South Africa which had the greatest potential for Islamophobia occurred when the same group of Muslims who tried to 'Islamize' the anti-apartheid struggle so as to justify an end game of an Islamic state, organized themselves into an urban terror group, threatening and assassinating gangsters and later businessmen and even *ulema* with whom they disagreed. Fear of this group became a genuine fear of Muslims. The Muslim leadership was able to dissipate this group and rally the Muslim community against them.

This points to the question of what sort of agency is taken. A critical insight from Rasool is that South African Muslims, throughout the periods of suppression and repression, and more importantly, despite these experiences, did not adopt 'the mantle of victimhood'. Islamophobia, and experiencing hatred towards you, can be an objective and real experience. 'When you internalise this objective reality, and suppose yourself a victim, you elevate your suffering above all other suffering ... It gives you the licence for self-pity and passivity, alternatively for what you may consider justified extremism' (Rasool, 2010: 153). Rasool asserts that South African Muslims, on the contrary, assumed agency, to insert themselves into the broader struggle:

> The clarity of such agency is that you recognise that what is done to you and your faith community is a variation on a theme of brutality done to all those considered the other and who purvey difference and opposition. This insight, that we are all victims of one source of brutality, but through methodologies specific to a varied conditions, allows, not victimhood, but agency in responding to the challenge confronting us.
>
> (Rasool, 2010: 153)

Rasool argues against elevating Islamophobia and hatred of Islam above the general impact of the negative consequences that come with globalization, such as poverty, conflicts or marginalization. Conferring a state of uniqueness on Muslim suffering lessens the possibility of collaboration with the millions of others who struggle.

So were these *Guidelines* elevating Islamophobia? Supporting Muslim exceptionalism? We tried to counter this by advocating a general rights-based approach which would tackle all forms of racism or sexism. As argued in the last chapter, a rights-based approach also allows for a degree of exceptionalism, in that the justification for, say, a prayer room in a state or Christian school would relate to the right to learn – something that enabled students to experience a learning environment conducive to their comfort and concentration. This is not a question of a religious right. Sticking to the conventions, the rules, enables distinctions to be drawn. Hence any accommodation to dress or food is acceptable, as long as it does not impede others' right to learn.

Robert Crane, in an article intriguingly titled 'Islamophobia, mimetic warfare and the bugaboo of shari'a compliance: Counter-strategies for common ground', rightly protests about the conflation of Islam with Muslim. Islam is a religion, and Muslims include people who commit crimes against humanity in the name of Islam. There is not a single Islamic regime in the world. This means that there is certainly no Islamic world, although arguably there is a distinct Muslim world in which the majority of people in 57 different countries are Muslims. Crane observes:

> As long as we fail to distinguish the difference between Christianity and Christendom or between Islam and Islamdom, or between Judaism and Jews, the chances of civilization surviving on earth for as long as eighty years is distinctly problematic.
>
> (Crane, 2010: 55)

I would add to this the difference 'between secularism and secularization'. Until people stop seeing secularism as a thing to fear, a 'secularophobia' on a par with Islamophobia, we will make no progress on how relations between state and religion can move forward. As Crane points out, the substance of war for extremists is to invent and instigate a clash of civilizations and to declare a holy war with the slogan 'No substitute for victory'. Debates about religion and secularism are not to be cast as a clash of civilizations, nor as secularism somehow proposing a global religion-free or at least religion-lite world. It is about worlds living together and intersecting, not about domination.

Given that the audience for the *Guidelines* was educators, we were concerned not to ignore the reality experienced by some of them. That reality included racism *by* Muslim students, as well as tensions between different branches of Islam (for example Sunni versus Shia) which got played out in the classroom or playground. Our thought was that teachers would feel patronized if the *Guidelines* simply told them to be sensitive and yet seemed not to acknowledge the complexity of their professional lives and of the intricate relations between students – in which religion was only one factor. But this part was removed – presumably on the grounds that it would offend Muslims or increase hostility. Yet, as Abdullah Faliq (2010) points out in the 'Editorial introduction' to a special edition of *Arches Quarterly* on Islamophobia, while there is evidence of Islamophobia or anti-Muslimism across much of Europe, and of a society that views this as acceptable:

> Conversely the Muslim civil society has to accept responsibility for its part in contributing to the rise of Islamophobia by a) not engaging adequately with wider society in fighting extremism and injustices across the board rather than only those which concern Muslims and b) the reprehensible actions and rhetoric of extremists within the community who are equally guilty of Westernophobia. Although Europe is considered a bastion of Islamophobic racism, we should not lose sight of racism among Muslims and racist policies peddled by Muslim governments.
>
> (Faliq, 2010: 7)

I think the *Guidelines* would have been stronger for recognition of this sort, instead of the constant portrayal of Muslims as victims. Nonetheless, it is to be hoped that the sections proposing much discussion and critical thinking in the classroom, with suggestions for both stimulating this and for managing it, would facilitate sensitive and controversial issues to be aired in a safe space. We included the usual ground rules for safe discussion, with examples such as:

- All participants must be treated with respect and courtesy.
- Only views can be attacked, not people.
- There must be a reason for a challenge: that is, a student or teacher cannot simply say 'that's rubbish' but must provide a reason for his or her opposition or query.
- All participants must be allowed to state their opinion without interruption. The use of a 'talking stick' whereby only the holder of that stick can speak can help.
- Participants should ask questions to help others develop their views.

Examples of ways in which students (and teachers) can examine their own prejudices were provided: in Canada, a nice one was a poster showing women, men and children from different backgrounds and with different clothes, engaged in various roles. The question is 'Who am I?' Students are first asked to identify those who are 'Canadian'. In most instances, it was the blonde-haired and fair-skinned people who were identified (even in multi-ethnic classrooms). Students are then asked to identify 'the Muslims' – picking in most cases darker-skinned people or women wearing hijab. Finally it is revealed that everyone in the picture is both Canadian and Muslim. A similar sort of exercise in the UK entailed a visit to a school by two men – one with spiky hair, a leather jacket and jeans, the other in full Muslim dress, with a beard and *taqiyah*. Students were asked which one was the imam and which the police officer. They were confounded when the young trendy man turned out to be the imam and the one in Muslim dress the police officer. The latter told stories of being stopped at the airport and having to show his police ID.

We also recommended resources such as *What Do We Do with a Difference? France and the debate over headscarves in schools* (Facing History and Ourselves, 2008). This has illuminating quotations from Tunisian and Algerian parents pointing out the hypocrisy of the French position – that there are schools or universities where there are no exams on a Saturday because it is the Jewish Sabbath; that there are meatless meals on Fridays because of the Catholics; and that 'the secular school doesn't miss celebrating Easter'. These parents did not mind such incursions of religion into the schools – it was the double standards they objected to.

One of the principles of a dynamic secularism is transparency on aims as well as feedback on strategy. What does banning 'ostentatious' or 'aggressive' religious symbols actually achieve? Wherever possible, accommodation is better than prohibition and is far more functional. As specified in the ODIHR Guiding Principles on the teaching of religion (2007), students should be able to opt out of the teaching of religion in the sense of religious instruction, although not of teaching about religion or religions in general, which may be compulsory. In sports, opt out may be a bit more complex. Hating sport, I would have loved an opt out provision. But the right to health might imply compulsory physical exercise, and the right to life might imply the need to learn to swim. As always, negotiation, discussion, dialogue and dynamism are key.

Preventing future insecurity

The mention of multiple voices brings us on to the third aspect of secure schools, that of foreseeing future insecurity, in particular of preventing extremism. I said a great deal about this in *Educating Against Extremism* (Davies, 2008). Some of my key points were about resisting absolutism, black and white answers and singular 'truths', and being comfortable with ambiguity and provisionality. This does present a challenge to some religious orthodoxy. I look now at some of the more recent work in challenging extremism, in order to bring to the surface the continuing debates as well as some of the energizing initiatives that are happening. I am mostly using examples from the UK, as this is the context I know best and have been most involved with.

Much of the educational work in UK schools is associated with the government's Preventing Violent Extremism (PVE) strategy, now called Prevent. Originally this drew some criticism, particularly from Muslim groups, as being about the targeting of Muslims and, in schools, about teachers being asked to be 'watchful' in spotting potential terrorists in their midst. However, there is now increasing sophistication about Prevent. The move has been from surveillance of suspicious-looking students to whole-school approaches around radicalization and extremism designed to reach all students (and staff). (I say more about the critiques of Prevent in the next chapter.) In 2008 the then Department for Children, Schools and Families launched *Learning Together to be Safe: A toolkit to help schools contribute to the prevention of violent extremism and the Government's 'Prevent strategy'*. I was involved in some of this preparation, and watched feedback with interest. By 2011 the focus had changed and the objectives were revised: to respond to the ideological challenge of terrorism and the threat from those who promote it; to prevent people from being drawn into terrorism and ensure that they are given appropriate advice and support; and to work with sectors and institutions where there are risks of radicalization. Research on *Learning Together to be Safe* included findings that:

- the toolkit was not really a toolkit, i.e. there were no actual resources to use
- some teachers felt lacking in confidence to deal with these sensitive topics
- there were concerns about where these subjects fitted into the demands of the curriculum and discussions on how Prevent could be covered within safeguarding frameworks.

As a result of research such as this, and demands from teachers, a number of resources have been developed for schools. The debates have not diminished but provide continuous learning and critical feedback mechanisms which fit our concerns about adaptability. These resources do not stay still.

The website Prevent for Schools (www.preventforschools.org, accessed 1 October 2012) catalogues and gives access to a number of different resources, including how to stay safe on the internet, theatre productions, students working as community ambassadors, producing films, making art exhibitions for the public, using computer simulations and touring prisons to show the grim reality – the whole raft of creative ideas. This chapter cannot go through all the resources, but it highlights some in order to tease out some points of learning from the evaluations that have been done. What they have in common is:

- the space for talking about controversial issues
- giving teachers confidence to do this
- critical thinking, debate, dialogue, challenge
- setting off emotions
- whole-school approaches

- linking with other curriculum areas
- localized understandings; the use of local personnel, such as police
- inputs to aid understanding and knowledge – not just discussion but information
- being agents of change – from making their own choices to trying to influence the community
- fun and laughs.

The obvious question is whether there is anything there that is not just part of good pedagogy. The answer is probably not – but an underpinning is the taking of risks. One school took a whole week off timetable for Year 10 students to make a film (see below). The theatre productions, such as *One Extreme to Another*, are very hard-hitting, as can be seen from the synopsis:

> Ali's got mixed up with an Islamic extremist. His former friend Tony is flirting with the far racist right and unemployment is rising. There's been another terrorist attack in London and a far right organisation is organising a march through Ali's neighbourhood. Will Tony march? Will Ali fight? Can his sister Sarah make him find another way? Will journalist Jessica use past relationships to get a scoop on the threatened riots, or will she put principles before her career to stop the clash and avert disaster?
>
> (Prevent, n.d.)

Performances are followed immediately by a hot-seating session where the audience is invited to ask questions of some of the play's key characters, and also to offer them some advice.

The *Tapestry* production from the Play House has a similar theme, of contrasting two different types of potential extremists – right-wing fascist and ideological religious extremist. Jason and Hassan have become involved with the Young Patriots and The Circle of Truth as a result of various events and circumstances in their lives. Threads of parallel stories are played out which cross community, religious, political and family lines to explore what divides us, what we hold in common, and what drives the few to consider taking matters into their own hands (Tapestry, 2013). Again, the audience is invited to talk to the actors in role and challenge their positions. Having watched performances in schools, it is clear to me that the exceedingly lively, sometimes humorous, and always localized treatment engages the students. *Tapestry* does not give moral messages or solutions but enables students to articulate their own responses. One of the great advantages is that the protagonists can be challenged for their views and actions, so that no one is 'offended' or feels liable to personal attack in the class. One boy said to a protagonist: 'If you did this in Muslim countries, you'd be tortured, killed, go to jail – you're enjoying the benefits of the West … .' One girl queried the mechanisms of violence: 'Has anything improved for me since you started using your fists?' Again, this production has unpredictable outcomes in terms of what students will engage with and what has resonance for them.

Not In My Name is another theatre production, this time performed by young people, with 75 per cent of the text made up of the words spoken by young people and community figures in the research phase. The play explores the aftermath of a terror attack on a small northern town. At the play's ending the audience learns that it was set a year into the future and the production then leaps back to the present day so that the audience can meet the attacker. Audiences were tasked with advising the young man on alternative steps he could take to make the difference he wants to see. In the evaluation the students appreciated the realism, if finding it daunting. They felt they knew more about Islam, about misinterpretation, and that not all Muslims were terrorists. They commented on 'The racism. I didn't think things were that bad'; 'The feelings from Asians in response to white people's comments'; 'I found out that it would be/is very hard to live as a Muslim.' Teachers also valued the approach: 'Outcomes met – made lots of audience uncomfortable' (Bartlett and Raffle, 2010: 8). Taking people out of their comfort zone is a fundamental strategy in awareness raising.

Learning and awareness come from not just watching but creating a production. In the PVE project in Colne Primet High School a group of Year 7 (first-year secondary) students devised an interactive theatre piece on Islamic extremism. The group – a mix of Muslims and non-Muslims – were chosen specifically because of their sometimes challenging attitudes around race and religion. They started with a series of short and intentionally provocative scenes to perform to each Year 7 class. These scenes included statements such as 'All young men are violent', 'All Asians are Muslims', and 'All Muslim women should cover their hair'. Following these short performances, each class engaged in discussion and it was the views expressed that informed the content of the final piece of theatre. What emerged from these classroom debates was the willingness of the pupils to openly discuss ideas which the adults found uncomfortable. They positively welcomed a forum in which they could ask questions around a subject which had previously seemed taboo. Questions such as, 'Is Islam a country?'; 'What does Jihad mean?'; and 'If a white person went to Pakistan would they be killed?' were all discussed. One highly significant point was raised from the account:

From the teachers' and creative practitioners' perspectives there was a realisation that much of the apprehension around approaching this topic was mainly down to our own fears; fear of offending and fear of our own ignorance, *states of mind which the pupils have not yet inherited.*[my italics]

(Curious Minds, n.d.: 20)

The fear of showing ignorance is definitely a block to exploration and sadly one that schools do not always dispel – in students or teachers. Teachers reported that they started to feel more comfortable with the subject: 'it is as if the box has been opened'. Their fears that Muslim pupils would find the area difficult to handle were unfounded: 'And perhaps we adults should listen more to our young people as they often express issues with a beautiful simplicity – for example, "Why do we think fighting will stop fighting?"' (Bartlett and Raffle, 2010: 20). The downside of live theatre productions is that they rely on the actors. An alternative has been the production of DVDs, as in Phase 2 of the Welsh Getting on Together (GOT) project. In their DVD *Challenging Extremism,* launched in May 2011, a number of televisual techniques were used – the use of archive footage, visual graphics, and the inclusion of a number of credible interviewees. The DVD includes a quotation from Martin Luther King: 'The question is not whether we will be extremists, but what kind of extremists we will be. ... The nation and the world are in dire need of creative extremists.' The DVD has been designed for maximum discussion afterwards – and, as the producer said, to get young people to talk openly and 'to express those views within the law of the land, as our democracy allows' (Yassine, n.d.).

DVDs are also used in Saudi Arabian Prevent-type programmes (of which more in the next chapter). One example was a television programme, based on a real story, that featured a character who was recruited for a terrorist attack. When this young Saudi man learned that this was to be a suicide attack, he refused to carry it out, but the extremists deceived him and detonated the explosives remotely. The character in the programme survived but was left severely disfigured. The message was clear: involvement with terrorists will result in tragic consequences for you and your family (Boucek, 2008). Yet Saudi programmes would be less likely to welcome open-ended discussion: Boucek also reports on how the government takes steps to retrain 'deviant teachers' who abuse their time with students by discussing extra-curricular issues such as politics and religion and by advocating extremist positions. It is not clear how the government distinguishes discussion and advocacy, but there is no doubt it wants to restrict 'unauthorised views' (Boucek, 2008: 9).

In the UK, other resources have been developed in concert with the police – again a contentious area for young people and for minority communities who feel scapegoated. 'ACT Now' (All Communities Together) is a well-known resource of four lessons, with the third being a table-top exercise delivered by external community facilitators with support from the police. It concentrates on supporting five crucial areas, with the aims that:

- the ideology sustaining violent extremism is discredited and alternative narratives/messages carry greater prominence and credibility
- vulnerable institutions and the public are able to identify and resist radicalization
- people can effectively address or rebut grievances that contribute to violent extremism
- there is understanding about how organizations such as the police gather, analyse and utilize information they receive
- there is understanding about how agencies such as the police communicate with the media, partners and communities and how this can be improved.

(ACT Now, 2009: 3)

The 'Social Storm' resource developed by Redbridge Council, on the other hand, is targeted at local schools to develop an understanding of online grooming by extremists and seeks to develop critical thinking in young people, encouraging them to critically analyse online propaganda. Significantly, local school pupils provided substantial input into the development of the resource. It follows a mythical conversation representing online grooming and propaganda, and the background notes perhaps sum up the whole contemporary approach to tackling violent extremism:

> The lesson does not seek to attempt to provide the 'right answer' to religious or politicised questions, but to introduce young people to the idea of analysing online material and debates by seeking additional sources which may provide alternative perspectives. As the teacher follows the progression of the mock online conversation the product itself provides the key messages students should consider. The strength of Social Storm is that the teacher does not have to provide theological or political answers that they may not feel skilled or knowledgeable about. The product aims to teach young people how to think and question information, rather than what to think or say.
>
> (ACPO, 2012a: 4)

This approach could constitute a perceived risk for some educators and schools, particularly if the teacher is seen to be the person who provides the answers, and even more particularly if there is a desire to have measurable 'outcomes'. As with discussions after the theatre productions, it is not known in what directions the students will go, and what they will make of 'additional sources'. (The benefits of schooling not having rigid end goals was discussed in the last chapter, and this fits well.) Yet this is the most exhilarating part of contemporary educational approaches to tackling extremism. A similar aim is found in 'Common Goals', which is a resource from Warwickshire for secondary school Years 7 and 8 students (age 11–13/14). The title sounds like one of those multifaith dialogues that seek to find shared understandings. However, it is the opposite, and warns of the dangers of seeming commonality. Its aims are to:

- identify the attractions of being part of a group
- identify ways in which radical/extremist groups attract members
- explain how radicalized/extremist groups use common goals to achieve their purpose.

The resource tackles not just online or other grooming but also the heady allure of membership of a group and its mindsets.

What is coming through from all these initiatives is the need for innovatory ways of embedding projects in the curriculum, not just as one-off events. 'Curious Minds' for example is a creative arts programme for Lancashire secondary schools which aims to address the objectives of the *Learning Together to be Safe* toolkit. The learning from the project has been that using creative, arts-based approaches increases the likelihood of open conversations both within the classroom and beyond. The localism is important, as well as alignment with the wider national curriculum, supporting the delivery of subjects such as citizenship, media studies, English, geography, art and religious education, so that is it not a bolt-on. However, reflections on the project showed that it takes time to get all partners on board. A number of schools initially expressed an interest in participating in the programme, but later withdrew because of concerns that parents or the local community might perceive the work to be inflammatory. It is seen as risky. Lancashire Partnership had to work hard with some schools to ensure their projects were challenging enough and were not solely focused on social cohesion but also looked directly at violent extremism. One key piece of learning, which supports my advocacy of a rights base for imaginative learning in this area, was presented on the Local Innovation Awards Scheme website:

Lynn Davies

It is crucial that schools understand the role they must play in challenging extremist messages both within school and in engaging with the wider community. This involves supporting individual pupils at risk, alongside developing a creative curriculum and strong ethos which upholds core values of democratic voice, pupil voice and human rights.

(www.localinnovation.idea.gov.uk/idk/core/page.do?pageId=17449227, Accessed 15 February 2013)

One head teacher (Mike Tull, Marsden Heights Community College, Pendle) on the 'Curious Minds' project went further, saying:

The fundamental difference between the imperative to forge and develop a cohesive learning community and the imperative to safeguard all members of that community is the level and nature of challenge. There are fundamental rights and wrongs which are not defined by religious, cultural and ethnic identity or culture. At every opportunity we must express the values that are incontrovertibly right and wrong, acceptable and unacceptable and it is our duty to ensure that our students are clear about these moral absolutes. If these absolutes are seen as being open to debate then this can open the door to extremist attitudes, including the justification for violence which may ultimately lead to the taking of life.

(Curious Minds, n.d.: 9)

I think there is a debate to be had about this. As devil's advocate, I could offer the opposite view – that positing incontrovertible moral absolutes actually opens the door to extremism. While I claim rights as the most secure underpinning for an educational institution, this is not because they are always absolutes. The point is for students to debate circumstances when a right that appears to be incontrovertible – the right to life, the right to education, the right to privacy, the right to speech – may not be upheld in some circumstances. This does not mean that rights are all adaptable, flexible, or relativistic. They are a security net, enabling daring things on the high wire. The security comes from knowing they are there to fall back on, not from their absolute nature for all time. Yet I fully understand the concern of Mike Tull, and respect his position on this as a head teacher. Distinctions do need to be made. I am comforted by the evaluation of the 'We Choose to Create' project, which said: 'By the end of the project pupils were clearly able to articulate the difference between strong beliefs expressed within a

156

human rights framework and ethos and strong beliefs arising from extremist ideologies'.

It is worth looking more at this particular project, to see how this was achieved. Rhyddings Business and Enterprise School wanted to develop a programme that would raise awareness of the issues surrounding violent extremism and bring together pupils and staff from across different curriculum areas – including performing arts, personal, social and health education (PSHE) and citizenship – for the benefit of future pupils. The outcome was a film, made when twenty Year 10 students came off timetable for a full week to work with staff and a professional film maker. In making the film, the students learned more about media and image as well as the reasons why people might turn to extremism. Pressure from peers, not having a voice and 'feeling that one's beliefs are constantly trashed in the media' were all emerging themes that pupils wanted to explore further. Although these students did not feel they could relate directly to the motives for extremist and violent behaviour, they did feel able to relate to some of the feelings that might be involved and could connect them with strong emotions and frustrations within their own lives. The resulting film had powerful personal narratives, with communication in modes such as dance. One student participating commented that 'young people need to be made aware of the message we are trying to get across because they are kept away from so much and they need to know about some of the negative things in the world.' This resonates with the findings of our study of teachers' and learners' needs from a Global Citizenship curriculum (Davies *et al.*, 2004), where students said they wanted to know more about war and the reasons for hate, and felt short-changed by teachers who did not want to discuss this area.

There would not be uniformity in the way that schools see and use the various products, and the various evaluations of programmes give clues to some of the underlying conditions or constraints. I conducted an evaluation of an interactive resource called 'Choices and Voices' produced by the Serious Games company, PlayGen, and supported by West Midlands Police (Davies, 2011). It takes the form of a computer simulation of social scenarios depicting tensions in community issues, where students have to make decisions about whether to participate and whether to use violence. Significantly, the resource does not talk about extremism or religion as such, but brings out issues of absolutism, peer pressure, adventure, secrecy, belonging, grievance, and following authoritarian leadership. As with all such resources, the eventual aim is to open discussion and bring controversial issues to the surface within a safe environment. Students mainly enjoyed playing the game, making decisions, and realizing they had a choice. The evaluation does however throw up pedagogical issues of how to provide stimulus materials. A couple of students were suspicious: 'The game is just trying to change the minds of the kids and it's full of bull. Really because you're just trying to make them take the easy option' (Davies, 2011: 8). Others thought it was a cool game that gets you thinking, 'that it is really good for people to go against bad things'. One said wistfully: '…I'd love to protest in real life. It seems awesome'. Overall there was reflection about beliefs and cultures, and extrapolations to other situations.

Having observed a number of sessions with different teachers or police officers facilitating the discussion after the activity, it was clear to me that the role and style of the teacher was critical in how the discussion went, and how directed or genuinely open it was. I noted that some students got sidetracked into the quality of the graphics and the degree of realism. Was throwing eggs or setting fire to things actually what would happen? As one experienced realist explained: 'One kid did arson. Should have just got him into a corner and hit him'. So should the resource have had more violence in it or less? Should it have signalled a concern with extremism upfront or not? The jury is out on this; the main lesson is to have a number of resources, a number of entry points. Perhaps the key comment was 'It's better than the usual stuff we do at school'.

Finally, an evaluation of a Prevent programme called 'Creativity, Culture and Education' (King *et al.*, 2010) threw up questions of identity and of encounter. On the creative writing project, 'My Voice', one author mentor encouraged their mentee to write the same story but for three different audiences. This exercise enhanced skills but also the ability to think empathetically about others. The notion of hybrid identities was supported: one outcome was to create resilience to the binary and overly simplistic understanding of communities (the 'us' and 'them' mentality) which is exploited by violent extremist rhetoric and radicalization processes. The evaluation found that participants' development in thinking around identity appeared to have been driven in part by engaging with creative media as a vehicle for self-expression but also by engaging with other individuals whom they would not normally meet in their daily lives. This underscores the argument in the last chapter about the value of close encounters with difference – not seeing others as aliens but rather recognizing that there are a range of viewpoints out there.

From ten in-depth case studies, the evaluation also provided insights into the sorts of teaching methods that help to build resilience to violent extremism, and I confess to being on the Expert Reference Group for this. The focus was on the prevention of radicalization rather than post-radicalization intervention (although as was pointed out, the process of radicalization is not a linear one). A number of key ingredients were found that would be generic for good teaching – lessons that are enjoyable, delivered by a teacher who models desired behaviours, producing something 'real' at the end of a project, and so on. In this area, external facilitators may be of benefit, with their specialized knowledge and experience in forming different sorts of relationships. There would be a debate about whether having external facilitators protects teachers from having to reveal their personal beliefs – or whether good pedagogy does mean teachers being honest about where they stand. This area points up the particular importance of adapting and amending practice, in that the ability to deal with challenging, controversial, or incendiary language has to be adapted in certain settings. Not all safe spaces are the same. Several factors are important for creating a safe space, including:

- the development, preferably with young people, of agreed ground rules which are easy to remember, and which provide a vital route of recourse if things become heated or if unsavoury things are said
- the ability of facilitators to ensure that sessions are inclusive and supportive to all, and to be able to deal with a young person saying something unpalatable, incendiary or offensive, while not being judgemental about them as persons
- tools and techniques which enable young people to facilitate sensitive discussions themselves, thereby taking ownership of the safe space.

Yet in the end, risks have to be taken about letting go of the discussion, and about finding an appropriate use of humour.

Conclusion

While dealing with seemingly disparate areas of schools and security, this chapter has identified 'the encounter' as providing a common thread. When trying to make schools safe from outside attack in countries such as Afghanistan, the community was seen to be central, not in making the school a fortress but in negotiating with insurgents or even government forces. This sometimes meant concessions in relation to teaching and learning objectives and syllabuses, agreeing to appoint teachers to monitor Islamic standards and values (e.g. in content and images in school textbooks). Elsewhere, the key to providing safety for religious minorities such as Muslims in a predominantly secular or Christian institution was to open up discussion, colliding with the experiences and feelings of those minorities and encountering one's own preconceptions and prejudices.

A similar philosophy was found in successful projects on preventing violent extremism, where students were confronted with controversial issues through drama, interactive technology, film making and creative arts – as with Islamophobia, thinking about the politics of the issues and simultaneously reflecting on their own emotions. Projects also considered how to engage with others in the wider community. None of these is without risk. Negotiating with the 'enemy' is the most obvious risk, but hazarding open-ended discussion in class with no notion of how it will end is, while on a different scale, worrying for teachers. Critiques of one's own and others' religion have to be permitted. Complex adaptive skill sets of negotiation, advocacy, conflict resolution, diplomacy, and choosing the way one uses language come to the forefront. In safe spaces, turbulence has to be created in order to investigate how it can be resolved – and whether even more or different sorts of turbulence are called for.

All is not anarchy, though. The chapter has also considered the enabling constraint of the law – whether in monitoring mechanisms for designating attacks on schools as war crimes or the international law on protecting education in insecurity and armed conflict. Knowing and using this law would be an enabling feature in disruption of conflict, in positive turbulence for peace.

Chapter 6

Learning and unlearning extremist behaviours

... The trouble is that in the modern world the stupid are cocksure while the intelligent are full of doubt.

Bertrand Russell

From the discussion of preventing violent extremism at school level, I move on to explore educational interventions for those already designated as extremist or seen as at risk. One consideration relating to secularism is whether the state should intervene in religious beliefs if these beliefs are seen to be contributing to potential violence.

There is a now a considerable literature on the background of extremists, and the chapter cannot hope to tackle all of it. Nor can it enter the whole field of counter-terrorism. As befits a book on education, what it does is look at some of those aspects which relate to learning: how religious ideologies are learned, but also what has been learned by those trying to counter extremism. This includes some illustrations of what we have learned about what *not* to do in terms of intervention, followed by some research on programmes of mentoring in different contexts.

What we have learned about extremists and terrorists – or should have

The first, obvious learning point is that people do change. Jihadists are not born as such, nor brainwashed from a very early age – the 'green diaper' theory of Islamic terrorism. As Sageman points out, jihadis are seldom well educated in religion. 'Their religious understanding is limited; they know about as much as any secular person, which is to say, very little' (Sageman, 2008: 51). And we have seen that madrassas are not the direct route to fanaticism. One problem for the idea that family can alert the authorities to their children's path to extremism is that family and friends do not believe that people change and become jihadists. 'Our memory remains frozen in time and we assume that people stay essentially the same' (Sageman, 2008: 4). Parents are usually the last to suspect their beloved child has become a drug addict – or a religion addict.

But accepting that people change is only the first step. We know, not just from complexity theory, that people's conversion is not linear, in spite of the analogies of 'pathways' into terrorism. It is an evolution, unpredictable, messy, a particular convergence of inputs in time and space. Similarly, Sageman warns us not to treat a terrorist organization as a unity but instead to look at how it came into being as a collective in the first place. We need to look at how terrorists evolve, how they interact with others, how they join groups, how they become motivated, how they are influenced by ideas and how they follow orders from faraway leaders. Whether individuals or networks, the key is seeing this as evolutionary. But while you can retrace a path, can you unwind an evolution?

It would be tempting to think there is some kind of terrorist personality, but this is not the case. Nor obviously is there a single cause, such as experience of racism – millions of second-generation children of immigrants are subject to prejudice yet very few become terrorists. However, it is tempting to look for patterns. Many have forayed into the educational background of jihadists, pointing out that the majority have studied technical fields such as engineering and medicine. Osama bin Laden was a civil engineer; Zawahiri was a physician. But the question is why such a high number from these fields? Sageman (2008) explores how engineering and medicine are the two most prestigious faculties in Middle Eastern countries like Egypt. Students, often from the middle class, idealistic, wanting to serve their country, are trying to reach the highest ranks. But as they reach the end of their formal education, they realize that the good jobs are available only through graft, corruption or nepotism. Engineers may also possess a specific frame of mind that draws them to Salafi ideas. Like mathematicians, they try to build from elementary building blocks, to construct arguments from foundations. Such structuring is similar for Salafis, who seek: 'to build an ideal utopia, return to the purity of the first community, that of the Prophet':

> This parallel is convenient. Since they are engineers and not Islamic scholars, they do not know much about 1,400 years of Quranic commentaries, They turn to Islam in their mid-twenties without a strong religious background that might have put into context the new religious arguments they encounter.
>
> (Sageman, 2008: 59)

Again, this turns on its head the notion of madrassas as the breeding ground. The fervour comes instead from the person's *lack* of religious training, which prevents them from evaluating their new beliefs in context. 'Had they received such training, they might not have fallen prey to these seductive Manichean arguments. It follows that more religious education for these young men might have been beneficial' (Sageman, 2008: 60).

I return later to the question of *more* religious education. The notion of brainwashing is also interestingly questioned in work on attempts to secularize people. As Froese (2008) points out, the popular notion of brainwashing as in the film *The Manchurian Candidate* stands in opposition to scientifically rigorous studies that show how social incentives and networks lead reasonable people to accept with full consciousness the teachings of highly deviant religious or political groups. Individuals cannot be forced to believe in ideas, concepts or leaders against their will. Instead, changing social and personal circumstances lead rational individuals to believe in things that appear irrational to others not in those circumstances. The Soviets did drastically change social incentives concerning religious decision-making. Yet this never produced the communist zombies of fiction. Importantly, as Froese reveals, 'While coercion can effectively curb behaviour, its impact on belief is erratic'. By limiting choices and creating massive incentives to lie about one's beliefs, the Soviet system 'did not brainwash its citizenry but rather produced a population teeming with halfhearted loyalists and silent malcontents' (Froese, 2008: 17).

Another non-linear issue is the evolution of different types of terrorist groups. Atran points to how the newer wave of jihadists in Saudi Arabia tends to be somewhat younger (and more likely to be single), less educated and less financially well off, less ideological, and more prone to prior involvement in criminal activities unrelated to jihad, such as drugs, theft and aggravated assault. They are much more likely to read jihadi literature in their daily lives than other forms of literature. They tend to look up to role models who stress violence in jihad, like the late Abu Musab al-Zarqawi, than to those who justify and limit violence through moral reasoning, such as the late Abdullah Azzam. So the new wave is more socially compatible with petty criminals. But although lack of economic opportunity often reliably leads to criminality:

> ... it turns out that some youth who have turned to crime for lack
> of better opportunities really don't want to be criminals after all.
> Given half a chance to take up a moral cause, they can be even
> more altruistically prone than others are to give up their lives for
> their comrades and a cause.
>
> (Atran, 2010: 208)

So here we see the idea of jihadism as a preferred alternative to a life of crime. Can this be tackled by the criminalizing of terrorist acts? Sageman (2008) would think so. For him, the most effective way to remove the glory from terrorism is to reduce the terrorists to common criminals. There is no glory in being taken to prison in handcuffs. No jihadi website carries such pictures, as opposed to the thousands of video clips of American military vehicles blowing up, or martyrs blowing themselves up next to Americans. Trials should be low-key demonstrations of the poverty of their ideas and vicious nature of their acts, with testimony from victims and families at the trials. This would fit the Demos argument for deglamorizing AQ (Briggs *et al.*, 2006). Trying to inculcate abhorrence of the impact of violence would also fit Ed Husain's account that one of the reasons he left jihad was his revulsion at the cold-blooded murder of a Nigerian fellow student, a Christian, who had been 'offensive' to Muslims, along with his serious misgivings about the London bombings. Husain's withdrawal was gradual, not a blinding light, and exposure to ideas from sociology and history were certainly part of it, as was exposure to the racism of Saudi Arabia (Husain, 2007). So Sageman argues for a 'subtle campaign' to influence the opinion leaders to embrace non-violence. This means placing emphasis on the mistakes made – bombing the wrong people, killing guests at weddings and so on. You need to capitalize on atrocities.

From their research on police–Muslim engagement for the purposes of counter-terrorism, Basia Spalek *et al.* (2009) note how Muslim populations largely adhere to the strict Quranic prohibitions on killing civilians and killing altogether outside a battlefield or the criminal justice system. As such, terrorist acts are seen as terrible crimes. The research shows that religious justification of terrorism caused initial conflict in some parts of communities, between religious doctrines of the sanctity of the human soul and the political argument used by AQ to gain support for what Muslims would normally see as crime:

> From a community security point of view, this confusion could be eliminated if terrorist acts are re-explained to the Muslim population as a pure crime – stripped of its political and religious propaganda. Many of our interviewees described how through clarifying the distinction between crime and ill-formed religious justification eventually led to their decision to take an active role in supporting counter-terrorism.
>
> (Spalek *et al.*, 2009: 74)

This mention of opinion leaders leads to the consideration of networks. As was outlined in Chapter 1, networks today operate horizontally and, whether criminal or ideological (or both), cannot be disbanded simply by picking off their presumed leaders. Atran shows us how in the Madrid bombings, plotters fell under the radar because they were *not* orchestrated by some 'Terror Central Organization', be it ETA or AQ. Instead, the plot was anarchic, fluid, and improbable. Political scientists and organizational theorists refer to this kind of structure as 'organized anarchy', which has four properties:

- 'fuzzy preferences' (ill-defined and inconsistent preferences, discovering preference through action rather than acting on the basis of preference)
- tinkered technology (trial and error learning)
- fluid structure and effort, varying over time
- being embedded in larger social networks rather than isolated from them.

The notion of 'organized anarchy' fits well with complexity theory. It is non-linear, with not just fuzzy, incoherent preferences, but also two-way feedback processes, discovering preference through action rather than the other way round. I will offer a prosaic case where I went with friends to greyhound racing. While I could understand the attraction of betting, I (fortunately) could not bring myself to gamble away much of the family income. We saw many families there, babies in buggies, 6-year-olds placing bets, grannies giving themselves heart attacks shouting at the dogs. This led to a debate among us as to whether introducing children to gambling so young was wrong, or whether the sight of so many people losing so much money would put them off for life. But you could certainly discover a preference by either betting on the favourite and getting a small return or blowing the whole lot on the 9:1 outsider *Foxy's Delilah*. This comparison between addictions (whether to drugs, gambling, or violence) is not trivial, as addiction can be part of an extremist position. In *Educating Against Extremism* (Davies, 2008) I describe the phenomenon of being addicted to Jesus – apparently the same parts of the brain light up as when being in love.

'Tinkered technology' is sometimes a lifeline for the world, as many jihadi attempts fail through an error in the bomb making. Worryingly, there will be trial and error learning as in any complex adaptive system, so we cannot be complacent that potential jihadists – as in the wonderful spoof film *Four Lions* – will remain incompetent idiots.

The fluidity and the embedding of networks within other networks are central to complex adaptive systems. Later I discuss more recent initiatives in police–community engagement which recognize that networks do not operate in a vacuum, nationally or internationally. We also now know the importance of friendship networks. If madrassas are at all implicated in joining JI or AQ, it is through not just exposure to the ideology but also through the patterns of friendship that develop. In the West, potential jihadist youth hang around by the mosque for companionship, but also socialize around meals in cheap local restaurants – the 'halal' theory of terrorism. Muslim student associations and study groups that form around radical mosques are oft-cited examples.

Lynn Davies

This also explains the gender difference: among immigrant parents, there is greater latitude for boys to go out and hang around. Girls would also have less hopelessness about getting jobs, as they would be sent back to the home country to get married – or they would stay at school to avoid just that.

But it is not just about a friendship network, not just Facebook or LinkedIn. Sageman talks of how, for his sample of extremist groups, the experience of faith and commitment was grounded in:

> ... intense group dynamics that completely transformed them in a process of group love. With the gradual intensity of interactions within the group and the progressive distance from former ties, they changed their values. From secular people, they became more religious.
>
> (Sageman, 2008: 87)

The 'progressive distance' is significant here, especially for our concern with deradicalization. There can be a double process of outside social isolation and internal mutual reinforcement, as former friends and acquaintances progressively avoid the radicalizing group. The group intensifies its loyalty and sees itself as the only true vanguard protecting *ummah,* the Muslim community. They start living in their own world. Christian fundamentalists follow the same pattern, as revealed in Ruthven's important work (2004).

The other side of the coin of ingroup love is outgroup hate. Amplification theory explains how grievances escalate and a conspiracy theory builds against the entire Western world. Sageman (2008) gives a humorous illustration of this process of blaming 'the enemy' for everything negative: when the toilet got clogged at the apartment in Hamburg where Mohamed Atta and his friends were living, witnesses reported that they started screaming at the Jews for having purposely done this to them.

Unlearning

Unlearning needs a complex intermix of inputs, just as learning does. What emerges from this brief foray into terrorism are the debates on targets. Do you focus on beliefs or behaviour? With animal rights extremists, it is often about behaviour – that you do not have to renounce your beliefs but you can find alternative ways of doing the political work. And it is not always easy to disentangle the beliefs anyway. I recall an interview with an animal rights extremist who had been attacking butchers' shops in the locality. On being asked whether he would attack halal butchers' shops, he replied, shocked, 'Oh no, that'd be racist, wouldn't it?' But with extremism that has, or appears to have, a religious underpinning, there is little agreement on the entry point.

Sageman rejects the religious dialogue idea. He thinks the entire effort to dissuade wannabes from joining the ranks of the Al Qaeda social movement by debating religious arguments and selective quotes from the Quran and Hadiths with them is misguided. Potential terrorists visiting websites would be bored with religious disquisition. They want 'jihadi cool'. Sageman even holds that a counter-terrorist focus on Islamic ideology is dangerous. 'We cannot afford to allow the terrorists to control the debate by framing the context of this war to their advantage. It is not the role of the West to tell Muslims what is Islam and what is not Islam' (Sageman, 2008: 157).

In another part of the West, this view would be supported by intelligence analysts such as Kamran Bokhari. In interview, Bokhari said 'If you do it from outside it's always going to be seen as a foreign imposition – Oh, they're going to change my religion for me' (Shephard, 2011). 'Change from within' is apparently a message often repeated by those who work in the field of deradicalization in Canada's Muslim communities. But what if the disquisition is engaged with by fellow Muslims? Perhaps there is a difference between prevention and rehabilitation. In the Middle East, traditional theologians visit imprisoned terrorists and bring a Quran along with them:

> They tell the prisoners that the holy book is the only arbiter of their dispute and then engage the prisoners by saying that they will debate them about their violent path. If the terrorists succeed in convincing them, then the theologians say they will join the jihad. If the prisoners lose, then the terrorists are invited to abandon violence.
>
> (Sageman, 2008: 37)

Is this a high-risk strategy? Certainly it is a concern in mentoring programmes that the mentee may convert the mentor in the end. (I return to this later.) Yet apparently the conversation between the theologians and the terrorists sometimes leads the terrorists, who do not have a deep understanding of their beliefs, to see that there is very little support in the Quran for their violent ideas.

Another area of debate is on the role of the internet and so-called 'online radicalization'. Rightly, there are programmes (discussed in the last chapter) to enable young people to be cautious about what they see on the internet. In *Terror on the Internet,* Weiman (2006) looked at 'passive' websites and assumed that the images found in them have intrinsic power to influence people to take up arms against the West. Sageman thinks otherwise. He maintains that people in general do not change their minds by reading newspapers or books: 'They usually read what conforms to their original bias and thereby only confirm their views, which were created elsewhere' (Sageman, 2008: 114). The internet is a marketplace of ideas, and while putative leaders could post suggestions in chat rooms, it is up to followers to pick and choose between them. Leaders have no way of enforcing their commands through the internet, as they might have in face-to-face groups, nor can they offer incentives except in an abstract way of promising future rewards in Heaven. I think a complexity approach would side with Sageman on this: as the reasons for radicalization have to be some highly intricate combination, no one route such as the internet is going to do it. There is no room for feedback and reinforcement. Unless you are a group of friends accessing the same site, there is no immediate network, no group love. There is the odd instance of someone who appears to have been radicalized just through the internet, but this is extremely rare. And we do not know the other circumstances which pushed them in this direction. However, this does not preclude the use of the internet in deradicalization programmes, which I look at later.

Whether providing alternative paths for group loyalty is the key is also debatable. The Boy Scouts have captured a lot of young people and kept them out of trouble. Sageman (2008) argues for a similar large and formal network of young Muslims, 'based on peaceful Muslim traditions', to give a sense of belonging. This would include a hierarchy of promotion that would recognize the talents and efforts of its members, as well as promoting local heroes to emulate. Yet this seems to be a very top-down form of organization, so does not fit what we know about the power of horizontal networks, and their fluidity and flexibility. I suspect they would attract only those who like this sort of thing, as did the Boy Scouts. As I argued in the previous chapter, where positive change occurs it seems to be in the *clash* of values, or in the encounters with difference. It would be better to encourage groupings of young people *across* different traditions and values, in pursuit of some common task which is nothing to do with their heritage, than to isolate young Muslims in some sort of Young Pioneer framework. The Hitler Youth did not prevent the rise of fascism – quite the contrary.

I would therefore endorse Paul Thomas's argument (2009) that the response to extremist Islamist ideologies is *not* to do more work with groups of Muslim young people, but instead to create programmes of integrated cohesion activity that move further and faster in altering the perceptions of young people of all ethnic and religious backgrounds by bringing them together for shared programmes of activity focused on fun, and on cross-cutting concerns. Good examples include the Youth Parliament Safe Space initiative, involving young people of *all* ethnic and religious backgrounds in political debate and processes relevant to young people (Thomas, 2009: 286). If you do discover your preferences through action, rather than the other way round, then it is necessary to change the action. The organization Demos is doing significant research to explore the reasons why young Muslims join terrorist groups. This research starts to suggest that political and social activism is an important outlet for youthful energy. They found that 'violent' extremists were less likely than peaceful extremists to have taken part in civic engagement and political protest. They also found that a number of young Muslims were diverted from violence when provided with peaceful, meaningful alternatives. Membership of one terrorist group in the UK went into decline when young Muslims joined the anti-war movement in large numbers and found an outlet for their frustration. Research from the US is finding the same thing – that political and social protest and activism act as a safety valve (Bartlett, 2010). And this would be across faiths and cultures, not confined to just one.

Can you wait for extremists to grow out of it, as some of the work on guns and gangs implies? Atran, talking to an ex-jihadist in Morocco, asked why he was no longer part of the jihad. 'Because I have less rage', he said. 'Because I have responsibilities. I have small children. But you know, when I talk about these things with people, with my friends, I forget this. Well almost' (Atran, 2010: 55). Here the new outlet for activity would be family rather than activism.

But this would be a risky process. Radical learning more often requires radical interventions or exposures. It is a bit like dieting. Gradual calorie reduction approaches do not work for many who are addicted to food. You do not convince the obese to eat less through moral messages and endless diet books. So for those who are addicted to extremism, does it have to be the gastric band approach – cutting off supply (and demand)? Or a different form of group loyalty, the deradicalization equivalent of Weight Watchers? I come back to these questions later.

Meanwhile here is my favourite prayer about temptation and behaviour:

A WOMAN'S PRAYER:

DEAR LORD
SO FAR TODAY, I AM DOING ALL RIGHT.
I HAVE NOT GOSSIPED
LOST MY TEMPER
BEEN GREEDY
GRUMPY

NASTY,
SELFISH OR
SELF-INDULGENT.
I HAVE NOT WHINED
CURSED OR
EATEN ANY CHOCOLATE.
HOWEVER
I AM GOING TO GET OUT OF BED IN A FEW MINUTES
AND I WILL NEED A LOT MORE HELP AFTER THAT.

AMEN.

Learning from the wrong avenues taken in prevention

Programmes such as Prevent have learned from errors. One has been the counterproductive emphasis on surveillance. In one London borough, those working with youngsters were told to add information to databases they held to highlight which youths were Muslim. They were also asked to provide information, to be shared with the police, about which streets and areas Muslim youngsters could be found in (Dodd, 2009). The classic blunder was the placing of covert security cameras at 72 sites in the predominantly Muslim Washwood Heath and Sparkbrook wards of Birmingham, ostensibly for general crime reduction, but financed through a counter-terrorism fund. This predictably caused a huge row, with the local MP threatening to raise it in the House of Commons. Bags had to be placed over the cameras and consultations with the community instigated. This sort of action vastly sets back community relations.

Some previous counter-terrorism strategies also contributed to deeply dividing British Muslims. Some organizations, such as the Quilliam Foundation, were accused of passing secret briefings to government against other Muslim organizations hitherto regarded as peaceful and moderate, and of alleging that such organizations were complicit in violent ideologies and practices (Dodd, 2010). A submission to the Home Office by the Centre for the Study of Radicalisation and Contemporary Political Violence drew attention to how such communication breaks down trust, with government sponsorship of organizations viewed with deep suspicion (Breen-Smith, 2010).

Jamie Bartlett (2010) strongly critiqued the view of Douglas Murray, the Director of the Centre for Social Cohesion, that Prevent does not address the real problem – Islamism. Prevent does need to be criticized, but Bartlett argues that Murray's solution – to fight all Islamism, not just the violent type – would make matters worse. Several important points are raised in his article, not least the perennial Liberal/Conservative tension: how to protect tolerance, equality and human rights while simultaneously rolling back the state. But what was also salutary was the statement: 'Back in 2005, Demos supported Prevent, on the basis that the root causes of terrorism needed to be tackled. We were wrong' (Bartlett, 2010). It is refreshing to see an organization admitting that it has learned from its mistakes.

In educational contexts, the errors have lain in asking educational institutions to look out for potential suspects. Not only has this been seen as akin to racial profiling, with Muslims being unfairly targeted and generally viewed with suspicion, but also as leading to escalating cases such as the notorious Nottingham University case in 2008. Here a master's student, Rizwaan Sabir, was arrested (along with a 30-year-old member of staff) under the Terrorism Act on suspicion of possessing extremist material. He was in fact studying terrorism for his dissertation, and had downloaded an edited version of the AQ handbook from a US government website. He had sent the document to the staff member because he had access to a printer. Both were released after being held in custody for six days. Academics all over the country expressed deep concerns about the implications for academic freedom if people are to be arrested for being in possession of legitimate research material. As someone commented on the Times Higher Education website on 29 May 2008: 'The funny thing about this is that UK and US governmental organisations will most probably reference that poor boy's dissertation when it's published in their analysis and creation of policy to tackle terrorism.' (*Times Higher Education*, 2008).

Thus not just Muslims themselves but academics and educators in general have protested. Fortunately, the tradition of satire has also mocked the surveillance attempts. The online satirical magazine *The Daily Mash* carried a nice spoof on the Home Secretary's request for GPs to watch out for signs of would-be suicide bombers. The headline was 'Doctors to check for anyone who looks a bit bomb-y':

> As [the Home Secretary] delved deeper into the bottomless pit of her insanity, doctors were told to carry out tests for blood pressure, heart rate and a seething hatred of liberal Western values … A GP said 'after successfully negotiating their way past my receptionist and spending a couple of hours in my waiting room reading a 1994 copy of *Take a Break* pretty much all my patients look like they want to end it all and take half the post office next door with them'.
>
> (*The Daily Mash*, 2011)

The *Daily Mash* explains that the plan is part of the government's £60 million a year Prevent programme, a counter-terrorism campaign 'that is considering a wide variety of ways to reduce extremism in the UK, except for Britain not acting as a right bastard in other people's countries' (*The Daily Mash*, 2011).

NewsThump similarly had a wonderful article headlined 'Top universities a "breeding ground" for Tories, warn Islamic groups'. It solemnly recounted how Islamic groups had accused top universities of complacency in tackling the number of people on campus expressing the sort of views normally associated with members of the Conservative Party. Universities were being identified where there was a 'particular risk' of people being recruited to the youth wing of the UK Conservative Party. A spokesman said there were numerous cases of 'people wearing barbour jackets' as well as 'hate incidents directed towards the unemployed, the sick and foxes' (*NewsThump*, 2011).

Learning about freedom of speech

The enjoyment of satire in the press is a hallmark of a civilized society. This relates to the whole question of freedom of speech. Religious organizations will sometimes call for greater protection against so-called defamation of religion. In the UK, however, measures already exist to deal with organizations that promote hatred and violence, under various sections of the Public Order Act 1986 and the provisions of the Criminal Justice and Public Order Act 1994 in relation to hate speech and the publication of material that incites racial hatred. New legislation is not needed, particularly if it starts to challenge freedom of speech or move towards what looks like a return of blasphemy laws. As Marie Breen-Smith points out:

> Crucially, the enforcement of such legislation must be seen to equally apply to those advocating violence from within violent jihadi tendencies and from within right-wing, sectarian and anti-Semitic movements. Currently, there is a perception that undue attention is paid to violent jihadis whilst other movements can spread their hate speech and propaganda unimpeded.
>
> (Breen-Smith, 2010: 7)

It is critical that religion is not privileged either way – either in having special categories of 'offence' in freedom of speech or conversely in having more attention paid to hate speech in religious ideology than in other types of hate speech. The issue is about the potentiality for violence, not about precisely what is said. Demos argues the importance of differentiating between radicals who are likely to use violence and those who are not.

Their opinion is that radical views must be engaged with in debate, with persuasive counter-argument rather than demonization, and that AQ must be deglamourized. Breen-Smith (2010) contrasts their approach with that of the Quilliam Foundation. Demos argues for greater transparency from government, the avoidance of conspiracy theories that foster distrust between government and certain communities, and investment in programmes that enable young people to think critically (see Bartlett and Miller, 2010). The Quilliam Foundation argument is that certain ideologies are dangerous and those espousing them ought to be marginalized. There may be less clear blue water between them than Breen-Smith implies, but banning, marginalizing and excluding has certainly not worked in the past, and it is questionable whether ideologies cause violent behaviour by themselves, as we have seen.

Complexity theory would support the Demos view: maximum connectivity in a society requires maximum trust, interaction and exposure to a range of views. Evolutionary theory might imply competition between species (and hence between humans) and therefore secrecy and lack of disclosure. However, in a human CAS, it is competition of ideas that counts, and these need airing, with a constant process of crediting and discrediting through participatory methods. In this regard, Bartlett and Birdwell quote John Stuart Mill's famous 'collision of truth with error':

> The peculiar evil of silencing the expression of an opinion is that of robbing the human race ... it robs those who dissert from the opinion still more than those who hold it. If the opinion is right, they are deprived of the opportunity of exchanging error for truth. If wrong, they lose, what is almost as great a benefit, the clearer perception and livelier impression of truth, produced by the collision with error.
>
> (Bartlett and Birdwell, 2010: 17)

A complexity approach might question whether 'truth' was ever to be arrived at, but the principle is indisputable: the important aspect is the collision. And the equally important aspect is the recognition that *everyone* loses if views cannot be aired. This is why debating societies are so valuable as a testing ground. I have seen young people transformed by taking part in Debate Mate (an educational charity that promotes debating in inner-city schools across the UK in areas of high child poverty). While initially hesitant, students have found a colossal boost from learning how to articulate ideas, having people listen to them, and having to predict what a counter-argument might be – a boost not just for their self-confidence but for realizing that there are a multiplicity of ideas out there and that you, as a modest individual or group, can have a go at them all. One boy revealed:

> I was really lazy, didn't apply myself, a real nuisance ... I got decent marks, but I wasn't involved. I felt left out. Then I got selected for Debate Mate, got picked out of G and T science ... it built my confidence ... it taught me how to listen as well, ... it turned me round.

> (Davies *et al.*, 2011: 13)

As Arun Kundnani, the author of *Spooked: How not to prevent violent extremism* (2009a), stressed in the context of expecting teachers and youth workers to identify extremists, trust is an essential ingredient in counter-terrorism. Young people need to be able to speak openly with teachers and youth workers about the issues they feel strongly about. If schools and youth clubs can no longer be relied on to provide such a venue, where will young people go? Kundnani reckons that the likelihood of their turning to those already committed to violence will only be increased:

> Ultimately, the real alternative to terrorism is not the official promotion of state-licensed British values but a democratic process that is capable of listening to the views that the majority may find offensive or discomforting. Unfortunately the Prevent programme is doing the exact opposite.

> (Kundnani, 2009b: 33)

Secularism is of course the antithesis to 'state-licensed British values'.

Police–community engagement

One important aspect of the state–religion relationship with regard to extremism is the work of the police within the community and its schools. This section examines the learning that has occurred in this area. Developments in policy and practice under the UK's Prevent strategy have suggested an increased focus upon the notion of community, in that the maxim that 'communities can defeat terrorism' has been incorporated into the strategy (Briggs *et al.*, 2006). Globally, there has been a great deal of debate about the role of police in PVE work, often relating to the question of how far a community trusts the police and how far police interventions actually increase the risk of radicalization. Currently in the UK the notion of community features as both object and subject of counter-terrorism policy: as object because the Muslim community is problematized and targeted by state policies and practices that place nation state security over community concerns; as subject because within counter-terrorism there is space for community members to be active participants in the delivery of outcomes, and to actively question and scrutinize counter-terrorism policies and practices (Spalek and Davies, 2012). These dynamics in what is seen as a community can at times conflict, as outlined earlier with regard to surveillance.

Terrorism legislation has increased the powers of the police, extended the limits of the law which govern policing, and has placed a burden on the police to assess and decide upon those thought to be at risk of committing acts of terrorism. The need for the police to assess risk has invariably led to sections of the population being subject to the sanctions of the criminal law on the sole basis of possessing certain identity characteristics (Walklate and Mythen, 2008). Within policing and security circles, identities viewed as being particularly 'at risk' of engaging in AQ-linked terrorism are religious and political identities which relate to Islam, notably Salafis and Islamists, plus specific ethnic groupings that intersect with Islam – in particular, Black Caribbean and African Muslim converts, and Pakistani and Somali ethnic Muslims. Schemes such as mentoring those deemed 'at risk' can, if inappropriately governed, comprise over-zealous and ill-informed flagging of individuals for 'vulnerability', ensuring the unnecessary collection of personal data.

The difficulty for counter-terrorism policy makers and practitioners lies in adopting a balanced approach that works within communities but does not target them in a clearly state-led way, involving covert policing models (McGovern, 2010; Spalek and McDonald, 2010a). Disproportionate state-led responses may play into the hands of terrorist strategists. Counter-terrorism policy should not help to create and sustain a sense of belongingness around issues of victimization and feelings of being targeted. If communities have shared meanings, it is likely that shared emotions underpin such shared meanings and so communities can also share emotions, whether of hope, fear or humiliation (Moisi, 2009). Struggles over the emotional-political landscapes of communities are global, as noted earlier with regard to Taliban-infused countries.

As a result of such awareness, the UK policing approach to preventing violent extremism has become more sophisticated. A 2011 report by the Universities Police Science Institute (UPSI), commissioned by the Association of Chief Police Officers (ACPO), found that the policing approach had *not* caused widespread damage or harm between Muslim communities and the police. In fact Muslim communities have a higher level of trust and confidence in the police than the general population. The report highlighted how communities are increasingly taking the lead in challenging violent extremism, working in partnership with the police (Innes *et al.*, 2011). Clearly, this has to be about building a relationship. As Sir Norman Bettison, ACPO Lead on Prevent and Chief Constable of West Yorkshire Police, said:

> You have a 365 day a year relationship with communities to encourage a conversation about problems that matter to the police. It's no good pitching up and saying that 'we want your help' if we have failed to respond to the day to day concerns of the community.
>
> (ACPO, 2011: 1)

The Kent Police Prevent engagement approach stresses the 'vulnerabilities' that a community might face, actual or perceived. Building up trust means understanding both types. They have found that as a result of this engagement activity, community leaders had, for the first time, approached them for assistance in resolving community tensions. These ranged from parking problems and assistance with planning applications to improve the welfare of local communities, to a request for drugs awareness training for young Bangladeshi youth groups (ACPO, 2012b: 4).

Spalek *et al.*'s (2009) research on police–community engagement recorded some good examples of empathy-building. They included initiatives that allow community members to learn about police perspectives, discuss and even engage in role play as police officers in hypothetical counter-terrorism case scenarios. Such partnership work was characterized by the absence of coercion – all parties were free to stop interacting as and when they chose.

Police working with schools have also had to overcome mistrust by youth and take care not to be seen as an additional discipline officer. As mentioned with regard to the 'Choices and Voices' project, the key has been enlisting the help of young people in tackling extremist attitudes, together with combating violence generally. In Birmingham, the language is now that of 'Community Safety Partnership', providing information to parents and carers about young people and (violent) gangs, why they join and how people can help them distinguish the fantasy from the reality of gang life. The words 'West Midlands Police' appear in very small print on their leaflet.

Yet, deeper philosophical as well as practical issues also arise. In the UK there are significant tensions between approaches that emphasize community cohesion, and those that emphasize freedoms associated with liberal democracy, particularly in relation to AQ-linked extremism. In community cohesion approaches, Muslim communities may be potentially problematized, for Islamic ideology is portrayed as dangerous and in conflict with 'Western values' so Muslims are viewed as not integrating with wider

British society (Jackson, 2005). Approaches that emphasize liberal freedoms, on the other hand, seek not to problematize particular communities but, rather, to enable individuals to draw upon features of a liberal democracy, such as social and political activism, so that a wider range of actions are considered legitimate and individuals no longer see violence as a means to pursue their aims.

Law enforcement agencies and their strategies are involved in both approaches. Neighbourhood policing can reduce insecurity and promote reassurance through a 'hearts and minds' strategy, designed to purposively impact upon people's beliefs and attitudes, so that they are less inclined to support – tacitly or explicitly – either the means or ends of those groups espousing the use of violence; and also through an 'eyes and ears' strategy – intended to persuade people to function as intelligence assets for the authorities (Goodey, 2008). Thus, neighbourhood police officers are expected not only to respond to ordinary, everyday crimes but also to take an interest in the ideologies circulating within communities, particularly where those ideologies endorse violence. Conversely, they may be engaged in partnership approaches with those community members who are involved in trying to redirect behaviour, not ideology – whether relating to gangs and guns, far-right groups, animal rights, or any extreme group. There are inevitably tensions and overlaps between these approaches, though.

In the US, a report from the Muslim Public Affairs Council (Beutel, 2010) argues for a domestic counter-terrorism enterprise centred on community-oriented policing. Interestingly, the report uses a market analogy: both terrorist groups and the community policing enterprises are similar to business firms. A terrorist business firm uses recruitment 'advertisements' to tap into a market of people experiencing identity crises. These identity-conflicted individuals are the labour pool or 'market for martyrs' that terrorist business firms recruit from. A community-oriented policing enterprise would compete against them in this market for martyrs, but requires a division of labour: law enforcement would focus on criminal behaviour while Muslim American communities deal with the ideological and social components which lead to violent extremism. Whatever one thinks about a business analogy, the four essential principles would make sense, particularly within a complexity perspective:

1. make decisions and assessments of Muslim communities on credible information

2. have respect for communities' civil rights and civil liberties (spying only adds to difficulties)

3. move away from a 'securitized' relationship – this just increases the isolation and alienation of communities

4. leave the counter-radicalization to Muslim communities.

(Beutel, 2010: 4–5)

These principles give insights into forms of secularism or separation – that the state manages crime and law enforcement and the (religious) community handles ideology. Nonetheless, it is a partnership, not a divide – a division of labour for greater coherence.

The report of the inaugural international workshop for the Police–Community Hub in Birmingham (2010) confirmed that the politicization of the security agenda, particularly in terms of the stigmatization of Muslim communities, had impacted negatively on achieving either state or human security: the conflation of counter-terrorism with issues of immigration, cohesion, national identity and values serves to isolate the very communities with which the state needs to engage. Islam – whether theology, personal belief or identity – plays a fundamental role in the prevention of violent extremism: the role of religious duty and ethical consciousness is key. However a level of unity within Muslim communities and schools of thought is seen as necessary. The attempt to define 'moderate' and 'radical' forms of Islam among some popular commentators, academics and policy makers, particularly in relation to Sufi and Salafi communities, undermines this coherent community response. Definitions of the term 'jihad' would be part of such community discussion, as jihad should not be conflated with terrorism. Importantly, the report stresses that risk-taking is part of intervention work with individuals vulnerable to or holding violent extremist ideologies. Just as in schools, the task is creating safe spaces – physical, emotional, virtual – in which all parties involved in the issues of terrorism and counter-terrorism, including community members, vulnerable individuals and practitioners, can explore issues and have those 'dangerous conversations' so often stifled in the public domain (Spalek and MacDonald, 2010b: 9).

Different forms of unlearning: Deradicalization, disengagement, desistence or debiasing?

In interventions to 're-educate' those at risk, I return to the pivotal question of whether mentoring in the area of violent extremism is about changing beliefs or changing behaviour (or both). It is possible to leave intact the goals of jihad, or of white supremacy, or of animal liberation, but to persuade people that violence is not an appropriate or valuable way to achieve them.

This would be strategic more than ideological. The distinction relates to different terminology used for processes of working with extremists. Ashour uses *deradicalization*, and defines this as:

> … a process of relative change within Islamist movements, one in which a radical group reverses its ideology and de-legitimises the use of violent methods to achieve political goals, while also moving towards an acceptance of gradual social, political and economic changes within a pluralist context
>
> (Ashour, 2009: 5).

A group undergoing a deradicalization process need not necessarily ideologically abide by democratic principles; it is more about attitudes to violence. 'Many deradicalised groups still uphold misogynist, homophobic, xenophobic and anti-democratic views' (Ashour, 2009: 5). There are three levels of deradicalization: first, simply abandoning the use of violence; second, a concurrent process of ideological delegitimizing of violence; and third, an organizational deradicalization and dismantling of armed units of the organization. Mentoring would relate far more to the first two, unless whole groups were being mentored at the same time. Ashour adds a fourth category of 'moderation' – a process of relative change mainly concerned with attitudes towards democracy, with peaceful participation in electoral politics, if allowed. Moderation can occur also in non-violent radical movements.

Fink and Hearne have different terms for these levels. For them, *disengagement* 'refers to a behavioural change, such as leaving a group or changing one's role within it. It does not necessitate a change in values or ideals, but requires relinquishing the objective of achieving change through violence' (Fink and Hearne, 2008: 1). *Deradicalization,* however, 'implies a cognitive shift', a 'fundamental change in understanding'. Cumulatively such processes can have a positive impact on global counter-terrorism by promoting the internal fragmentation of violent radical groups, and delegitimizing their rhetoric and tactics in the eyes of the broader public. Bjorgo and Horgan's (2008) book *Leaving Terrorism Behind: Individual and collective disengagement* documents efforts from various countries towards these ends.

Another term in current use is *desistance.* The term has been coined as the opposite of 'persistence' in a deviant or criminal trajectory or life, and is simply defined as 'going straight' (Maruna *et al.,* 2004). 'Desistance' is usually applied to criminal rather than ideological mindsets, but the psychology of desistance has some potentially fruitful connections. Research found that the reform narrative of desisting ex-prisoners revealed three basic examples: first, that the criminal behaviour 'was not the real me' – who was, underneath, essentially good; second, that of 'tragic optimism' – that what seemed like a wasted life could be put to good use by counselling others; and third, that of preserving some continuity by making desistance a 'rebel act' – getting out of the system which traps ex-offenders in a cycle of crime and prison, breaking out of the chains of social control.

While these stories may not resonate with deradicalization accounts, the significant feature is that of recognizing 'self-narratives', that is, the stories we humans carry with us, stories that are not created in a vacuum. They are rational adaptations, and it is others who construct some stories as tellable and others as marginal or subnormal. Maruna *et al.* (2004) point out the problem of the probation practice discourse being dominated by a deficit approach of 'risks' and 'needs', of assessing clients' endless range of social, psychological and moral deficits and 'treating' or 'targeting' them. This has the danger of reifying and internalizing the deficits in the client's self-identity. (Complexity theory would talk about lock-in here.) Instead, future-oriented, alternative narratives of the self should be the goal. The message is also about recognizing the broader social contexts and conditions required to support change. 'Thus where being office-focussed encourages practice to be retrospective and individualised, being desistance-focussed allows practice to become prospective and contextualised' (McNeill, 2003: 155–6). This too would have implications for where mentoring takes place, physically and mentally, in space and time.

Debiasing is another concept within psychology which has been applied to ideological extremism and armed conflict (Lilienfield *et al.*, 2009). The bias most pivotal in this is 'confirmation bias', the tendency to seek out evidence consistent with one's views, and ignore, dismiss or selectively reinterpret evidence that contradicts them. Cults and extremist movements fan the flames of confirmation bias by presenting only one point of view and assiduously insulating members from all others. Yet according to Lilienfeld *et al.*, we know far more about people's cognitive biases than we do about debiasing. 'Critical thinking' apparently does not transfer across domains nor tackle selective perceptions of 'evidence'.

Shermer (2002) has conjectured that highly intelligent people possess especially effective 'ideological immune systems' because they are adept at generating plausible counter-arguments against competing claims. This will be of significance for the skills of people engaged in discussing and challenging views. Lilienfeld *et al.* (2009) state that the goal of debiasing techniques is to help people grasp and appreciate alternative points of view, not necessarily to accept them as equally valid or moral. Techniques within this area are of 'perspective taking' to diminish outgroup stereotypes and 'consider-the-opposite' or 'consider-the-alternative' strategies. It is thought however that some debiasing efforts may succeed only if participants can be persuaded that their biases result in poor decisions of real-world consequence to them. It is also conceded that it is extremely unlikely that ideological extremism is underpinned only by confirmation bias and other purely cognitive 'errors'. Because ideological extremism contains a marked 'hot' (affective) component of hatred that contributes significantly to its intensity, purely cognitive methods of debiasing may take us only so far. Yet the perception of enemies in sharply polarized ways may be challenged a little. And as Shneour (1998) argues, instilling even mild doubts can often attenuate the intensity of fanatical beliefs and open the door to further questioning of these beliefs. It may also render ideological extremists less willing to act on their convictions.

Whichever 'D' word is being used, a further question is whether the reasons for radicalization proximate the factors encouraging deradicalization. That is, if people were drawn to violent extremism primarily through the strength of the theological or political argument, then is that where successful delegitimation occurs? If they were drawn by the peer group, by bonding with others, then are alternative social networks the answer? If they wanted excitement and recognition, then will avenues for non-violent work in the community and beyond fulfil such needs? The problem however is that the reasons for joining extremist movements and groups can be a complex mixture, even within one individual. The factors encouraging disengagement are not necessarily those that projected people into the initial behaviour and mindset. Horgan (2009) argues that the reasons for *becoming* a terrorist, *staying* a terrorist, and then *disengaging* from terrorism are often different and context-specific. Decisions to withdraw may be voluntary or coerced. Githens-Mazer and Lambert are clear on this – on what they call the persistence of a 'failed discourse' on radicalization:

> ... approaches to counterterrorism and/or counter-radicalisation that assume the existence of simple 'root causes' or 'pathways' that, when addressed will systematically stem terrorism's occurrence are not only naïve but may actually be counterproductive.
>
> (Githens-Mazer and Lambert, 2010: 900)

Once more we see the challenge to linear approaches, whether in adopting or desisting from radicalism. Yet while 'root causes' cannot be stereotyped, Fink and Hearne (2008) did find from their research common patterns which encouraged disengagement. These are first the 'push' factors of social environment, disillusionment with group leadership of activities, stress and exhaustion from living a clandestine life, and revulsion at violent acts. Second are the 'pull' factors of longing for a normal life (triggered by age or pressure from partners and families), and desire for an alternative occupation less threatening to long-term socio-economic prospects. Sometimes there is a 'cognitive opening' from such disillusionment, stress, trauma or revulsion – and this can be facilitated by education, social and economic assistance and counselling. Such an opening is particularly important for our concern about intervention. Yet given the complexity of disengagement, mentoring may admittedly be only one factor; or the client may have come to mentoring predisposed to change, with other factors in their life more salient than what actually happens during the mentoring.

How and why learning and relearning occur may also be determined in different international contexts by the positioning of the client or target. In Indonesia, Singapore and Malaysia government-sponsored deradicalization programmes were aimed particularly at mid-ranking commanders as well as the grass roots of the Jemaah Islamiah (JI), to convince them to abandon violence and delegitimize it ideologically, This was said to remove 'tens of thousands' of former militants from the ranks of Al Qaeda supporters (Ashour, 2009).

Saudi Arabia is well known for its 're-education' programmes for ex-prisoner extremists as well as online mentoring (Davies, 2008). The online dialogue with extremists, called the *Al-Sakinah* (tranquillity), used some forty *ulema* and 'propagators of Islam' (male and female) with internet skills to enter extremist websites and forums and converse with the participants. The educators counted 130 Al Qaeda and associated websites, and studied their focal ideas and the principles that guided them in online recruitment and mobilization. 'We saw positive signs during the conversations ... We did not demand that the people with whom we spoke renounce their views by 100 per cent – this would have been a false hope' (Yehoshua, 2006). The most effective strategy was to draw people into side discussions from the main public dialogues and exchange views with them at that point. In both the analysis and then use of the internet, there was thus a direct link between the forums for radicalization and the forums for deradicalization. Yet as Stevens and Neumann (2009) point out in their study of *Countering Online Radicalisation*, radicalization is only a 'virtual' phenomenon in part, and any attempt at countering it needs to be anchored in the 'real world'.

It is significant that the broad Saudi deradicalization experiment has moved on, and the rehabilitation programme is constantly being adapted and reviewed. In 2008 Boucek was able to report that the 'soft' approach of the three interconnected areas of prevention, rehabilitation and post-release care (PRAC) was generating very positive and intriguing results. Recidivist and re-arrest rates were extremely low. This might have been partly because it dealt mostly with minor offenders. 'It is still a work in progress' (Porges, 2010). Since its inception in 2004, the programme focused initially only on inmates who were not directly involved in terrorist attacks, but later included repatriated Guantanamo detainees and Saudi self-styled 'freedom fighters' returning from Iraq, treating these groups in a separate centre. The initiative is overseen by committees of clerics, psychologists and security officers who handle religious, psycho-social, security and media-related programming. Based on their study of results with early programme participants, Saudi rehabilitation experts have begun increasing the disengagement-focused elements. They still stress the importance of religious dialogue to address a detainee's understanding of Islam, 'a strategy critical for a government that relies on religion for legitimacy' (Porges, 2010: 2). But recent changes suggest new emphasis on educational efforts aiming to modify a detainee's behaviour, not to change his religious beliefs. Boucek had also recognized that:

> Success of the program also is based in part on the recognition that being radical is not inherently a bad thing. Acting on radical beliefs with violence, however, is, and that is the behaviour that needs to be modified. The fact that the vast majority of prisoners who complete the programme are not acting on their previously held beliefs can be interpreted as a sign of success, regardless of whether their repentance is ultimately sincere.
>
> (Boucek, 2008: 23)

Teachers now offer a wider range of programmes, to include classes and counselling on sharia law, psychology, vocational training, sociology, history, Islamic culture, art therapy and athletics. Family members are increasingly involved, and highly individualized approaches are taken, which are time-consuming but have long-term benefits. The authorities still want to shape thoughts, but also to reintegrate prisoners into Saudi society. Through updated classes on history and culture, the programme has countered AQ efforts to manipulate the history of the Arabian Peninsula. An interesting aspect with regard to information and feedback is how success is measured – it used to be just according to the recidivism rate, the number of detainees who 'go back to the fight'. This painted a positive picture early on, when the Saudis claimed a 100 per cent success rate. But then they had to admit that at least 11 former Guantanamo detainees had returned to terrorist activities after graduating from the programme. They now use responses gained from the larger prison-based initiative, for example the response of 297 previous members, over

220 of whom have been released, The adjustments also reflect lessons learned from working with the most hardened ideologues who, the Saudis admit, do not respond to rehabilitation and are unlikely to successfully complete the programme. What is particularly valuable in terms of learning and adaptation is the trial and error approach, the willingness to keep learning about what is effective in deradicalization and rehabilitation. This transparency and meta-learning is helpful for all, not just the Saudis.

It certainly might help the UK efforts. A BBC report in 2010 said that the use of imams in the prison service to deradicalize jailed Islamic extremists was failing. Imams are viewed as puppets, and as failing to challenge core beliefs. The report quoted Dr Peter Neumann from the Centre for Radicalisation at King's College London, who had researched deradicalization efforts in 15 countries and found that a larger imam service would help but that ex-inmates needed more support outside prison. This fits the Saudi experience. Neumann argued for a post-release network 'to allow them to escape jihadist activities' (Champion, 2010). So much depends on the nature of the counselling and how this is 'experienced' by the receiver.

Mentoring those 'at risk'

These different '4Ds' are put into context if we look at research on the actual processes of, and impact of, mentoring, which I was involved in (Spalek *et al.*, 2010; Spalek and Davies, 2012). The project arose from a concern that there was a shortage of easily accessible and quality-assured, accredited and vetted mentors who could provide one-to-one support to people assessed to be at risk of violent extremist behaviour. This encompassed Al Qaeda influenced, extreme right wing, and animal rights extremism. The initial focus of the project was to design a structure for selection and recruitment of a suitable pool of mentors, with agreed professional daily rates, as well as to develop a governance plan to sustain the programme after the first phase of recruitment. A team from the University of Birmingham was engaged to conduct an evaluation of the pilot phase of the project. We looked at the managerial structure, the concept of mentoring, the support and training needs of mentors, risk and risk management, the measurement of success, and how the project would enhance understanding of radicalization and deradicalization. We interviewed mentors as well as those on the project and steering boards. This research was in the context of a dearth, also, of empirical research on mentoring in sensitive contexts such as extremism. It is a highly controversial strategy, both in questions of identification of 'clients' and in measurement of 'effectiveness'. It carries high levels of risk in itself – for example in whether the process of mentoring acts to cement people's views rather than change them, or even whether mentors themselves can become radicalized. The risk of alienating communities is ever present, as discussed above. I pick out two areas of interest here: whether mentoring against extremism is unique, and how success is measured.

How far is mentoring for violent extremism unique?

It can be argued that mentoring around violent extremism carries distinctive features, and can be distinguished from mentoring in other areas of criminal behaviour or in drug and alcohol use. Working within fields of ideology requires specific skills or backgrounds not always found in agencies such as the Probation Service or in counselling services. The generic considerations that cut across all mentoring processes, such as building a relationship, trust and confidentiality, take on new meanings when they are confronted by deeply held views and very different logics. Yet the participants in the study did not always agree about the focus of intervention. As one summed it up: 'Do we seek to rid ourselves of violent extremist ideology or do we seek to make people less vulnerable to it?' Mentors who work across a range of clients (for example, those with addiction or criminal behaviour as well as extremists) saw parallels in their strategies and relationships across that range. Clients were seen as 'vulnerable' and the primary concern was the risk to themselves, almost before the threat to society. A focus on the individual led to concepts such as 'rehabilitation', helping them to work through the issues that have influenced them for their own benefit. The notion of 'vulnerability' was often repeated, and of 'support': 'We're not in the business of policing people's thoughts … but we have to be in a position to provide some support to vulnerable people who have been made vulnerable by adverse influences.' From this aim of 'support' come objectives of enhancing self-esteem and confidence or of providing ways to reduce vulnerability such as helping with housing, jobs or training. The client is seen as someone who has needs which can be addressed directly or indirectly by the mentoring process. One mentor talked of mentoring being about 'whole person issues':

> This isn't just about quoting lines from a particular holy book or a particular tradition, it's about understanding the individual you're faced with, and what that individual may have gone through may be far more complicated than actually a theological argument. Theology might be a very small part of it. Theology might be just a way of that individual expressing other issues that may have happened in their lives.
>
> (Spalek and Davies, 2012)

This articulates with the RecoRa report *Recognising and Responding to Radicalisation* (Meah and Mellis, 2009), which talks of two parts of intervention – first 'binding' the individual to society through guidance to work, apprenticeship, education or other means of a structural association with 'others', and second, or preferably at the same time, an ideological intervention by a key figure capable of challenging the radical narrative. They also highlight the key elements of successful intervention as building strong neighbourhood and religious networks that can provide targeted support in relationship and confidence building (Meah and Mellis, 2009: 10). Networks are part of complexity.

Those mentors working specifically with AQ extremists, however, would on the other hand highlight the unique nature of the ideological component. For both credibility and skill in debate, AQ mentors were seen to need highly specific knowledge of all branches of Islam and all levels of jihad:

> I don't think you can challenge extremist ideology with employability. You need an articulation of the counter narrative, you need to deliver that in a fashion that retains your trust and credibility with the person but they have to go from point A to B because I do not see flirting with point A as the result of the intervention. There has to be a viable theological alternative, accept the covenant of security, accept that non-Muslims have the same rights as Muslims, accept that the UK is not in a state of war (The mentor is referring to the concept of *dar al-harb*.)
>
> (Spalek and Davies, 2012)

'Covenant of security' is a term used in the media when referring to Al-Muhajiroon, which is now a proscribed terrorist organization. It was often cited by group members as an informal agreement between the British authorities and leaders of Muslim communities which entailed a high degree of toleration in exchange for self-policing by the communities. Many commentators felt that this covenant was breached after the terrorist attacks of 7 July 2005. This mentor pointed very clearly not just to the technical difficulties of changing beliefs but the political ones as well:

> I obviously sit back and I go OK, what we're actually doing is trying to challenge people's prevailing theological understandings and replace them with newer ones, why don't we just be honest. … Now I put on the civil servant hat. Me and you know … there's

no government on the planet that would able to stick its political reputation on the line by telling Muslims what to believe.

(Spalek and Davies, 2012)

Yet in some ways this is precisely the debate. As Thomas points out, the UK government has taken an inherently judgemental 'values-based' approach to PVE, giving the impression that the government is overtly intervening to shape religious practice (Thomas, 2010: 446). Mentors themselves accepted the distinctive nature of mentoring in ideological fields, and that it does touch on belief:

And ideological beliefs are quite difficult to work with because you're addressing a person's soul really aren't you? ... [We're saying] their faith is not what they think it is. Their faith is actually something else and not what they believe it to be.

(Spalek and Davies, 2012)

Rather than giving 'support', mentoring here seems to be pushing people in directions they themselves may not see as necessary or as fulfilling anything for them. Sometimes this was overtly directive, providing the 'right' view:

With offenders they know they're doing wrong, with these people they don't. It's about providing them with an alternative belief but one that's the right one in relation to the ideology as opposed to the twisted one.

(Spalek and Davies, 2012)

This relates to the view of a prison mentor, Imam Ahtsham Ali, who says they had to combat those who take verses from the Quran as a way of promoting extremism. 'We have thought of 13 different theological points that an extremist narrative may have. We are trying to create a manual that will theologically go through the Koran to counter these views' (Ford, 2012: 65). Yet for another mentor in our project, it was *not* about 'conversion', or the 'correct' views, and more about asking questions:

If I say 'we need to bring you to the correct Salafi understanding', I've just reinforced the same ideology. Compulsion, coercion, imposition, you must do this. Instead, I say, 'Brother, you must wake up'. 'Wake up from what?' 'I don't know, ask yourself'.

(Spalek and Davies, 2012)

Measures of success

One challenge with such an open-ended approach is the evaluation of success. The research participants themselves saw benefits in how evaluating the mentoring process would give helpful insights into 'what works'. Yet they acknowledged the complex issues around 'indicators' and played around with an extensive range, linked to their own theories of the purpose of mentoring discussed above – whether reducing vulnerability or disengaging an individual.

One mentor made a distinction between such short-term prevention or rejection and the longer-term acceptance of real alternatives in action. 'For me, a viable alternative to physical jihad is not "okay I won't do it today"'. Rather than postponement, success in mentoring would be real emotional and community-based resilience which would continuously mitigate the threat of terrorism.

One mentor gave the example of a 'sort of convert' who actually did not know how to pray and had to be taught basic behaviour as a Muslim. 'If doing that reduces somebody's vulnerability, then it's done its job'. He (and others) said they were not trying to create the perfect person – 'that isn't what we're about, that's social engineering'. Participants agreed it was not about total transformation:

> You don't have to change somebody's mindset entirely … They don't have to go to Disney World in Florida, but could reconcile the animosity they feel towards the West and look for some rationality.
>
> (Spalek and Davies, 2012)

The measure was more about 'distance travelled', how far a client had moved on. Terms used by different participants were 'standing on their own two feet'; 'self-reporting of feeling happier about their life'; 'visible changes in their lifestyle'. The possibility of drawing up or using a Channel-type risk assessment was mentioned, to determine how many of the risk factors had been reduced. (Channel is a British programme aiming to identify those deemed 'at risk' of violent extremism and, using a multi-agency approach, to provide them with interventions, including mentoring.) It was acknowledged that it was more difficult than assessing 'reoffending' under probation, but that activities and behaviours could be logged. A compilation of indicators drawn from a number of respondents would include:

- no longer sending money and equipment abroad to help a fight
- no longer donating money to (extremist) people who collect at the door

- not being part of grooming processes such as trips to the Lake District
- reduction or change in the sorts of things they were saying and doing.

A more specific outcome, albeit perhaps longer term, is renouncing membership: 'But ultimately when you know that that person is part of HUT [Hizb-ut-Tahrir] and he's actually officially left, that's … outright.' For one member of the Project Board, success and risk were closely linked. There was a need for an initial risk assessment in terms of risk to society, and then this could be used as a measure of progress.

> To use the Palestinian example again, what he's saying, what he's doing, where he's going, what he's viewing. Clear intentions to do all that. All of which pose a risk. If we then do a set of actions, maybe including a mentor, and then an assessment is made of him that says actually, he's now not looking at the internet as much. His foster parents say he's much easier to cope with. He's still saying he wants to go to Pakistan. He's still saying that if he had the chance he'd fight Allied Forces. But actually you can see that there's some effect, isn't there?
>
> (Spalek and Davies, 2012)

This participant had looked for suitable tools but had been unable to find any. Success was not just measuring activity. 'And I think we won't be doing ourselves any favours if our measurement of success is 52 successful encounters this year'.

In contrast to – or in parallel with – the reduction in negative behaviours were the indicators of more positive behaviours, becoming active members of society. This means looking for the positive steps an individual would be taking around improving their prospects. Here can be observed the 'futures' orientation mentioned earlier under 'desistence'. Such futures would include entering education and training, gaining work or community involvement, 'reinvesting' in their family, taking responsibility for themselves, and these activities 'becoming more important than perhaps a slightly selfish politically led or extremist agenda'. An obvious signal was the situation of 'poacher turned gamekeeper': 'People come to the mosque and want to be helped to change. Then two years down the line doing the same job as you, out there challenging. Very positive indicator that a person's changed'.

For one mentor, however, it was just the process of discussion which would be an indicator of success. He contrasted the client who remained silent, switched off – 'that feels a bad indicator'– with:

the person that keeps coming back and is actually arguing with you as well, so that means that he's actually taking out from his thoughts, his arguments and the doubts and putting them out on the table and saying 'Give me the answers to these'.

(Spalek and Davies, 2012)

Here we see a connection to the 'debiasing' techniques mentioned above of promoting alternative arguments. It is part of the whole thrust of this book about encounters, voicing opinions and doubts, about asking questions, having them listened to and responded to.

Yet an interesting and probably contested view was expressed around who takes responsibility for change:

We're always told this, it's not a numbers game. Guidance isn't in our hands, it's in the hand of God. So if that person's sincere enough to want to change, and he's asking God sincerely, then he will see the light. Whether that happens in our life or not …

(Spalek and Davies, 2012)

One mentor had a different – and intriguing – experience:

I spoke to a Muslim who had been radicalised, he was a member of a group associated with AQ and he said the reason he stopped was he just getting bored really, he didn't want to go to meetings any more, he'd rather go to the cinema.

(Spalek and Davies, 2012)

Much depends of course on 'how far in' someone is when the mentoring starts, whether 'you start mentoring someone who is just about to buy his cub uniform or just about to put the bomb on his back. … How long does that take to get them out? How far will they come out? Will it be easy for them to go back in?'

Timing is key. The STREET project (Strategy to Reach, Empower and Educate Teenagers) works with young people in gangs, Pupil Referral Units (PRUs), and others referred to them by statutory services or families. In interview in 2010, the director, Alyas Karmani, made the key point that when dealing with radicalized or high-risk audiences the teaching methods that aim to deconstruct propaganda must sit within a wider package of interventions – a comprehensive programme to build resilience and address the wide spectrum of risk factors. Core theological exploration and deconstruction should only be attempted when those individuals hold informed extremist views. There must be careful triage at the initial stages to provide a bespoke package of support, i.e. there is no point going into the detail of extremist ideology (and effectively 'educating' young people about it) if this is not something which is an active risk factor for that individual. 'It's really important to think "how deep do we need to go?" I mean how many 14-year-old ideologues are there really?' (OPM, 2010: 1)

Once again the debate arises on methods and on how important theology is. Do you have ex-extremists or imams coming into schools or well-trained teachers who can equip young people with the tools to deconstruct myths and propaganda techniques? It is thought AQ-inspired messages need to be seen within the context of a more informed understanding of global geopolitical issues (OPM, 2011). STREET also relies on established local social networks where trust and reputation are crucial. For instance, it appeals not to Muslims' sense of Britishness but rather to their sense of being Londoners, and to a common possession of 'London roots'.

Conclusion: Is secularism the answer?

Githens-Mazer and Lambert critique the conventional wisdom of radicalization which boils down largely to an assertion that a sense of Islamic difference (variously explained in terms of a lack of integration, a lack of secularism, the existential threat posed by Islam to the West, or external Islamic influences from Saudi Arabia and the wider Middle East) has the dangerous potential to mutate issues of differing identities into support for violent 'Islamo-fascism' (Githens-Mazer and Lambert, 2010: 890). Everything in the media gets bound up with community cohesion and what constitutes 'reasonable behaviour' among British Muslims. For writers such as Gilles Kepel (2005) the clear solution is the wholesale adoption of the French model of 'radical secularism' which has, he claims, by a programme of social control including most notably a ban on all religious symbols in schools, conscious integration and a preventive security policy, led to France being spared terror attacks for the past decade. Githens-Mazer and Lambert rightly question this conventional wisdom. Is it provable in fact? And what does it say about the way the media, policy makers and academics are currently engaged in using labels such as 'radicalization' and 'radicalized'? Their in-depth research casts doubts on the conventional wisdom about 'Salafi inspired' jihadism and the complexities of who might take up a radical stance. The Brixton Salafis and the Salafi-run STREET project directly confronted the threat of radicalization, but government came under substantial pressure from commentators and the media for treating with reactionaries. The notion that shared values and beliefs will be a counter to terrorist threats is a political claim rather than one driven by real-world security concerns.

Therefore a radical secularism that attempts to forge such shared values under some nationalist umbrella, as in France, misses the point. Policies deriving from dynamic secularism, in contrast, either let communities do their own deradicalization, or at least engage with and acknowledge the complex sets of histories and belief patterns already existing in a community. Rather than preventing their expression, symbolically or otherwise, the task is to surface them and work with them. In schools, it is reasonable to let the Prevent agenda be run by anyone who has the skill to promote and manage the debate. In deradicalization, when views and orientations appear more fixed and the risk is nearer, at least one component has to be the ideological, which must be treated as such. The division of labour is not so much the privatization of the spiritual, but accepting that the state and the police need to treat terrorism as criminal and engage with all aspects of the vulnerability of communities, while the ideological and individual aspects are dealt with by a person who knows something about theology.

The first lesson that's been learnt in working in the area of actual or suspected radicalization is that trust is key. This applies whether working with communities or working with individuals deemed to be at risk. Until there is trust, the dialogue, dangerous conversation and mutual collaboration to prevent extremism will not happen. The jury is out on whether you try in such dialogue to change beliefs or just behaviour, but anyway a non-linear perspective will confirm that it will not be possible to assume a long-term change. As we saw in the previous chapter about preventing attacks on schools, the role of the community is crucial. That community is not homogeneous, and may or may not have 'shared values', but these values cannot be imposed by outside. It will be equitable partnerships between communities and the state that enable understandings and resilience.

Chapter 7

Positive insecurity, turbulence and change

> *Never doubt that a small group of thoughtful, committed citizens can change the world. Indeed, it is the only thing that ever has.*
>
> Margaret Mead

This chapter pulls together the conclusions from the previous ones to celebrate the basic paradox: that for security, there needs to be turbulence. For change to occur, there needs to be positive insecurity. Just as we talk about positive and negative peace, we can talk about positive and negative insecurity. My argument is that a complex, inclusive, secular system – a dynamic one – will foster the turbulence needed for progress in a society, while safeguarding the basic workings of that society.

Dynamic secularism

I summarize the ten basic tenets of dynamic secularism as explored in this book before looking at the connections to complex adaptation and emergence within and through education.

First is the basic order of a separation of state and church in terms of those goods which the state provides or controls: law, police and the military as state institutions; and then the state regulation of basic goods for all, such as transport, water, health and education. Just as tribalism, partisanship and cronyism are antithetical to political order, religion is never neutral. It constitutes a group, a tribal identity, and represents a danger for a common political order. A religion's supernatural ideals derived from ancient texts should not be a constituent of the daily, earthly workings of governance.

Second, and leading logically from this, is a framework of common human rights to underpin law and the various workings of the economy. Economically, all analyses of why some countries developed and became rich and others did not will point to this secular regulation and system of accountability. Accountability to God is not enough. Markets need institutions to work in. For human development and human security, common rights for all that cut across religions are a prerequisite. As a secular system, these can be critiqued, developed and updated, but they are always indivisible and cannot be taken away from people. Children's rights also form a secular value system for a school, cutting across all religions and none.

Third, religion is acknowledged as important to large segments of society and can be part of the diversity of views which enrich the constant dialogue needed for a society to evolve. It provides personal security for some. Religious organizations can, because of their values, enhance other sorts of security through aid work and charitable work. Religions should not be banned or discouraged or driven underground. However, they should not receive state financial support *as religions*, but only in the same way as any organizations which engage in development work but do not proselytize.

Fourth, religion is not to be privileged over other movements, groupings or cultures. There should be no politics of automatic representation. Competition provides one of the levers for evolution: religions must compete equally in the marketplace of ideas and of influence. Religions do not have rights; people do. Religious discrimination is covered by basic human rights law, and the state has a duty to protect those who experience discrimination in jobs, housing or education because of their beliefs. It also has the duty to protect people if they suffer harm *within* their religion, if this contravenes rights as enshrined in law, for example with questions of gender equality or age of marriage. In this sense, the state can intervene in religion. For many people, religion is only part of their identity, and the acknowledgement of hybrid identities gives the fluidity and creativity needed in a complex society. Singular identities are not to be prioritized above hybrid ones. It is accepted that we have multiple, recombinant identities, and these combinations are part of our adaptability. A frozen singular identity presents a grave risk to both self and society.

Fifth, religion is not however privatized in the sense of not participating in public life. Religious groups are free to lobby, influence, be consulted and even form a political party – as long as this is transparent and as long as that party does not threaten or intimidate. In that sense, dynamic secularism underpins the basic ideals of democracy. The question of political participation is always contextual, with the growth of Islamist parties presenting problems in Arab states. But the answer cannot be to ban parties unless they contravene other parts of the law, such as denying freedom of religion for others, or engaging in hate speech, or using violence. The distinction between what parties say they will do and what they actually do applies to all politics. It cannot be legislated for in advance.

Sixth, there should be freedom of religion and freedom of religious expression. People must have the right to hold religious beliefs, as well as the freedom to exit from a religion. Religious expression, such as in dress or the display of religious symbols, is permitted, just as any other expression of tribal or group identity, whether T-shirts with political slogans or a poster of Che Guevara on the wall. As with the politics of recognition, it is important not to elevate religious expression above other sorts of expression, so making it a *cause célèbre* and amplifying difference and conflict.

Seventh is the basic general right of freedom of expression. This includes a free press and free scientific enquiry, which are not only hallmarks of a civilized society but, history tells us, underpinned massive shifts such as the Industrial Revolution. Argument, encounter, discussion and dialogue are central to this: freedom of expression is not just a right but becomes a way to learn – whether in schools or as part of a deradicalization process. This freedom of expression includes the freedom to criticize religion – just as we have the freedom to criticize Marxism, or the idea of global warming, or homeopathy. Like everything else, this is within the framework of legal prohibitions on incitement to hatred, or libel laws. But religion does not occupy some sort of special, protected place in public debate. In fact, it is crucial for social emergence as well as equity that religion and sacred texts are scrutinized and any basic flaws or contradictions revealed. Adaptation requires the rupture of locked-in perspectives.

Eighth, the flexibility in a CAS means that there can nonetheless be 'reasonable accommodation' of religious requirements, as long as these do not harm others and mean greater inclusion rather than less. It is on the same level as accommodating vegetarianism or providing a smokers' room. It is *not* however on the same level as the provision of disabled toilets, as that relates to basic rights and is of a higher order. Religious accommodation is not a right but a strategy in a dynamically secular state, up for negotiation. This has to be seen contextually: the erection of a mosque does not in itself harm, but the noise from it might legitimately be questioned by those not taking part – as with a night club. The number of public holidays is another question, as having too many may harm the economy. Gender segregation in public meetings, as sometimes demanded by more orthodox Muslims and Jews, is debatable, unless it really leads to parity in participation rights rather than preventing it. But providing a prayer room in a school, or halal meat, or a different sort of uniform, or a Christian Fellowship club can be part of ensuring students feel comfortable and included in the institution. This carries the equal risk of exclusion and difference, of course, so ongoing judgements have to be made about the value of accommodating minority interests. And there has to be mutual reciprocal accommodation, as discussed later in relation to religious opposition to gay–straight clubs in schools.

Ninth, in educational terms, in a plural society the state should not fund educational institutions of diverse religions, as segregation is harmful for the connectivity needed for emergence and basic cohesion. When there are competing religions, state-provided schools should be secular in their management and control. However, in a monotheistic society, all schools may be 'religious' and the state will be involved in their support. The question in that case concerns regulation and moderation, so that there is a broad curriculum, employment opportunities, gender equity and non-violence. The same regulation would apply to private faith institutions in any society: they should be permitted but should adhere to the basic principles of rights and freedoms.

Finally, religious education should feature in a core curriculum. In a DSS this is obviously not doctrinal but is tackled within social science, political science or philosophy. Comparative religion is less about surface features of rituals and ceremonies and more about a critical, analytic dissection of the role of religion in a society – for good or ill. It would cover religious tension and discrimination, and their causes. It would enable critical discussion of sacred texts and their origins and implications. It could also tackle some of the values underpinning the narratives: as the atheist children's writer Philip Pullman argues, 'The good Samaritan' is a great story and should be included in the literature children read. A rights-based approach covers most things, and research shows that children in rights-based schools do become nicer to each other; but it does no harm to underpin this with direct messages about basic kindness. Getting people to perform a daily 'random act of kindness', without thought of reward either now or in the hereafter, has quite powerful escalatory power. So education about religion can be viewed as a considerable learning resource: for skills, debate, morality, and understanding of political conflict and revolution. I would say 'milk it' – with sufficient critical distance and disrespect where appropriate.

It is worth repeating that these principles are actually conducive to religion. In a religiously plural society, a dynamic secular state acts as an umbrella protection without showing bias to any one faith. When states start funding religions, they are also going to want to control them; this means *less* freedom for a religion or religious organization. While a religion may have its own law such as sharia, people will be calling on the national common legal framework to ensure their basic rights in that society. Freedom to critique a religion means dynamism for that religion, so that it evolves and better fits the contemporary world.

While these ten guidelines for a dynamic secular system may seem, when presented as a list, to be parallel to a set of religious injunctions or secular prohibitions, the point is that each contains the seeds of dynamic change rather than conservative control. They are flexible, provisional, and context bound. Even human rights are contextual – which is why we have human rights lawyers. The underpinning rationale is adaptability.

I have toyed with various analogies for dynamic secularism (not quite an umbrella, not quite a protective suitcase) and the nearest would be the institution of restaurants. In complexity terms, there is a multiplicity in any country. There is no Master Chef in the Sky who directs operations. Instead there is provision for all tastes and a great deal of learning, interaction, creativity and fusion across different cookery styles. Immediate feedback enables a restaurant to respond to the clientele. From the state there is basic health and safety protection, inspection of kitchens, protection for workers, possible noise and parking regulation, but otherwise restaurants are allowed to get on with it. They will compete, but the state does not favour one chain over another. The food industry will lobby government relentlessly, but others will take them on (with protests about Starbucks and McDonald's), so there is constant dynamism. So why can't religions be more like restaurants? The latter give succour if not to the poor at least to those with a modicum of cash. They provide a social space to meet. And they save, if not souls, at least washing up.

I use this analogy because it is better than seeing religion and secularism as oppositional, or even as operating somehow in parallel. Complexity theory warns us against simple binaries, of either/or; and work on extremism will warn us of dualisms, of good versus evil. The secularism which I have been promoting throughout this book is not an alternative to religion but an encompassing arrangement which can enable religious adherence to continue and even to flourish if it does not harm.

Change in a complex, adaptive, dynamic secular system

This last point leads to the ultimate concern of the book: how change occurs in the directions we want it to. I now want to map these ten tenets of dynamic secularism onto complexity ideas to examine how DS can underpin change. The Taliban is an almost perfect complex adaptive system – networked, constantly evolving, self-organizing, with effective feedback loops in its performance against the activities of both government and occupation forces, as well as of the population. It has integrated an education commission into its quasi-government parallel structures – providing and controlling schools, not just destroying them. We can learn from the Taliban – but also improve on them.

Put simply, there are two aspects of theories of change: *what* we are focusing on (in what ways we see education as linking to security); and *how* we are strategizing (our assumptions about how change best occurs). The first is not really generalizable – every context has a unique relation to conflict. A focus on vocational education in order to integrate unemployed youth can be successful in countries where jobs or self-employment are available, but less effective or even counter-productive in contexts where qualified youths are then without a sense of purpose and where joining armed militias is more attractive or lucrative. An attempt at cultural recognition by providing minority languages or culture in the curriculum may work in Guatemala but would be almost disastrous in the Balkans, where language policy is used and manipulated by nationalist groups and where learning only in mother tongue hinders access to higher education or employment. Linear assumptions about interventions creating a chain of events which eventually lead to conflict transformation are highly dubious. In Chapter 1 and Chapter 5 I cast doubts on the securitization of aid, and on Western suppositions about the processes towards security for so-called fragile states.

More generalizable perhaps are the *how* questions – what we now know about how change occurs in complex adaptive systems, or how social systems can move towards greater adaptability. To develop this, I present some seemingly oppositional categories in summary form in the table opposite. These do not represent religion versus secularism, but two theories of change/stability. The contenders are 'Unsafe Gods' versus 'Turbulence for security'. The left represents hindrances to change, while the right presents the complexity mindsets which enable progress towards the sort of positive security we might want, human, societal, or national. I would have to say that religion is in danger of falling more into the Unsafe Gods category, but not exclusively so.

Let me explain and exemplify these a little.

1. Non-linearity

An intriguing theory proposed by Edward de Bono in 2000 was that Arab–Israeli aggressiveness was due in part to low levels of zinc found in people who eat mostly unleavened bread without yeast. Therefore shipping them out jars of Marmite would bring peace to the region. (For non-UK readers, Marmite is a dark-brown yeast extract in an iconic and equally dark-brown jar.) But the Marmite theory is unsafe – not just empirically, but because yeast extract is highly salt and large quantities are likely to provoke heart disease.

	Unsafe Gods	Turbulence for security
1	Linear assumptions – utopian visions, notions of the end-time, actions now meaning rewards in heaven, long-term chains of causation, grand goals	Change through multiple interactions, acceptance of unpredictability, comfort with short-term goals, amplification of small interventions
2	Lock-in: rigid secularism as well as rigid sacred texts which promote conformity	Flexibility, creativity, adaptation, constant revision and review through feedback and critique
3	Top-down authority – religious and hard-line secular leaders and commandments	Self-organizing systems, horizontal networks and possibilities, modelling, community engagement
4	Strong singular identities	Hybrid, multiple, shifting identities – or no identity at all
5	Inner peace, love and tolerance	Outer rights, non-violence and intolerance of social injustice
6	Respect (indiscriminate) for all others, and silencing of voice	Freedom of expression and critique
7	Learning about other cultures; celebrating diversity and difference	Ignoring otherness of cultures in order to work together; making boundaries less important
8	The politics of recognition	Not privileging any religion, culture or lifestyle
9	Indicators of success; examples of transferable good practice	Indicators of failure; learning from bad practice and mistakes
10	Seriousness and taking offence; rage and revenge	Satire and turning ridicule to one's advantage; accommodation

More in keeping with complexity would be hummus, a signature dish in *The Arab–Israeli Cookbook* by Robin Soans. This book was a spin-off from his 2004 play of the same name based on interviews with ordinary Israelis and Palestinians caught up in a conflict they never wanted. They have much in common, not just the foods, about which they are passionate. One they share is hummus, even if the recipes are different and even the spelling. The book and the play reflect 'the shared culture and centuries of history when Jews and Arabs lived together in harmonious symbiosis' (Soans, 2004: 7). Soans says that talking about food now stops either side from getting propagandist. This actually seems a highly promising approach to breaking boundaries, on the lines of the West–Eastern Divan Orchestra.

The Marmite theory however is a linear theory, of single causation and mitigation. Similarly, Howard Jacobson wrote a slightly tongue-in-cheek article on who is likely to be recruited into extremist groups – susceptible students, who are just about able to read, have too much time on their hands, too few girlfriends, a handful of university chums similarly vague in their comprehension of world events, and a computer at their disposal. Religion is only the smokescreen. 'The great atheist tyrannies of the last century recruited their foot soldiers in an identical manner – targeting partially educated, preferably pampered, but certainly crestfallen young men for whom the usual safety valves of dissoluteness have for some reason failed to open'. Jacobson therefore proposes lots of booze and sex as the answer:

> Whatever you think of the pure in mind, beware, reader, the pure in body ... If you stopper the compulsion to procreate, where does the energy go? ... It seems that if you can't replenish the human race, depleting it is the next best thing.
>
> (Jacobson, 2010: 23)

Great theory but the problem is the solution that would be inferred from it. I would be more than happy with extra booze and sex, but it is hardly a short-term, let alone a long-term generalizable policy proposal.

Unlike linear religious concepts of the end time, of the second coming, of the millenarian Utopia, theories from complexity do not specify long-term goals nor quick fixes. As Stacey pointed out in the context of management:

> In management context most textbooks focus heavily on techniques and procedures for long-term planning, on the need for visions and missions, on the importance and the means of securing strongly shared cultures, on the equation of success with consensus, consistency, uniformity and order. [However, in complex environments] the real management task is that of coping with and even using unpredictability, clashing counter-cultures, dissensus, contention, conflict, and inconsistency. In short, the task that justifies the existence of all managers has to do with instability, irregularity, difference and disorder.
>
> (Stacey, 1996: xix–xx)

This would apply equally to education managers.

2. Interrupting lock-in

This question was exemplified best in Chapter 4 when I looked at how religious women are deconstructing sacred texts – whether Jewish, Islamic or Christian – to critique their patriarchal basis. We saw how the women's efforts elicit a counter-defence and attack from those holding themselves as more expert, or closer to God; but there is no doubt that their struggles will have an amplifying effect. If sections of these texts can be seen as in need of revision, then why not all of them?

Rigid secularism can be interrupted too. A nice example from our research on pupil democracy in Europe (Davies and Kirkpatrick, 2000) was in a school in the Netherlands that wanted to ban headscarves for Muslim girls. The student body thought this outrageous and so devised a strategy whereby they all turned up the next day wearing headscarves, boys and girls alike. This was both about solidarity and the demonstration that what you wear makes no difference to how you learn. The school backed down on its policy.

3. Leadership

Here the shift is from change coming from leaders and (often self-styled) authorities to the realization that change comes from self-organization. We saw this in community-based schools and in community resistance to the Taliban, protecting schools from attack as well as protecting girls' education. We saw it too in police engagement as partners with a community, not as figures of 'authority' but as equals in the challenge to radicalization. This relates to the notion of community neighbourhood practices of self-security mentioned in Chapter 1.

Once one moves away from leadership, there are many ways in which new behaviour is modelled. The phrase is: 'What would it be like if?' Apparently, people are twice as likely to litter if their environment is dirty (Goldstein *et al.*, 2007). This resonates with the broken window theory for communities and schools, that a broken window should be replaced right away, before the whole environment is seen as broken and treated as such. Modelling is not the same as leadership. Tarouk Masoud talks of the 'myth of durable authoritarianism' (quoted in Mason, 2012: 27), that one cannot assume support for dictatorships. Paul Mason also reveals how Anthony Giddens declared in an essay that Gaddafi was a follower of the Third Way and Libya was on the road to becoming the Norway of North Africa. Respect for leaders is highly risky (Giddens, 2007).

Admittedly, querying authority leads to dilemmas of top-down regulation. One classic instance is the imposition on schools in the UK of the

Duty to Promote Community Cohesion. Although this is no longer inspected, the government believes it necessary to retain the duty 'given the current proliferation of faith based schools and the consequent loss of opportunities for students to spend their formative years in multi-cultural environments' (Rowe *et al.*, 2012: 105). From research, schools did feel more benefit than burden, with negativity largely around the imposition and inspection. The duty encouraged and gave teachers 'permission' to look at some of the holistic issues surrounding teaching and learning, to examine their work with community, to feel a 're-focusing of the official policy away from the narrowly instrumental approach that has driven the "test, tables and targets" culture' (Rowe *et al.*, 2012: 106). Change here is not about 'leadership' from government, but about giving legitimacy to an area that teachers may think important anyway, and giving them space. In fact, authority might be seen not as changing behaviour, but as enabling it.

4. Identities
This book has alluded often to the problem of seeing people as singular representatives of their religion. Far more functional is the creative display of hybrid identities. Illustrations of 'interpretive diversity' were cited, such as secular Jews, 'Aussie Mossies', secular Christians, and the organization British Muslims for a Secular Democracy. History is full of identities being imposed upon people, whether in the Balkans or Rwanda or Germany or South Africa. There is an old joke in Northern Ireland that when someone says they are an atheist, they are asked 'But are you a Protestant atheist or a Catholic atheist?'

The question of security is central here. As Walzer asserts: 'When my parochialism is threatened, then I am wholly, radically parochial ... and nothing else. Under conditions of security, I will acquire a more complex identity than the idea of tribalism suggests' (Walzer, 1993: 8). Celebrating hybridity in views is also very valuable. Martin Rowson in *The Dog Allusion* draws on the White Queen in Lewis Carroll's *Through the Looking Glass* who famously declared 'Why sometimes I've believed as many as six impossible things before breakfast':

> But still, if your political bent is not totalitarian, or you're not blinded by Manicheanism or substitute racism, in this context you should have no problem whatsoever in sympathising, or maybe even empathising, with poor and beleaguered Muslims and their families while still deploring the narrowness and short-sightedness

of their self-selected spokesmen, while simultaneously supporting the efforts of Muslims in Muslim countries using whatever methods they can to free themselves of the corrupt and incompetent despots who rule them, even if you deplore the wider implications of the political Islamism they resort to, while at exactly the same time utterly deploring the crass interventions of Western powers to bolster these despots, but also actively supporting, advocating and defending the Western way of life to the death.

(Rowson, 2008: 99)

Uncannily this is my position to the letter. But there is a purpose in such complicated positionings. As Rowson points out, this is human. It may not display consistency, but if we had done that we would still be amoebae. We are far more complicated than is presented in most monotheistic religions. Complexity and emergence does not just tolerate such tangled webs but actively demands them. Students occupying colleges and universities to protest about student fees have sprayed Debord's aphorism: 'Be realistic – Demand the impossible'.

5. Inner peace

It may seem counter-intuitive to list this as an Unsafe God, but I offer the example of Sri Lanka (see Chapter 4). With conflict between Tamils and Sinhalese, spreading the notion of inner peace used to be very much part of the national policy on peace and social cohesion. It was convenient for government to conceptualize conflict in Sri Lanka as a problem of ethnic prejudice rather than a political question of land and rights. Hence if people all had inner peace and knew about the ways of life of 'others', then long-term harmony would be possible. The people, rather than government policy, could be blamed for the continuation of strife. The problem is that inner peace is a well-known Buddhist concept, and is linked with the promotion of Buddhist ethno-nationalism rather than something which really unites people. Inner peace, and the acceptance of your lot, has always been a control feature of both religion and domination.

More turbulent is looking outwards to identify social injustice in the society. This was mentioned in the section in Chapter 5 on Islamophobia, where students were exposed to the discrimination and racism which prevailed (or which they were part of) and were encouraged to challenge this when they met it.

6. Respect

This is another thorny question. Respecting others seems incontrovertible but, as noted in Chapter 4, it loses its meaning if applied to whole identities rather than to actions. Rights are to be respected, not necessarily their holders. The notion of 'respecting diversity' is even more woolly, a code for tolerating 'others'. Instead, a rights-based focus in schools gives a means to know what to respect and what not to respect, what to tolerate and what to challenge or critique. Total acceptance of everything and everybody as worthy of respect is anathema to complex adaptation and learning. The counter to fear of offence and disrespect is freedom of speech and enquiry, within the usual boundaries of prohibitions on hate speech or deliberate offence. There are clearly huge debates around issues such as the cartoons depicting the prophet Muhammad that were published in a Danish newspaper in 2005. A complexity approach would ask, what is this gratuitous offence trying to achieve? What change does it want to make? Did the experiment work? If this cannot be identified, then lampooning does not help adaptability. In contrast, satires on government policy can have the effect of alerting people to the fact that they do not have to accept it as serious.

7. Celebrating diversity

Chapter 4 drew attention to how the educational efforts around peace in Sri Lanka have been critiqued for a stereotypical multicultural curriculum which constantly emphasized difference in prayer or artistic expression between Sinhalese, Tamil, or Muslim. The focus in contact initiatives has fortunately now shifted from observing alien others to joint programmes of contact, to engage in common problem-solving and community research. Child rights clubs and Interact clubs now bring students together for tasks. One Hindu student talked to us about a day when students from five different places 'worked as friends, forgetting our religion, forgetting our family background'. In this context, forgetting religion would seem more productive than dwelling on it. Descriptions of fundamentalists use the phrase 'dwellers rather than seekers', that is, that fundamentalists seek safety rather than new spiritual vistas (quoted in Davies, 2008).

In terms of making boundaries less important rather than emphasizing them, I turn to an interesting example from the Philippines. Based on her ethnographic research, Lindsey Horner (2012) discusses the work of a radical Christian NGO, Malikha Bridge, which had the mission of 'Godly transformation'. But this was not evangelical, rather a transformation into social progress within the hybridity of the Mindanao society. They worked to challenge the harsh treatment of ethnic Muslim gay men. They connected wealthy Christians with poor Muslims on projects – for a water tower, toilets or pre-school facilities, supporting the communities' wish for children to learn about Islamic values. In line with non-linearity, peace was seen as open-ended and diverse. Their praxis was based around the notion of 'faith as uncertainty' (the tradition of Christianity to surpass itself, to be open to learning, here learning in particular from Muslim brothers and sisters). They used extensive networking. There was fluidity, as they were freed from having to evangelize. Peace was seen as a process and as aspirational. A key phrase was 'occupying the spaces in between', managing the tensions between strong beliefs and uncertainty.

What is salutary is the remarkable uncertainty about, and constant scrutiny of, one's faith. This enabled the NGO to gain trust as well as solid results of community improvement and shifts in homophobic attitudes. This is a great fit for complex adaptivity.

8. The politics of recognition

As soon as one religion is privileged, either over other religions or over other types of representation, then ironically this can lead to greater hostility or problems, rather than less. In Chapter 3, I tackled the question of automatic recognition of minority religious groups in politics and argued that this is unsafe for politics, and for the religion too. As with the funding of faith schools, either all religions have to be recognized or there has to be some sort of official list. Neither is tenable in a democracy.

And 'representation' is a very Unsafe God indeed. A recent example in the UK is Lord Ahmed. Nazir Ahmed was elevated to the House of Lords in 1998 as the first male Muslim peer and 'a voice for the Muslim community' (Norfolk, 2013). In 2007 he killed a 28-year-old man by driving into him just after texting, and received a prison sentence, though he was freed on appeal two weeks after sentencing. He later claimed that his sentence was evidence of a Jewish conspiracy, the result of pressure on the courts by Jews who own newspapers and television channels, though he later retracted the accusation. Maajid Nawaz of the Quilliam Foundation made an excellent comment on the case and the fact that Muslims are disproportionately represented among the purveyors of anti-Semitic prejudice and attacks:

> Perhaps we should not be surprised that this is the case when so-called 'community leaders' such as Lord Ahmed give vent to such obnoxious views or host book launches in the House of Lords for

anti-Semites. His respectable veneer gives space for a tiny minority to pretend that their extremist views are mainstream.

This is the whole problem with 'communalism' – the approach to ethnic minorities taken by authorities over the past couple of decades. People are ennobled as if they were local chieftains who can represent this community or that religious group. This can quickly descend into the poisonous world of identity politics in which, in order to retain credibility as local leaders, they have to pander to the most vocal, most organised minority within the 'community' – and for many Muslim peers, that means Islamists. That's why communalism only causes mistrust between communities.

(Nawaz, 2013: 28)

Nawaz points out how Ahmed's reported outburst against Jews reinforces the stereotype that all Muslims secretly harbour medieval anti-Jewish, homophobic and misogynistic views. This only increases discrimination against Muslims and Pakistanis. Everyone loses: Jews and Muslims alike. Nawaz's analysis is spot on in terms of the huge dangers of identity politics and communalism.

9. Learning from mistakes
This was exemplified in the discussion in Chapter 6 of the UK government's Preventing Violent Extremism strategy. The heavy focus on surveillance of Muslims in schools and universities and the gross error of placing security cameras in a predominantly Muslim district acted to increase the alienation of Muslims from the state and its law enforcement. The shift to partnership work and building trust rather than suspicion has enabled some healing. So has recognizing people in the community as active agents in promoting security and not just as either victims or collaborators in terrorism. An ideological but contested shift has been from community cohesion to safeguarding – that it is not the role of the state, nor that of the police, to bring people together.

10. Automatic seriousness and offence
Here the shift is from the Unsafe God of a default position of revenge, retribution and taking offence, to a political maturity that lets the law deal with definitions and infringements of rights. The American satirical organ *The Onion* published a cartoon in 2012 under the banner 'No One Murdered Because of This Image'. The cartoon depicted Moses, Jesus, Ganesh and Buddha doing indescribable things to each other (*The Onion*, 2012). Hugo

Rifkind says that at first he thought it was too shocking and they should not have published it, whatever the rationale. 'Then I realised that my reaction was the whole point. Because what I didn't think, at any time, was "… and the best way of settling this would be by killing somebody or storming an Embassy"' (Rifkind, 2012: 21). Under the cartoon was a spoof news report: 'Though some members of the Jewish, Christian, Hindu and Buddhist faiths were reportedly offended by this image, sources confirmed that upon seeing it, they simply shook their heads, rolled their eyes and continued on with their day.' The war-time slogan 'Keep calm and carry on' has a lot going for it.

The Christian website *Ship of Fools* is a splendid example of a religion being self-critical and satirizing itself. The aim is to strengthen the Christian faith by being able to stand back and critique or mock it where necessary. Readers write in with reviews of sermons, like restaurants, and look out for the more eccentric interpretations of Christianity, such as:

> The King James Bible is celebrating its fourth century, but apparently there are some believers who think that other versions come from Satan and should be burned. Amazing Grace Baptist Church in Waynesville, North Carolina, has an annual book burning night every Hallowe'en, where members destroy copies of any Bible apart from the King James, along with country records and the works of liberal heretics such as Billy Graham. Too extreme, or not extreme enough? Steve Van Nattan of the serene-sounding Blessed Quietness Journal says: 'If you do not burn your NIV, NASB, New KJV, or whatever other slop hog filthy piece of excretion you are reading instead of the King James Bible, YOU ARE GOING TO HELL. I am delighted too.'
>
> (Tomkins, 2011)

As the *Ship of Fools* comments, 'Proof indeed of the blessings of quietness'. One reader found that in their local W.H. Smith you could get an autographed copy of the Holy Bible. But my favourite example is from the Bethel Lutheran Church in Willowick, Ohio:

EVENINGS AT 7
IN THE PARISH HALL

MON	ALCOHOLICS ANONYMOUS
TUE	ABUSED SPOUSES
WED	EATING DISORDERS
THU	SAY NO TO DRUGS
FRI	TEEN SUICIDE WATCH
SAT	SOUP KITCHEN

SUNDAY SERMON
9 A.M.

"AMERICA'S JOYOUS FUTURE"

I wish all religions – and secular societies – had such websites. If Muslims routinely produced their own cartoons and satirized any weird versions of Islam, there would be no need for others to point them out. The comedian Shazia Mirza does this, but she is unusual. I treasure a wonderful book of cartoon illustrations of women in face-covering burkas, with the accompanying text written by Jamila Mujahed, president of the Afghan Women's Association. The text talks of the female oppression in Kabul under the Taliban; the illustrations are all of the surreal situations that arise from wearing the burka. One burka-clad woman photographs four identical others, saying 'Smile please'. Another says to her friend, 'Sorry I'm late, I didn't know what to wear'. Yet another shows a distraught small boy running around a group of identical burka-clad women crying 'Maman'. The only thing it seems good for is playing poker. The juxtaposition of the disturbing accounts of being imprisoned in the burka with gently humorous illustrations is much more powerful than either would be alone (Bassano di Tufillo and Mujahed, 2008).

Humour is particularly suited to complexity and emergence because it transgresses boundaries and juxtaposes non-equivalences. I liked the story of the woman who said she was divorcing her husband over religious differences: 'He thought he was God and I didn't'.

Illustration: Shared classes in Northern Ireland

What with ten principles of secularism and ten ways to avoid Unsafe Gods, this all seems a bit fragmented and 'listy'. One example which seems to me to pull together many of the features discussed is that of shared classes in Northern Ireland. Schooling divided by Catholic and Protestant faith has long been seen as contributing to sectarian tension. Yet while the ideal of integration receives support, only 7 per cent of schools are integrated, and evidence of impact on the rest of the sector is slight. Parents like the *idea* of integrated schools but when they make their actual choice, they tend to send their children to the 'best' schools, that is, Protestant or Catholic according to their faith. The project of collaborative networks of schools was designed to present a workable alternative to full integration, with students meeting in shared classes for core curricular areas. At the time of writing, there are about three thousand such classes across 12 partnerships.

There have been a number of evaluations and these continue (Gallager *et al.*, 2010; Duffy and Gallagher, 2012; Gallagher, 2012; Hughes *et al.*, 2010). Apparently, project leaders had been advised by key figures in education at the start of the project that cross-sectoral collaboration on any meaningful basis was either impractical or risky. Concern was expressed that bringing large numbers of young people from different schools together on a regular basis might simply provide opportunities for sectarian incidents or problems. In the event, the number of such incidents was low and when they occurred they were handled in a constructive and positive way by the schools – the teachers had received training on handling such diversity. In the past, it is likely that such incidents would have been brushed under the carpet and any collaborative work halted: during the project the few incidents that did occur were addressed directly and publicly, and the collaborative work continued.

The project thus broke through the barriers of reticence (that it was not workable) and concern (that it would worsen sectarian tensions). The 12 partnerships varied according to their locality, legacies of local violence, and religious demographics. Among the pupils surveyed, as many as two in five had never met someone from a different religious community prior to their involvement in the Sharing Education activities. The majority of the students said they found these activities to be enjoyable and positive: they enjoyed the opportunity to meet with students from other schools; they reported that their confidence had increased and they had become more comfortable with the idea of contact with students from other communities.

Participants argued that the experience of sharing and cross-sector collaboration mitigates the impact and challenges of living in contested space by providing more opportunity for reciprocal movement across that space and for sustaining relationships through learning about each other (Duffy and Gallagher, 2012). This is very much a refinement of contact theory, far more complex than just bringing people together, and depends on how it is nested within the community and its history (Gallagher, 2012). One crucial finding for this book is that many pupils considered religion as less important than shared interests when they were making friends. The central idea is to leave borders where they are but make them less important (as in Europe).

A number of features of this project make it a near-perfect example of complex adaptation. First, there was no utopian vision: instead it was moving from best practice to next practice – building up new solutions between fully separate and fully integrated schooling, with people not sure how it would go. The driving principle is that the future is there to be made – and it may involve moving towards integrated schools or it may mean staying with shared ones. Second, there was experimentation: teachers had to find creative ways of overcoming the logistics of transport, timetabling and finding spaces to teach and learn. Linked to this was, third, a philosophy of being tolerant of failure, trying things out, and accepting that it did not matter if things did not work. Fourth, and leading from this, was learning from mistakes, using brutal honesty with self and partners. In the words of one teacher:

> So that has been the best way for us to learn, by unpicking it ourselves and going maybe we could have done that differently [sic]. ... I think being allowed to make those mistakes was a valuable part of the experience. ... The learning curve itself was enough and we were granted that at least. So I have to say that [it] is important that people feel comfortable and trust the process and that [it] is ok to make mistakes as you go along.
>
> (interview in Duffy and Gallagher, 2012: 17)

Fifth, and again linked, this was a bottom-up venture: bureaucracies thrive on predictability and cannot do innovation, so project organizers ignored the officials. Teachers were trained in network analysis and in working as networks, sharing problems and ideas horizontally (Gallagher, 2012).

The turbulence features then are many: interrupting lock-in (both of religious sectarianism and of the conviction that there is no solution to it); experimentation and taking risks; using feedback and mistakes for constant review and adaptation; horizontal networking; and the amplification of small effects, building up the pilot work gradually.

Amplification of change

This case study can act as an entry point for thinking about how amplification of change happens in the ways we want. There are clearly many routes to achieving this. In Chapter 2 I presented an amplification spiral for how religion may make conflicts more intransigent and escalatory. From the discussions in this book, it is possible to present the counter to this spiral, a benign amplification process, as shown below:

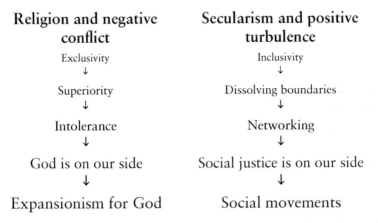

Religion and negative conflict	Secularism and positive turbulence
Exclusivity	Inclusivity
↓	↓
Superiority	Dissolving boundaries
↓	↓
Intolerance	Networking
↓	↓
God is on our side	Social justice is on our side
↓	↓
Expansionism for God	Social movements

This is equally turbulent, but the intensification is not based on physical violence. The process works as follows.

Inclusivity

Rather than being locked into an exclusive religious identity, inclusivity comes from a common rights basis, as indicated throughout the book but examined in detail in Chapter 4 when looking at human rights as a basis for a secular school value system. In UNICEF UK's Rights Respecting Schools, a growing movement, the whole ethos revolves around the Convention on the Rights of the Child. All students, staff, parents and governors learn about the convention and what it means for relationships. This means massive shifts in relationships between teachers and students, as teachers have to treat students with dignity and patience, as they would adults. Students reciprocally understand why they should respect the teacher's right to dignity. All students know of their right to learn, so know not to prevent others' rights to learn. This has impacts on discipline and behaviour. Research demonstrated students showing much increased inclusivity across religious and ethnic lines, and challenging racism if they met it inside or outside school.

Common rights also give people leverage for action. The international legal systems of rights and protections that were examined in Chapter 5 also provide security, as in humanitarian law and the laws on protection of schools in conflict. While they may take time to be enforced, they give a platform for people to demand security. The pro-turbulence factors here would be an authority taking risks by according rights to people of all ages and seeing how they made use of them.

Dissolving boundaries

This comes from the notion of encounters and of contact. Chapter 5 looked particularly at different sorts of encounters – with dissimilar people, with divergent ideas, and with sacred texts. Encounters with other people first rub up against the divides and then, if working for common tasks, act to make those boundaries or divides less important. Encounters with texts and the critique of locked-in anachronisms such as gendered inequality act to find new narratives of being and living, for self and others. Chapter 6 looked at the power of encounters that the radicalized (or those seen as at risk of radicalization) had with mentors, and examined the debates about whether changes of belief or changes of behaviour were the ultimate aim – and whether it mattered, as long as violence was not done. Central to all encounters is freedom of speech, being able to voice views, however unpalatable, in order to have them challenged and unpicked. In schools, this means a safe space as well as ground rules for discussion. But it may also mean shock tactics, as seen with the Prevent projects, to flush out those disturbing views.

Encounters are not about increasing stereotyping by superficial meetings and greetings, by one-off visits to the gurdwara. They have to be about challenge. This may be in examining identity, or in parking that identity for a while to engage in a common endeavour. Encounters may initially be uncomfortable. (Humour can sometimes be uncomfortable too, when it mocks the more outlandish parts of a religion or ideology.) Sometimes this is applied to encounters with 'the enemy', as was explored in communities negotiating with the Taliban over keeping schools open. Communities also have to negotiate with religious authorities and government. It is skilled and developmental work.

Networking

This leads to discussion of the contemporary phenomenon of networking. Clearly, the power of networks works for negative as well as positive social undertakings. We can learn from violent and criminal networks as well as the benign; as we saw when looking at criminal networks and Taliban networks, these are self-organizing. They shift, adapt and morph. This ability to change is an inherent part of their business model. Decapitating a network by removing its leader has little impact. Transnational organized crime mitigates risk by placing a high priority on the social networks of ethnicity, religion and family to conduct business. They depend on effective communication, adaptability and flexibility, but also on trust.

So what we learn, as we learned with the Arab Spring, is that horizontalism is the key to change. In schools, it is no longer enough – if it ever was – to nurture visionary educational leaders and school principals. They may be able to kick-start a process, but the sustainability will depend on the networks they create as well as those they do not, that already exist or that spring up in response. Conclusions on educational leadership in countries like Angola reveal that sending school principals off for training does not create sustained change but that networks or clusters of schools, teachers and students exchanging ideas and problems might (Davies, 2013b). Complexity-aware head teachers I know in the UK have worked with contemporary social media rather than complaining about its ill effects, encouraging student blogs about homework and about the school, networking across schools to exchange ideas and even trying to embed Twitter as part of the process of Continuing Professional Development.

To understand the power of such seemingly disparate phenomena as crime networks and student blogs, network theory helps. This shows how the greater the number of people who use a network, the more useful it becomes to each user. This 'network effect' is the creation from two people's interaction of a 'third thing' which comes for free. As Paul Mason points out in his book *Why It's Kicking Off Everywhere: The new global revolutions*, 'Everyone who uses information technology understands that they are – whether at work, on Facebook, on eBay or in a multiplayer game – a "node" on a network: not a footsoldier, not a bystander, not a leader, but a multitasking version of all three' (Mason, 2012: 74). Mason is optimistic about networks – that the democracy of retweeting filters out the trash as people respond and comment. Truth can travel faster than lies and all propaganda becomes instantly inflammable. Spin can be inserted, but the instantly networked consciousness of millions of people will question it, acting like white blood cells against infection. I agree up to a point – young people doing their research homework on Wikipedia and other sites are used to looking at the associated comments and dialogues to check veracity. Mason points out that governments cannot turn the internet off without harming their economies, and as Mubarak, Gaddafi and the Bahrain royals discovered, even turning it off does not work. He reckons a network can usually defeat a hierarchy. There can be 'swarm' tactics even when the hierarchy has greater strength and a better information system. The network is better at adapting to a situation where the quality of information is crucial to success, but where information itself is 'fluid'; a

213

hierarchy is best if you are only transmitting orders and responses, and the surrounding situation is predictable.

Activism for social justice: Violence, disabled toilets, or singing?

The final amplification question is: when does a network become a social movement? Investigation of the motives for joining extremist groups suggests it is at least partly for excitement. Is peace boring? Atran apparently thinks so: 'In peace, there is calm and ultimately boredom. I suspect that boredom's role in generating war over the ages is considerable' (Atran, 2010: 324).

So there is a need for excitement, and antidotes to boredom need encouraging, not closing down. The rewriting of the definition of terrorism under the Blair government to include animal rights and environmental activists was very problematic. The risk of violence was overstated:

> Does anyone seriously believe that Climate Camp or Climate Justice Action ... plan to use violent methods? This particular bunch of activists are wedded to non-violence: the idea that they would plan to hurt anyone deliberately is nonsensical. These people have disabled toilets and fire exits at their camps, for God's sake.
>
> (ven der Zee, 2009: 43)

I suspect it is not just about fear of violence but fear of power. Horizontalism provides the most useful methods for people with no power. Paul Mason quotes the activist Eva Jasiewicz, who believed the social media have been the key to turning a niche, lifestyle form of protest into an accessible method for everybody. She said:

> The anti-road movement of the late 1990s didn't ask you to sign up to an ideology, just to put your body in the way of a JCB. The difference is that then, we didn't have a media strategy ... social media says to people who are alienated and disparate: you are like me; these things (capitalism) are everywhere.
>
> (Mason, 2012: 56)

Mason also agrees with her view that the social media are not the central thing: 'The things that are central are off the radar: social interaction, relationships, building trust. Talk to people. Trust is explosive'.

Here is the notion of trust again, and I like the idea of trust being explosive. It is usually distrust which foments aggression. But what happens in networks is what has been called 'the strength of weak ties', a phrase also used by Gallagher in the context of the shared classes in Northern Ireland outlined above. It is the paradoxes in complexity that are the exciting and dynamic features. The Web, paradoxically, helps to forge intimate emotional ties among people who might otherwise physically put one another off if they met (Atran, 2010).

The blurring of public and private that has occurred through social media is significant. It redefines the individual as someone who is participating in the sharing of information, not just receiving it, and whose image of themselves is thereby shifted or transformed. What happens is that being in a movement changes people almost permanently. Meyer writes:

> By engaging in the social life of a challenging movement, an individual's experience of the world is mediated by a shared vision of the way the world works and, importantly, the individual's position in it. By engaging in activism, an individual creates himself or herself as a subject, rather than simply an object, in history and … is unlikely to retreat to passive acceptance of the world as it is.
>
> (Meyer, 1999: 186)

So the educational task is to build habits of engagement, seeing oneself not just as a member of society, nor even just as a participant but as an actor in shaping what goes on. An Office for Public Management briefing *Changing Behaviour* records that social norms and social values such as loyalty, commitment and reciprocity play an important role in behaviour change, and:

> … to participate in solving collective problems, people need to feel part of a wave of change, rather than isolated or powerless. Harvard sociologist Robert Sampson terms this 'collective efficacy': we need to know not just what is right or even in our self-interest but also that our participation will make a difference.
>
> (Goss, 2010: 1).

People have to feel they are part of a movement, that their contribution is worthwhile.

This is where we come back to the power of resistance through non-violent cultural means. Syria has spawned a vast output of satire, arts and cultural productions against the regime, captured in a six-month-long exhibition at the Prince Claus Fund Gallery in Amsterdam in 2012. In the accompanying 80-page publication there is a debate about whether satire breaks the 'fear wall' of expressing opinions or whether humour and satire are too slight and insignificant to challenge the regime politically. But Donatella Della Ratta argues in her article that Syrians are 'reappropriating creativity' which had been monopolized by the regime. This is a 'user-generated' creativity, a 'read/write culture' as opposed to a 'read-only' culture (Della Ratta, 2012:

11–12). It undermines the disciplinary efforts of the leader's rule. Protesters broadcast a revolutionary song *Ya Haif* from a minaret – revolutionary in itself, not only because, according to Islamic traditions, minarets are only for calling the faithful to prayer, but also because the iron grip of the Syrian secret services bans any activities emerging from mosques apart from those for religious purposes. The broadcast obviously refuted the cheap lies of the regime that activists were Islamic extremists, since no fundamentalist would allow anything other than the devotional call to prayer to be issued from a mosque. *Ya Haif* stood at the top of the Syrian revolutionary hit parade as the first song specifically written and recorded for the uprising in March 2011. The song soon paved the way for dozens of songs and musical pieces, which glorified the insurgency and energized activists. What helped in spreading these songs was their repetition in the daily demonstrations. There was a refusal to be swayed or divided by sectarianism. Some posters in the university had the slogan 'My God, enhance my revolutionary actions' – a take-off on the Quranic verse: 'God, enhance my education.' Women also appear on many of these posters (Della Ratta, 2012: 34).

Activism and civic engagement in schools

But are schools good at collective efficacy? Warwick *et al.*'s (2012) study of young people's community engagement uses complexity theory to look at the ecosystem surrounding young people, the complex ecologies of young people's lives. They talk of the motivation for civic action that happens through a sense of 'preferable futures'. But their overriding experience was meeting young people who reveal how difficult it is to acquire the responsibility, skills, resources, support and space that civic engagement actually requires. A key challenge for the 'civic pedagogue' is to let go of control to some extent and find authentic ways to support young people as active citizens. This means finding out what they care about but also giving them opportunities to influence and lead. The authors cite a study by Pye *et al.* (2009) that over 2 million young people in the UK might consider volunteering on a regular basis if they were simply asked. A lack of awareness of what it might involve was the key barrier. An international study found a direct correlation between students' knowledge of their civic community and their actual level of engagement in it (Schulz *et al.*, 2009).

This has implications for religious education. Understanding and researching whether and how religion operates in a community, and understanding how it intersects with ethnicity, gender and heritage, would contribute to this civic knowledge. Learners can create maps of their own communities and see where religion impacts on how people live their lives –

or where it seems less important than other features. Community mapping has long been a feature of community empowerment techniques within adult literacy programmes based on Freirian principles. Participants make maps, matrices and calendars which reveal who does what and when, who has power, where services and opportunities are, and where any human rights violations occur (Archer and Cottingham, 1996). The equivalent religious mapping would be much more interesting, political and immediate than learning 'about' religions in a disembodied or generalized ideal philosophical space.

Complexity theory helps us to understand the power of information. The Arab Spring seems – and is – a world away from community engagement around a school. Yet the drivers are similar. Paul Mason (2012) describes how in other countries there have been 'spontaneous horizontalists' – students protesting about fees and occupying buildings. A spontaneous international horizontalism seems to have happened, showing up the similarities of youth across borders. Mason talks about how young people spoke and dressed, about the music they listened to, and about how they used social media. The year 2011 saw a cultural revolution, a loss of fear of the dictatorships in North Africa, a loss of apathy among educated youth in Europe, Latin America, and the US. There was mass rejection of the values of twenty years of free market capitalism. Mason's work seems to imply that there are parallels between the Arab Spring and the Occupy movement, although he finds the slogan 'we are the 99%' more potent than the Egyptian 'bread, freedom and social justice'. The Occupy movement did not have a replacement for capitalism, but might be seen to be successful in its way.

Networking and activism are releasing the lock-in of the religion/power nexus. In their report on education for citizenship in the Arab world, Faour and Muasher (2011) reveal how whole generations in the Arab world were ingrained with the notion that allegiance to one's country means allegiance to the ruling political party, system or leader, and that diversity, critical thinking and individual differences are treachery. The authors think that current educational reform will do little to remedy this notion. Furthermore there is an 'unwritten alliance' between governments on the one hand and authoritarian political parties and religious institutions on the other (the two major political forces in the Arab world), against any radical education reform. Both sides want their version, their interpretation of history, religion and values to be the only one imparted to the next generation so as to keep a monopoly on what students are taught. Students are not supposed to question, think about, analyse or consider any other interpretations.

This appears to be classic lock-in. Yet what then accounts for the Arab Spring and student revolution? For Faour and Muasher, the lock-in is not absolute. As they point out, 'if the objective was to create and maintain docile societies, what has been achieved, in fact, is the very opposite. The recent uprisings have irrefutably demonstrated that Arab publics are no longer willing to be silent about the failure of their political systems in providing both freedom and bread' (Faour and Muasher, 2011: 20). This is well illustrated by the cultural satirical movement in Syria instanced above.

Three amplifying movements

I give just three examples of movements related to religion and education which are likely to act as amplification mechanisms.

E-learning in Iran

Mariam Memarsadeghi said eloquently:

> One of the ironies of political repression is that a people suffering under it can be far more appreciative and sensitive to the transformative power of education than those living in open societies. They yearn for and cherish the value of open, democratic learning that affirms free thinking and individual rights.
>
> (Memarsadeghi, 2013: 2)

Consequently Memarsadeghi set up Tavaana, which is the E-learning Institute of Iranian Civil Society. She found people in Iran had probing, exhaustive critiques of the educational system and an insatiable hunger for intellectual growth, civic values and knowledge about the architecture of democracy and democratic transition. In Tavaana, the curricular themes guard against political themes not being inclusive, turning violent, or being prone to takeover by extremist or radical elements. Her important point is that providing these curricula post-transition may be too late. Memarsadeghi talks of 'unlearning tyranny' (which resonates with the notion of unlearning radicalism in Chapter 6). Iranians were and are highly engaged in civic discourse and free association, if only in the private sphere and the virtual public realm. She found students were demoralized but quickly became energized. 'The creation of civic education opportunities by and for others who live under repression, including about civic responsibility and personal virtues, is itself an ethical act of defiance against the immorality of a totalitarian regime' (Memarsadeghi, 2013: 4).

She quotes Hannah Arendt prescribing this as the only ethical option for those living under totalitarian rule. Yet this option and the creation of an alternate, competing liberal public realm has only recently been made possible because of the discursive openings of the internet. It is the internet which is the key to unlock ideas in an increasing number of repressive regimes and contexts. Tavaana students experience live courses, participate in a weekly 1.5-hour live lecture with interactive PowerPoint presentations, and have discussion sessions with an instructor and fellow classmates. They also complete assignments, quizzes, tests and asynchronous discussion. The e-learning platform allows for a live video stream for the instructor. Students' cameras are switched off for security reasons and students have a fake identity and do not know each other, but there are microphones for all, real-time polling and quizzing, web tours, multiple ways for students to show their thoughts, questions and feelings, including raising hands, using emoticons and clapping others' good ideas. Students frequently comment that they are surprised about the extent of dialogue and that they get more out of their virtual learning experience than the traditional classroom experiences they have had.

Again, this supports the emphasis throughout my book on dialogue and connectivity across a wide range of people and their ideas. Tavaana's students include the country's most prominent civil society activists, journalists and human rights defenders along with clerics, physicians, mental health workers, teachers, professors, community service organizers, musicians and artists. There are strong partnerships with a range of other institutions for civic education and also the New Tactics Program of the Center for Victims of Torture.

Like the Iranian educationist Saeed Paivandi, Memarsadeghi argues for institutional building blocks of democracy, including the separation of religion and state, and for fully remembering our past, exploring culpability, and openly telling the history of gross human rights abuses. Tavaana has trained more than one thousand students, 95 per cent from inside Iran. But one student equals many more – the student may have a family of 25 listening – or whole classrooms or whole villages. Such is the amplificatory power.

Such e-learning is of course not unique, and one could mention the Iran Academia, an online university with the objective of enabling Iranian youth from all political, religious and ethnic backgrounds to access higher education and develop and apply critical thinking skills to a range of social justice, political, and human rights issues. These are seen as indispensable to Iran's process of democratization, but are nevertheless excluded from the country's higher education curriculum (http://iran-academia.com). The Iran Academia is still at the early stages, but they recognize that the Iranian government will likely resort to cyber-surveillance techniques to curtail and interfere with students' access to the courses, and a variety of technological counter-measures is being considered. Significantly, Tavanaa has also developed a Cybersecurity for Activists Manual. What is happening in these endeavours, though, is dramatically increasing the possibility space for learning, and it will be impossible to contain it.

I am Malala

The now well-known story of Malala Yousafzai illustrates another way of amplifying change. The Pakistani schoolgirl was shot on the school bus by the Tehrik Taliban Pakistan (TTP), for her advocacy of girls' education. Malala became a heroine of the opposition movement after the Taliban took control of Swat in 2008. Aged 11 she campaigned against laws that prevented girls from attending school. She had an anonymous blog – *Gul Makai*, or 'flower face' – for the BBC Urdu website, detailing life under the Taliban. Yet in complexity terms we can see that she was not acting in isolation. Malala was strongly backed and influenced by her father; and thanks to a mixture of chance and networks she had access to the BBC. She was chairperson of the District Child Assembly in Swat. The *New York Times* made a documentary about her life. What appears is a confluence of networks at a particular time. The individual, the name becomes important and iconic – but she did not bring about change single-handed, nor, in spite of thousands of followers, does she necessarily exemplify leadership in conventional terms.

Yet it is exciting to see Malala's case as a 'critical juncture'. Pakistan's foreign minister hopes it will be a 'turning point' in public perceptions of the TTP. Commentators say things like: 'If the murder of Martin Luther King was a world historical event, so, in its way, was the moment a posse of TTP gunmen boarded Malala's school bus in Swat' (*The Times*, 2012c). It is held that the strength and unanimity of Pakistan's reaction has been a revelation to the TTP and to the secular world it rejects, but the fear is that the common response may not hold for long. Thousands offered to give blood; tens of thousands marched through Karachi in her name on the weekend following the shooting, but voices from the religious right are already alleging that the story is being manipulated by 'outsiders'. Trials will need to set new standards for transparency and due process. A group of fifty Islamic clerics has issued a fatwa against those who tried to kill her. Yet spirals of violence can occur: Malala has rightly resisted schools being named after her, for fear of yet more reprisals.

Internationally, the ripples are spreading. Gordon Brown launched a UN petition using the slogan 'I am Malala' – a very significant phrase, similar to that used at the start of the Egyptian revolution – 'We are all Khaled Said' (the man beaten to death by police in Alexandria). The UN Youth Advocacy Group (YAG) has taken up the case, helping to secure 2.5 million signatures in response to the petition. Those signatures resulted in the Pakistani government establishing a $10 million Malala Fund and suggestions that the percentage of Pakistan's GDP devoted to education might increase from 2 per cent (one of the lowest rates in the world) to 4 per cent. The YAG then worked to gather signatures for a petition calling on the Indian government to eliminate all forms of child labour, which at the time of going to press had been agreed by the cabinet but not yet put before parliament. The Brookings Institution account says:

> In an increasingly interconnected world, young people – as early adopters of technology and social media – are well-positioned to mobilize their global networks in support of campaigns to address barriers to education.
>
> (Greubel and Robinson, 2013)

This is a great example of amplification, in both the impact and spread of a single event, and in the strengthening of those who join a campaign and whose success then empowers them to take on other issues. We do not yet know the outcome of the huge international campaign in support of Malala, and whether this will change attitudes in Pakistan and in the Pakistani Taliban. But it has to make a dent. Of marked significance for this book is that Malala Yousafzai was shortlisted for the 2013 Secularist of the Year prize in the UK; the prize was donated 'in her honour' to Plan UK, whose 'Because I am a Girl' campaign promotes girls' access to education. On her sixteenth birthday on 12 July 2013, she gave a speech at the United Nations which was streamed across the Western world.

Gay–straight alliances in Canada

A very different but equally inspiring case is that of the student activism which contributed to a piece of legislation in Ontario which had its third and final reading in June 2012. Bill 13, the Accepting Schools Act, is an anti-bullying intervention that includes the specific provision that students be allowed to start gay–straight clubs or alliances in schools. There is considerable homophobic discrimination in Canada. Alberta passed a law four years ago allowing parents to pull their children from any class in which sexual orientation would be discussed. Opposition to the direct naming of such clubs had been fierce – students were told that they could call them 'Rainbow clubs' or other such euphemisms, but not mention the 'G' word. But the pressure from students and supporters of lesbian, gay, bisexual and transgender (LGBT) rights meant the legislation went through, and clubs are now permitted and can be named as such.

Amplification is now evident in a proposed similar anti-bullying law in Manitoba, Bill 18, which aims to promote equality based on gender, race and sexual orientation. It is again the section that would require schools to allow gay–straight alliance groups (GSAs) if students wished them which has drawn the most criticism from religious leaders. They claim that it infringes their constitutionally protected right of freedom of religion. Catholics, Mennonites, Orthodox Jews and Muslims have all opposed the bill (although others within the same religions have supported it). The grounds are that the Bible and the Quran reject homosexuality, so any apparent sanctioning of it is wrong. Therefore, a curious inversion of tolerance is invoked: that 'it would be the height of intolerance to ban a religious group from teaching and practising as it believes' (Lambert, 2013). The bill would allow schools to respond to bullying that takes place after hours, including through text messages and social media, and GSAs – clubs for all kids who support LGBT rights – would specifically be permitted. However, the local pastor argues that the bill 'protects gay kids more than religious ones'. (This is why inclusive secularism is so important – it is not either/or. Nor is it clear what position the pastor would take on the rights of a gay Catholic. ....) He said in a sermon that 'It's going to be the beginning of an incremental attempt to destroy the Christian church', likening same-sex intercourse to adultery, bestiality, and paedophilia (Wingrove, 2013).

Evan Wiens, a 16-year-old student at Steinbach Regional Secondary School has become the face of Bill 18 in the city where it is most strongly opposed. He is the only student who has come out as gay and says he is fighting for those who cannot speak out:

> 'They should not have to feel ashamed, and they should not have to feel like they have to hide themselves'. He was shy at first about his fight. 'But then I thought about it, and I thought if a church is allowed to vocally oppose a bill, what's so bad about me standing up for my rights?
>
> (Wingrove, 2013)

Go Evan! Go Malala! Go Mariam! And go the Education Minister Nancy Allen who congratulated Evan and stated: 'This is about safe schools, young people reaching their potential'. Here is someone who understands education and human security.

These three examples seem very different, but they do have some commonalities: an individual concerned to bring about change, to create turbulence, but being themselves in – or becoming part of – a network. Their underpinning is rights – the right to critical learning, the right to girls' education, the right to freedom of expression. Above this driver of rights there are different mechanisms – setting up an institute, generating international petitions, making changes in the law. What they have in common is having to deal with opposition – from repressive clerical-government authorities, from the conservative Muslim religious right, from the conservative Christian right. But, as in the natural world, it is learning to deal with such opposition or competition that enables progressive movements to evolve and to counter-attack. A constant process of learning, unlearning and relearning is evident.

What they share too is the power of networking across various media, where learning occurs all the time. As Sageman (2008) revealed, even during the course of the Iranian uprising of 2009, the ways of using social media visibly evolved. Protesters called the process 'wave creation', using emails, blogs and SMS to evolve the protests in real time. They launched 'Googlebombs' against President Ahmadinejad. The new technology makes possible new relationships among protesters themselves, and between protesters and the mainstream media. It gives protesters increased leverage over NGOs, multilateral bodies, and guarantors of international law.

But, as intimated earlier, social media do not provide the whole solution. There is a continuing debate over how the social media brought hope in the Arab Spring but may not have achieved real reform. Online information was hugely powerful – without the internet, people in Egypt would not have known that an uprising in Tunisia had taken place. Online debate brought people together, and the revolution seemed unstoppable. Yet it is now being confronted by old-fashioned brute force in Syria. Are leaders and personalities still needed against such repression – not to mention international aid for the opposition? Also, government loyalists in Syria are fighting back over Twitter, launching smear campaigns against opposition figures. As Hugh Tomlinson wrote in 2011, 'social media could become a tool of repression as quickly as they became one of liberation' (Tomlinson, 2011: 8) and this remains a danger. The tweets and the blogs broke open the lock-in; but this viral spread is not neatly contained. What has happened too is the takeover or at least infiltration by Islamists. Do you still need traditions of scholarship and books to surround the sound bites? Suddenly, formal education takes on an urgent role again.

Conclusion: Certainty and doubt

Just as I complete this book, there has been a horrific event in Woolwich, South London, where a soldier was beheaded in the street by two UK-born Islamic extremists – Michael Adebolajo, 28, and Michael Adebowale, 22. Adebolajo came from a Christian family but converted to Islam in 2003.

After the beheading, he engaged in a long tirade to justify his actions, revelling in the publicity and posing for the cameras. His rant was a curious mixture of Islamist rhetoric, Christian Old Testament vengefulness, revolutionary political bombast and rap argot. He swore to Almighty Allah but invoked 'an eye for an eye and a tooth for a tooth', which is Biblical, not Quranic. 'Remove your government, they don't care about you' he said. 'You think David Cameron is going to get caught in the street when we start bustin' our guns?' He tried to conjure up insecurity for the British people: 'We will never stop fighting you until you leave us alone. Your people will never be safe. The only reason we have done this is because Muslims are dying by British soldiers every day' (Owen and Urquhart, 2013). He appeared to be unaware that the order to withdraw the troops had already been given.

As always, newspapers and social analysts have been poring over the backgrounds of the extremists to find clues to their actions. Both men had been to the University of Greenwich, Adebolajo studying sociology – which should have been protective. But after his conversion to Islam he had links with the outlawed Islamist group Al-Muhajiroun and had a history of involvement in radical Islamist activities. This was not lone-wolf-type activity, but rather had significant support in the UK and internationally. Radical clerics in the UK such as Anjem Choudary refused to condemn the attacks, blaming UK government policy. Adebolajo had been radicalized in part by the cleric Omar Bakri Mohammed – who has been secretly filmed stating that decapitation of the enemies of Islam was permitted. This cleric told the *Independent* newspaper that he could understand the feeling of rage that had motivated the attackers and that what they had done could be justified under certain interpretations of Islam. 'To people around here [in the Middle East] he is a hero' (Sengupta, 2013).

It is clear that formal education had provided no protection against extremism or its logics and heroics. Nor, significantly, had Christianity or Islam. What characterizes the extremists is their threefold certainty: of their ideological position, of the absolute requirement for extreme violence, and of a subsequent reward in heaven. In contrast, the key task of a secular education is to instil habits of doubt, to question the definitive messages from ideological leaders – spoken or written. This does not mean simply replacing such messages with some new recombinant certainty, a horrible mixture, as in the case of Michael Adebolajo. It means skills in discourse analysis and also political analysis of what will be achieved.

Unsurprisingly, there has been a spate of counter-reactions, ranging from racist comments on Facebook to Islamophobic bullying of Muslim women in the street to attacks on mosques and Islamic schools. The very people Adebolajo seeks to defend are under threat. History, social science and religious education have to work in concert to enable students to examine how spirals of revenge and retribution occur, and how they can be interrupted.

The perennial dilemma has to be admitted of wanting young people to be idealistic and to participate in the political life of society, yet wanting this to be a critical idealism, not one that follows a trajectory culminating in violence and an absolute, certain belief that your god wants you to wage war on others.

People seek inspiration as well as certainty in a variety of forms. The musician Sidney Harrison talked amusingly of the role of religious certainty in music and in being a composer of religious music:

> Since nobody can make a masterpiece out of *I doubt if my Redeemer liveth* you had better have a religion. A cynic may smile at the notion of praising God for a successful battle, never blaming him for an unsuccessful one, but only bloodshed can lead to a *Te Deum*, a *Messe des Morts* or a *War Requiem*. No war; no requiem. … Whether there is something about a requiem that is conducive to the next war is a question that no composer cares to answer. Nobody, after all, can hope to set to music
> '*The trumpets do not sound*
> *The marching feet are still*
> *No foe is to be found*
> *There's nobody to kill*'.

(Harrison, 1964: 36)

(I am reminded of Woody Allen's quip about how he can never listen to too much Wagner without getting the urge to conquer Poland.) As said, the genius of Bach was certainly inspired by his devout religiosity, and if only for that reason, a dynamic secular society has to accommodate faiths and their productions. It is the cycles of certainty 'conducive to the next war' that need to be treated with caution.

This book is about what can happen when religion represents a risk, when it leads to the events that inspire a *War Requiem*. Or when it results in a decapitation. The risk is to national security and to the complex adaptive society which will survive and evolve. I have to admit that dynamic secularism is also a risk, in that (apart from ground rules) it is open-ended and not locked-in, allowing a multiplicity of world views whereby the supernatural ones compete more or less equally with the earthly ones in the public space.

The book is also about change and emergence, about revolutions big and small. The Arab Spring brought hope and promise of new societies.

But the various oppositional groups in Arab Spring countries are facing sectarianism in their midst, in particular political Islamism. Christian and other fundamentalisms block progress towards equality in other parts of the world. Education becomes an Unsafe God when it does not try to protect against the takeover of progressive social movements by forces that want to return society to mythical old ways rather than foresee new progressive ones.

Education's role is to foment doubt and be a place for vigilance, not for complacency about its benign impact. As in the Northern Ireland example presented earlier, it is a sort of middle way, here between end-time mission statements and anarchic activity. It is about preventing the lock-in of rigid ideology and providing the enabling conditions for learning towards positive change, without necessarily specifying or even knowing what this change might be. These enabling conditions are six-fold: human rights, non-violence, feedback on learning and teaching, connectivity, encounters and fun. As well as essential basic literacy, schools can nurture the skills of dialogue, debate, argument, productive satire, and the challenge to orthodoxy and frozen views. Education can foster the deconstruction of texts, whether sacred, extremist, political, economic, or *Hello!* magazine. Clearly, it has to operate within the power of social media and what is, as I write, still called 'new' technology. But after providing these enabling conditions, rather than everything being reduced to 'outcomes', education has to accept some unpredictability. Just as we saw the concept of faith-as-uncertainty being effective in change for good, we can usefully live with the idea of learning-as-uncertainty. The enabling conditions can safely generate turbulence, amplification of small effects, critical junctures, spontaneous horizontalism, interpretive diversity and collective efficacy – as well as generating musicians, layabouts and future academics.

I end with the words of Mahatma Gandhi – the great secularist. 'I want all the cultures of all lands to be blown about my house as freely as possible. But I refuse to be blown off my feet by any.'

References

Acemoglu, D., and Robinson, J. (2012) *Why Nations Fail: The origins of power, prosperity and poverty.* London: Profile Books.

ACPO (2011) 'New research indicates Muslim communities welcome engagement' (Press Release 10 April). Online. www.acpo.presscentre.com/content/Detail. aspx?ReleaseID=219&NewsAreaID=2 (accessed 28 August 2013).

— (2012a) *Community Engagement*, Issue 13 (September). London: Association of Chief Police Officers.

— (2012b) *Community Engagement*, Issue 14 (November). London: Association of Chief Police Officers.

ACT Now (2009) *'Terrorism'*: Teachers Notes. All Communities Together Now. North West Regional Prevent Team.

Adams, S. (2012) 'The World's next genocide'. *International Herald Tribune,* 17 November, 8.

Ahmad, I. (2012) 'Muslim educational backwardness: Competing pressures of secular and religious learning'. In Sleeter, C., Bhushan Upadhyay, S., Mishra, A.K., and Kumar, S. (eds) *School Education, Pluralism and Marginality: Comparative perspectives.* New Delhi: Orient Black Swan.

Akyol, M. (2011) 'Westerners, put your faith in the "Islamic Calvinists"'. *The Times,* 28 December, 22.

Alami, M. (2013) 'Syria's Foreign Legions'. *Sada Journal,* 28 February. Online. http://carnegieendowment.org/sada/index.cfm?fa=show&article=51071&solr_ hilite=Alami (accessed 28 August 2013).

Allen, C. (2010) *Islamophobia.* Farnham: Ashgate.

Anderson, W.T. (1995) 'Four ways to be absolutely right'. In Anderson, W.T. (ed.) *The Truth About the Truth: De-confusing and re-constructing the postmodern world.* New York: Tarcher Penguin.

Annan, K., with Mousavizadeh, N. (2012) *Interventions: A life in war and peace.* London: Penguin.

Apple, M. (2006) *Educating the 'Right' Way: Markets, standards, God and inequality.* 2nd ed. New York: Routledge.

— (2013) 'Gender, religion and the work of homeschooling'. In Gross *et al.,* 2013.

Appleby, R.S. (2008) 'Building sustainable peace: The roles of local and transnational religious actors'. In Banchoff, T. (ed.) *Religious Pluralism, Globalization, and World Politics.* New York: Oxford University Press.

Archer, D., and Cottingham, S. (1996) *Reflect Mother Manual: Regenerated Freirian literacy through empowering community techniques.* London: ActionAid.

Asad, T. (2006) 'Trying to understand French secularism'. In de Vries, H., and Sullivan, L.E. (eds) *Political Theologies: Public religions in a post-secular world.* New York: Fordham University Press.

Ashour, O. (2009) *Votes and Violence: Islamists and the processes of transformation.* London: The International Centre for the Study of Radicalisation and Political Violence.

Atran, S. (2010) *Talking to the Enemy: Violent extremism, sacred values and what it means to be human*. London: Allen Lane.

Bader, V. (2007) *Secularism or Democracy?: Associational governance of religious diversity* (IMISCOE-AUP Series). Amsterdam: Amsterdam University Press.

Bart, G.R. (2010) 'The ambiguous protection of schools under the law of war: Time for parity with hospitals and religious buildings'. In *Protecting Education from Attack: A state of the art review*. Paris: UNESCO.

Bartlett, A., and Raffle, A. (2010) *Not in My Name: Comparative report for all areas*. London: Theatre Veritae.

Bartlett, J. (2010) 'Let the big society fight terrorism'. *The Guardian,* 7 July. Online. www.guardian.co.uk/commentisfree/2010/jul/07/big-society-terrorism-july7-islam (accessed February 2013).

Bartlett, J., and Birdwell, J. (2010) *From Suspects to Citizens: Preventing violent extremism in a big society* (Demos Report). London: Demos.

Bartlett, J., and Miller, C. (2010) *The Power of Unreason: Conspiracy theories, extremism and counter-terrorism* (Demos Report). London: Demos.

Bassano di Tufillo, S., and Mujahed, J. (2008) *Burqa!: Ma vie en Kabul*. Paris: Editions de la Martiniere.

Benn, T., Jawad, H., and Al-Sinani, Y. (2013) 'The role of Islam in the lives of girls and women in physical education and sport'. In Gross *et al.*, 2013.

Bennett, R. (2012) 'The day all hell broke loose at Christian football match'. *The Times*, 24 September,12.

Bergen, P., and Pandey, S. (2006) 'The madrassa scapegoat'. *The Washington Quarterly*, 29 (2), 117–25.

Berkey, J. (2007) 'Madrasas medieval and modern: Politics, education and the problem of Muslim identity'. In Hefner, R., and Zaman, M. (eds) *Schooling Islam: The culture and politics of modern Muslim education*. Princeton, NJ: Princeton University Press.

Bernard, C., Jones, S., Oliker, O., Thurston, C., Steams, B., and Cordell, K. (2008) *Women and Nation-building* (RAND Monograph Series). Santa Monica, CA: RAND Corporation.

Beutel, A. (2010) *Building Bridges to Strengthen America: Forging an effective counterterrorism enterprise between Muslim Americans and law enforcement*. Washington: Muslim Public Affairs Council.

Bhargava, R. (2009) 'Political secularism: What can be learned from India?'. In Levey, G.B., and Modood, T. (eds) *Secularism, Religion and Multicultural Citizenship*. Cambridge: Cambridge University Press.

Bhatterai, T. (2010) 'Children's clubs and corporal punishment'. In Cox, S., Robinson-Pant, A., Dyer, C., and Schweisfurth, M. (eds) *Children as Decision-Makers in Education*. London: Continuum.

Bickmore, K. (2005) 'Teacher development for conflict participation: Facilitating learning for "difficult citizenship" education'. *International Journal of Citizenship and Teacher Education*, 1 (2), 2–16. Online. www.citized.info/pdf/ejournal/vol_1_no_2.pdf (accessed 28 August 2013).

Bierce, A. (2002) *The Unabridged Devil's Dictionary*. Originally 1911. Athens: University of Georgia Press.

Biesta, G. (2007) 'The education-socialisation conundrum or "Who is afraid of education?"'. *Utbildning & Demokrati* 16 (3) 25–36.

— (2008) 'Pedagogy with empty hands: Levinas, education and the question of being human'. In Egéa-Kuehne, D. (ed.) *Levinas and Education at the Intersection of Faith and Reason* (Routledge International Studies in the Philosophy of Education). London: Routledge.

Bjorgo T., and Horgan, J. (2008) *Leaving Terrorism Behind: Individual and collective disengagement*. New York: Routledge.

Black, A. (2001) *The History of Islamic Thought: From the Prophet to the present*. Edinburgh: Edinburgh University Press.

Blakemore, C. (2012) 'If scientists are silent, loony ideas will win'. *The Times*, 5 November, 26.

Blanchard, C. (2008) *Islamic Religious Schools, Madrasas: Background* (Congressional Research Service, Order Code RS21654). Washington, DC: Library of Congress.

Blumör, R. (2012) *Haben die Taliban eine Bildungsstrategie? Zur Mikrobildungspolitik einer Aufstandsbewegung (Do the Taliban have an educational strategy?)* Kabul: unpublished paper.

Boler, M. (1997) 'The risks of empathy: Interrogating multiculturalism's gaze'. *Cultural Studies*, 11 (2), 253–73.

Borchgrevink, K. (2010) *Beyond Borders: Diversity and transnational links in Afghanistan religious education* (PRIO Paper). Oslo: Peace Research Institute.

Boucek, C. (2008) *Saudi Arabia's 'Soft' Counterterrorism strategy: Prevention, rehabilitation and aftercare* (Middle East Program Number 97). Washington, DC: Carnegie Endowment for International Peace.

Boudre, S. (2006) 'After the tsunami, Aceh plays host to first ever lifeguards'. *Terra Daily*, 15 August . Online. www.terradaily.com/reports/After_The_Tsunami_Aceh_Plays_Host_To_First_Ever_Lifeguards_999.html (accessed 28 August 2013).

Breen-Smith, M. (2010) *Submission to the Home Office Review of Counter-terrorism and Security Powers*. Aberystwyth: University of Aberystwyth Centre for the Study of 'Radicalisation' and Contemporary Political Violence.

Briggs, R., Fieschi, C., and Lownsbrough, H. (2006) *Bringing it Home: Community-based approaches to counter-terrorism*. London: Demos.

British Muslims for a Secular Democracy (n.d.) 'About us'. Online. http://bmsd.org.uk/index.php/about-us/ (accessed 28 August 2013).

Brown, C. (2000) *Religion and State: The Muslim approach to politics*. New York: Columbia University Press.

Brown, N. (2011) *Post-Revolutionary Al-Azhar* (The Carnegie Papers: Middle East: September 2011). Washington, DC: Carnegie Endowment for International Peace.

Buchanan, R., and Hurst, G. (2013) 'Gove gets full marks from top historians'. *The Times*, 27 February, 1 and 8.

Burde, D. (2010) 'Preventing violent attacks on education in Afghanistan: Considering the role of community-based schools'. In *Protecting Education from Attack: A state of the art review*. Paris: UNESCO.

Burke, J. (2013) 'Al-Qaida: How great is the terrorism threat to the West now?' *The Guardian*, 29 January. Online. www.theguardian.com/world/2013/jan/29/al-qaida-terrorism-threat-west (accessed 7 February 2013).

Buzan, B. (1991) *People, States and Fear*. Boulder, CO: Lynne Rienner Publishers.

Byrne, D. (1998) *Complexity and the Social Sciences*. London: Routledge.

Campbell, M. (2012) 'I tapped, Mubarak toppled'. *Sunday Times*, 15 January, News Review 2–3.

Carabelli, G. (2012) 'Engaging with youth in Mostar through art practice: The case of (re)collecting Mostar (2010–2011)'. Paper presented at workshop 'Ethnicity and Education: The challenge of diversity and social cohesion', Exeter Centre for Ethno-Political Studies (EXCEPS), 11–12 July.

Carabello-Resto, J. (2010) 'Contentions in the making: Discussing secularism among Scottish Muslims'. In Marranci, G., and Turner, B. (eds) *Muslim Societies and the Challenge of Secularization: An interdisciplinary approach*. Dordrecht: Springer.

Carm, E. (2012) 'The role of local leaders in cultural transformation and development'. *Compare*, 42 (5), 795–816.

Casanova, J. (1994) *Public Relations in the Modern World*. Chicago: University of Chicago Press.

— (2009) 'Immigration and the new religious pluralism: A European–United States comparison'. In Levey, G.B., and Modood, T. (eds) *Secularism, Religion and Multicultural Citizenship*. Cambridge: Cambridge University Press.

Castells, M. (1996) *The Rise of Network Society*. New York: Oxford University Press. Vol.1 of *The Information Age: Economy, society and culture*. 3 vols. 1996–8.

Champion, G. (2010) 'Prison is "not taming" Islamist radicals'. *BBC News*, 13 April. Online. http://news.bbc.co.uk/1/hi/uk/8615390.stm (accessed 28 August 2013).

Clark, K. (2011) *The Layha: Calling the Taleban to account* (Thematic Report 6/2011). Kabul: Afghanistan Analyst Network.

Clayton, J. (2012) 'Nation "on brink of religious war" after prayer-time attacks kill 200'. *The Times*, 23 January, 30.

Clemens, W. (2010) 'Ethnic peace, ethnic conflict: Complexity theory on why the Baltic is not the Balkans'. *Communist and Post-Communist Studies*, 43 (3), 245–61.

Coghlan, T. (2012) 'Are the locals up to it? No. Afghanistan analysis'. *The Times*, 3 February, 5.

Collier, P. (2009) 'Post-conflict recovery: How should policies be distinctive?' *Journal of African Economies*, 18 (1), 99–131.

Communitarian Network (2002) *The Diversity Within Unity Platform*. Drafted by Amitai Etzioni. Online. http://communitariannetwork.org/diversity-within-unity/ (accessed 22 June 2011).

Connolly, W.E. (1999) *Why I Am Not a Secularist*. Minneapolis: University of Minnesota Press.

Coulson, A. (2004) *Education and Indoctrination in the Muslim World. Is there a problem? What can we do about it?* (Cato Policy Analysis Number 511). Washington, DC: Cato Institute.

Council of Anglican Provinces of Africa (CAPA) (2010) *Securing the Future, Unlocking our Potential*. Report of the All Africa Bishops' Conference II, Entebbe, Uganda.

Council of Ex-Muslims of Britain (CEMB) (2012) Online. http://ex-muslim.org.uk/2012/12/council-of-ex-muslims-of-britain-expresses-concern-at-the-exclusion-of-muslim-women-from-demands-for-gender-equality (accessed 10 December 2012).

Covell, K., and Howe, R. (2005) *Rights, Respect and Responsibility: Report on the RRR Initiative to Hampshire Education Authority.*

Crane, R. (2010) 'Islamophobia, mimetic warfare and the bugaboo of shari'a compliance: Counter-strategies for common ground'. *Arches Quarterly*, 4 (7), 54–61.

Critelli, F. (2013) 'A world beyond the veil: Pursuing gender equality in Pakistan'. In Gross *et al.*, 2013.

Curious Minds (n.d.) *The Art of Prevention: A creative approach to supporting schools in their contribution to the prevention of violent extremism.* Online. www.preventforschools.org/download/file/TheArt%20of%20Prevention.pdf (accessed 29 August 2013). Liverpool: Curious Minds.

Daily Mash (2011) 'Doctors to check for anyone who looks a bit bomb-y'. 7 June. Online. www.thedailymash.co.uk/news/war/doctors-to-check-for-anyone-who-looks-a-bit-bomb-y-201106073916 (accessed 29 August 2013).

Daily Telegraph (2010) 'Iran to forbid universities from offering "Western" subjects'. 24 October. Online. www.telegraph.co.uk/news/worldnews/middleeast/iran/8084411/Iran-to-forbid-universities-from-offering-Western-subjects.html (accessed 29 August 2013).

Daly, M., and Wilson, M. (1988) *Homicide.* Hawthorne, NY: Aldine de Gruyter.

Darby, P. (2009) 'Rolling back the frontiers of empire: Practising the post-colonial'. *International Peacekeeping*, 16 (5), 699–716.

Davies, L. (1984) *Pupil Power: Deviance and gender in school.* Lewes: Falmer Press.

— (2004) *Education and Conflict: Complexity and chaos.* London: Routledge.

— (2008) *Educating Against Extremism.* Stoke on Trent: Trentham.

— (2009) *Capacity Development in Education in Fragile Contexts.* Briefing paper for ETF/GTZ/INEE.

— (2011) *Choices and Voices: An evaluation of the interactive resource for schools for Preventing Violent Extremism.* Birmingham: Centre for International Education and Research, University of Birmingham.

— (2012a) 'Sri Lanka's national policy on education for social cohesion and peace'. In *Education for Global Citizenship.* Doha: Education Above All.

— (2012b) 'Educating the Roma: Towards a human rights based approach'. In Sleeter, C., Upadhyay, S.B., Mishra, A.K., and Kumar, S. (eds) *School Education, Pluralism and Marginality: Comparative perspectives.* New Delhi: Orient Black Swan.

— (2013a) 'The challenges for education of protracted displacement in Sri Lanka'. In Smith Ellison, C., and Smith, A. (eds) *Education and Internally Displaced Persons.* London: Bloomsbury.

— (2013b) 'Angola: Fostering teacher professionalism and safe schools'. In Clarke, S., and Donogue, T. (eds) *School Level Leadership in Post-conflict Societies.* Abingdon: Routledge.

— (2013c) 'Fundamentalist religion and gender: The case for an inclusive secular education'. In Gross *et al.*, 2013.

Davies, L., Bischoff, T., and Williams, C. (2011) *Learning the Language of Compromise: An assessment of the relationship between 'student voice' and learning.* Birmingham: Centre for International Education and Research.

Davies, L., Harber, C., Schweisfurth, M., Williams, C., and Yamashita, H. (2009) *Educating in Emergencies in South Asia: Reducing the risks facing vulnerable children*. Birmingham: Centre for International Education and Research/ UNICEF South Asia.

Davies, L., Harber, C., and Yamashita, H., (2004) *Global Citizenship: The needs of teachers and learners*. Report of DFID funded research project. Birmingham: Centre for International Education and Research, University of Birmingham.

Davies, L., and Kirkpatrick, G. (2000) *The EURIDEM Project: A review of pupil democracy in Europe*. London: Children's Rights Alliance.

Davis, B., and Sumara, D. (2006) *Complexity and Education: Inquiries into learning, pedagogy and research*. Abingdon: Routledge/Taylor and Francis Group.

Davis, W. (2009) *The Wayfinders: Why ancient wisdom matters in the modern world*. Toronto, ON: House of Anansi Press.

Dawkins, R. (2006) *The God Delusion*. London: Bantam Press.

DCSF (2005) *Learning Behaviour: Lessons learned*. The Report of The Practitioners' Group on School Behaviour and Discipline, Chair: Sir Alan Steer. Nottingham: DCSF Publications.

de Bruxelles, S. (2012) 'Women! Know your limits (and only speak if hubbie is with you)'. *The Times*, 6 December, 14.

Della Ratta, D. (2012) 'Peer creativity and user-generated contents: Towards active citizenship in Syria'. In Halasa, M. (ed.) *Culture in Defiance: Continuing traditions of satire, art and the struggle for freedom in Syria*. Publication produced for Prince Claus Fund Gallery Exhibition. Online. www. princeclausfund.org/files/docs/2012%20Culture%20in%20Defiance.pdf (accessed 31 March 2013). Amsterdam: Prince Claus Fund for Culture and Development.

Dennett, D. (2005) *Breaking the Spell: Religion as a natural phenomenon*. New York: Viking Adult.

De Poli, B. (2010) 'Muslim thinkers and the debate on secularism and laïcité'. In Marranci, G., and Turner, B. (eds) *Muslim Societies and the Challenge of Secularization: An interdisciplinary approach*. Dordrecht: Springer.

DFID (2012) *Faith Partnership Principles: Working effectively with faith groups to fight global poverty*. London: Department for International Development.

Diamond, J. (1998) *Guns, Germs and Steel: A short history of everybody for the last 13,000 years*. London: Vintage.

Dingley, J. (2009) 'Religion, truth, national identity and social meaning: The example of Northern Ireland'. *National Identities* 11 (4), 367–83.

Dodd, V. (2009) 'Anti-terrorism strategy "spies" on innocent: Data on politics, sexual activity and religion gathered by government'. *The Guardian*, 17 October, 1.

— (2010) 'List sent to terror chief aligns peaceful Muslim groups with terrorist ideology'. *The Guardian*, 4 August. Online. www.theguardian.com/uk/2010/ aug/04/quilliam-foundation-list-alleged-extremism (accessed 28 August 2013).

Dolan, J., Golden, A., Ndaruhutse, S., and Winthrop, R. (2012) *Building effective teacher salary systems in fragile and conflict-affected states*. Reading: Brookings.

'Dr G.D. Agrawal (Swami Gyan Swarup Sanand): Ganga Tapasya 14th Jan 2012 till now' (2012). In *Gangapedia*. Online. http://gangapedia.iitk.ac.in/?q=content/dr-gd-agrawal-swami-gyan-swarup-sanand-ganga-tapasya-14th-jan-2012-till-now-0 (accessed 13 August 2012).

Duffield, M. (2010) 'The liberal way of development and the development-security impasse: Exploring the global life-chance divide'. *Security Dialogue*, 41, 53–76.

Duffy, G., and Gallagher, T. (2012) *Collaborative Evolution: The context of sharing and collaboration in contested space*. Belfast: School of Education, Queen's University Belfast.

Durkin, S. (2012) 'From "Educating for peace and human rights" to "delegitimising violence": Recent developments in peace education in the Basque Country in the context of a conflict in transition'. Paper presented at workshop 'Ethnicity and Education: The challenge of diversity and social cohesion', Exeter Centre for Ethno-Political Studies (EXCEPS), 11–12 July.

Dyer, C. (2012) 'Education and social (in)justice for mobile groups: Re-framing rights and educational inclusion for Indian pastoralist children'. In Schweisfurth, M., and Harber, C. (eds) *Education and Global Justice*. London: Routledge.

Facing History and Ourselves (2008) *What Do We Do with a Difference? France and the debate over headscarves in schools*. Brookline, MA: Facing History and Ourselves Foundation.

Faliq, A. (2010) 'From the editor'. *Arches Quarterly*, 4 (7), 7.

Faour, M., and Muasher, M. (2011) *Education for Citizenship in the Arab World: Key to the future* (Carnegie Papers). Washington, DC: Carnegie Endowment for International Peace.

Faulks, S. (2009) *A Week in December*. London: Hutchinson.

Fest, J. (2012) *Not Me: A German childhood*. Originally 2006. London: Atlantic Books.

Fink, N., and Hearne, E. (2008) *Beyond Terrorism: Deradicalization and disengagement from violent extremism*. New York: International Peace Institute.

Firth, R., and Wheeler, A. (2009) '"Sustainable Schools" and initial teacher education: Thinking in complexity about education'. In Inman, S., and Rogers, M. (eds) *Papers Presented at UK Conference July 2009 on Developing Critical Perspectives on Education for Sustainable Development Global Citizenship in Initial Teacher Education*. Proceedings of a conference held at London South Bank University, 9 July 2009. UK TE ESD/GC Network.

Ford, R. (2012) 'Dealing with the rising tide of Muslims in our prisons'. *The Times*, 13 January, 65.

Foresight Future Identities (2013) *Final Project Report*. London: The Government Office for Science.

Fraser, N. (1999) *Justice Interruptus: Critical reflections on the 'post-socialist' condition*. New York: Routledge.

Froese, P. (2008) *The Plot to Kill God*. Berkeley: University of California Press.

Gallagher, M. (2008) 'Foucault, power and participation'. *International Journal of Children's Rights*, 16, 395–406.

Gallagher, T., Stewart, A., Walker, R., Baker, M., and Lockhart, J. (2010) 'Sharing education through schools working together'. *Shared Space: A research journal on peace, conflict and community relations in Northern Ireland*, 10, 65–74. Online.www.community-relations.org.uk/fs/doc/chapter-five.pdf (accessed 28 August 2013).

Gallagher, T. (2012) 'Recognising difference while promoting cohesion: The role of collaborative networks in education'. Paper presented at workshop 'Ethnicity and Education: The challenge of diversity and social cohesion', Exeter Centre for Ethno-Political Studies (EXCEPS), 11–12 July.

Galtung, J. (1969) 'Violence, peace, and peace research'. *Journal of Peace Research*, 6 (3), 167–91.

GCPEA (2011) 'Briefing note June 24, 2011: Expanding the monitoring and reporting mechanism (MRM) trigger'. Online. www.protectingeducation.org/news/briefing-note-june-24-2011-expanding-monitoring-reporting-mechanism-mrm-trigger (accessed 28 August 2013). New York: Global Coalition to Prevent Education from Attack.

Geyer, R. (2003) 'Beyond the Third Way: The science of complexity and the politics of choice'. *British Journal of Politics and International Relations*, 5, (2), 237–57.

Ghani, A., and Lockhardt, C. (2008) *Fixing Failed States*. Oxford: Oxford University Press.

Giddens, A. (2007) 'My chat with the colonel'. *The Guardian*, 9 March. Online. www.theguardian.com/commentisfree/2007/mar/09/comment.libya (accessed 28 August 2013).

Gillespie, J. (2012) 'Trigger happy: Snipers are the most cheerful soldiers'. *The Sunday Times*, 5 December, 9.

Githens-Mazer, J., and Lambert, R. (2010) 'Why conventional wisdom on radicalization fails: The persistence of a failed discourse'. *International Affairs*, 86 (4), 889–901.

Giustozzi, A., and Franco, C. (2011) *The Battle for the Schools: The Taleban and state education* (Thematic Report 08/2011). Kabul: Afghanistan Analyst Network.

Glad, M. (2009) *Knowledge on Fire: Attacks on education in Afghanistan: Risks and measures for successful mitigation*. Online. www.care.org/newsroom/articles/2009/11/Knowledge_on_Fire_Report.pdf (accessed 28 August 2013). Atlanta: Cooperative for Assistance and Relief Everywhere (CARE).

Gledhill, R. (2012a) 'Church women in protest at women bishops'. *The Times*, 21 May, 6.

— (2012b) 'We're losing our religion as we become "nones"'. *The Times*, 10 October, 21.

Goldstein, N.J., Martin, S.J., and Cialdini, R.B. (2007) *Influence: 50 secrets from the science of persuasion*. London: Profile Books.

Goodey, J. (2008) 'Racist violence in Europe: Challenges for official data collection'. In Spalek, B. (ed.) *Ethnicity and Crime: A reader*. Maidenhead: McGraw-Hill.

Goss, S. (2010) *Changing Behaviour*. London: Office for Public Management.

Govinda, R. (2012) '"*Didi*, are you Hindu?" Politics of secularism in women's activism in India: Case-study of a grassroots women's organization in rural Uttar Pradesh'. *Modern Asian Studies* 47 (2), 612–51. Online. http://dx.doi.org/10.1017/S0026749X12000832 (accessed 19 December 2012).

Graham-Harrison, E. (2012) 'Clerics issue repressive rules for Afghan women'. *The Guardian*, 6 March. Online. www.theguardian.com/world/2012/mar/05/afghanistan-women (accessed 28 August 2013).

Granovetter, M. (1983) 'The strength of weak ties: A network theory revisited'. *Sociological Theory*, 1, 201–33.

Greubel, L., and Robinson, J. (2013) 'Youth are central to shaping global education policy'. 7 January. Online. http://tinyurl.com/mnozbzk (accessed 14 January 2013). Washington, DC: Brookings Institution.

Gross, Z., Davies, L., and Diab, A. (eds) *Gender, Religion and Education in a Chaotic Postmodern World*. Dordrecht: Springer.

Hallum, A. (2003) 'Taking stock and building bridges: Feminism, women's movements and Pentecostalism in Latin America'. *Latin American Research Review*, 38 (1), 169–86.

Halpin, T. (2012) 'Pussy Riot uproar'. *The Times*, 18 August, 1.

Harber, C., and Davies, L. (2002) *School Management and Effectiveness in Developing Countries: The post-bureaucratic school*. London: Continuum Press.

—(2003) 'Educational decentralisation in Malawi: A study of process'. *Compare*, 33 (2), 139–54.

Harris, E. (2007) 'The cost of peace: Buddhists and conflict transformation in Sri Lanka'. In Broadhead, P., and Keown, D. (eds) *Can Faiths Make Peace? Holy wars and the resolution of religious conflicts*. London: I.B. Tauris.

Harris, S. (2004) *The End of Faith: Religion, terrorism and the future of reason*. New York: W.W. Norton.

Harrison, S. (1964) *The Artless Musician*. London: Pelham Books.

Hashash, S. (2011) 'The Muslim Brotherhood spreads fear from the wings'. *The Sunday Times*, 30 January, 19.

Hausler, K., Urban N., and McCorquodale, R. (2012) *Protecting Education in Insecurity and Armed Conflict: An international law handbook*. London: British Institute of International and Comparative Law/Doha: Education Above All.

Haynes, J. (2005) *Comparative Politics in a Globalizing World*. Cambridge: Polity.

— (2007) *Religion and Development: Conflict or cooperation?* Basingstoke: Palgrave Macmillan.

— (2009) 'Conflict, conflict resolution and peace-building: The role of religion in Mozambique, Nigeria and Cambodia'. *Commonwealth and Comparative Politics*, 47 (1), 52–75.

Hitchens, C. (2007) *God is not Great: How religion poisons everything*. New York: Twelve.

Holloway, R. (2012) 'Time for the charge of the doubt brigade'. *The Times*, 28 May, 21.

Holyoake, G.J. (1896) *Origin and Nature of Secularism*. London: Watts & Co.

Hopkins, E. (2010) 'Classroom conditions for effective learning: Hearing the voice of Key Stage 3 pupils'. *Improving Schools*, 13 (1), 39–53.

Horgan, J. (2009) *Walking Away from Terrorism*. London: Routledge.

Horner, L. (2012) 'Chasing peace in Mindanao'. Paper presented at workshop 'Ethnicity and Education: The challenge of diversity and social cohesion', Exeter Centre for Ethno-Political Studies (EXCEPS), 11–12 July.

Howson, C. (2011) *Objecting to God*. Cambridge: Cambridge University Press.

Huddleston, T. (2012) 'Civic education in south-east Europe and Turkey: Reflections on recent policy and practice'. Paper presented at the Legatum Institute conference 'The Future of Iran: Educational Reform', London, 12 November.

Hughes, J., Donnelly C., Hewstone, M., Gallagher, T., and Carlisle, K. (2010) *School Partnerships and Reconciliation: An evaluation of school collaboration in Northern Ireland 2010*. Belfast: Queen's University Belfast.

Human Rights Watch (2006) *Lessons in Terror: Attacks on education in Afghanistan* (Volume 18, Number 6 (C)). New York: Human Rights Watch.

Human Security Report Project (2012) *Human Security Report 2012: Sexual Violence, Education, and War: Beyond the mainstream narrative*. Vancouver: Human Security Press .

Hunter, I. (2009) 'The shallow legitimacy of secular liberal orders: The case of early modern Brandenburg Prussia'. In Levey, G.B., and Modood, T. (eds) *Secularism, Religion and Multicultural Citizenship*. Cambridge: Cambridge University Press.

Husain, E. (2007) *The Islamist*. London: Penguin.

Hussain, M. (2008) *Oxford Muslim Students Empowerment Programme*. Windsor: Eton College.

Ibrahim, N. (2011) 'An insider account of EIG's partnership with the Egyptian state security'. Paper presented at the conference 'Political Transitions, Policing and Counter-Terrorism: Power, partnership and community', University of Birmingham, 27–8 July.

Ilaiah, K. (2006) *Why I am not a Hindu: A Sudra critique of Hindutva philosophy, culture and political economy*. Calcutta: Samya.

The Independent (2012) 'Top Israeli Rabbi urges prayers for the destruction of Iran'. 27 August. Online. http://tinyurl.com/9jpd5ek (accessed 29 August 2013).

Innes, M., Roberts, C., and Innes, H. (2011) *Assessing the Effects of Prevent Policing*. Cardiff: Universities' Police Science Institute, Cardiff University.

Islamic Relief (2012) *Building a Better Future*. Online. http://issuu.com/islamicreliefcanada/docs/magazine_2012_allfinalv3 (accessed 28 August 2013)

Ivens, M. (2011) 'Don't cheer yet for revolution in Egypt'. *The Sunday Times*, 30 January, 23.

Jackson, R. (1990) *Quasi-States: Sovereignty, international relations and the Third World*. Cambridge: Cambridge University Press.

— (2005) *Writing the War on Terrorism: Language, politics and counter-terrorism*. Manchester: Manchester University Press.

Jacobson, H. (2010) 'Twenty-two, male and introspective – of course he should have been on a no-fly list'. *The Independent*, 2 January, 23.

Jeffrey, C., Jeffery, R., and Jeffery P. (2008) 'School and *madrasah* education: Gender and the strategies of Muslim young men in rural north India'. *Compare*, 38 (5), 581–93 .

Johnson, N. (2008) 'Complexity in human conflict'. In Helbing, D. (ed.) *Managing Complexity: Insights, concepts, applications*. Berlin: Springer-Verlag.

Johnson, S. (2001) *Emergence: The connected lives of ants, brains, cities and software*. New York: Scribner.

Jones, L.I. (2013) 'Women's theologies, women's pedagogies: Globalization, education and liberation in Nicaragua'. In Gross *et al.*, 2013.

Jones, L., and Reiss, M.J. (eds) (2007) *Teaching about Scientific Origins: Taking account of creationism*. New York: Peter Lang.

Kavakci Islam, M. (2010) 'Sole protector, of what? Unpacking Turkey's anti- Muslim policies'. *Arches Quarterly*, 7 (4) 75–81.

Kawahashi, N., Komatsu, K., and Kuroki, M. (2013) 'Gendering religious studies: Reconstructing religion and gender studies in Japan'. In Gross *et al.*, 2013.

Kelly, J. (2012) 'Taleban have victory in their sights as dejected Afghan troops swap sides'. *The Times*, 1 February, 6–7.

Kepel, G. (2005) *The Roots of Radical Islam*. London: Saqi Books.

King, E., Holloway, S., Brown, K., and Sawar, S. (2010) *Creativity and Education in the Prevent Agenda: A review of policy, theory and evidence: Report to Creativity, Culture and Education*. London: Office for Public Management.

Knowles, D. (2008) 'Sarah Palin: Iraq war "God's will"'. *Politics Daily*, 2 September. Online. www.politicsdaily.com/2008/09/02/sarah-palin-iraq-war-gods-plan/ (accessed 28 August 2013).

Kosmin, B.A. (2007) 'Contemporary secularity and secularism'. In Kosmin, B.A., and Keysar, A. (eds) *Secularity and Secularism: Contemporary international perspectives*. Hartford, CT: Institute for the Study of Secularism in Society and Culture, Trinity College.

Kundnani, A. (2009a) *Spooked: How not to prevent violent extremism*. London: Institute of Race Relations.

— (2009b) 'Trust made meaningless'. *The Guardian*, 19 October, 33.

Kurtz, L. (1995) *Gods in the Global Village*. Thousand Oaks, CA: Pine Forge/Sage.

Kuru, A. (2009) *Secularism and State Policies toward Religion*. Cambridge: Cambridge University Press.

Kymlicka, W. (2004) 'Citizenship education: Anti-political culture and political education in Britain'. In Lockyer, A., Crick, B., and Annette, J. (eds) *Education for Citizenship: Issues of theory and practice*. Aldershot: Ashgate.

Lambert, S. (2013) 'Religious leaders battle Manitoba anti-bully bill'. *The Globe and Mail*, 15 March. Online. www.theglobeandmail.com/news/national/religious-leaders-battle-manitoba-anti-bully-bill/article9845049/ (accessed 19 March 2013).

Lambeth Palace (2012) 'Full list of recommendations compiled from inputs of individual speakers'. Conference, *Education for Children Affected by Armed Conflict*, London, 3 September.

Lane, H.S. (2012) *A Study of the English Defence League: What draws people of faith to right-wing organisations and what effects does the EDL have on community cohesion and interfaith relations?* Online. http://faith-matters. org/images/stories/edl%20report.pdf (accessed 28 August 2013). London: Faith Matters.

Larsson, G. (2010) 'Yusuf al-Qaradawi and Tariq Ramadan on secularisation: Differences and similarities'. In Marranci, G., and Turner, B. (eds) *Muslim Societies and the Challenge of Secularisation: An interdisciplinary approach*. Dordrecht: Springer.

Lefort, C. (1986) *The Political Forms of Modern Society: Bureaucracy, democracy, totalitarianism*, ed. and trans. J.B. Thompson. Cambridge: Polity.

Levey, G.B. (2009) 'Secularism and religion in a multicultural age'. In Levey, G.B., and Modood, T. (eds) *Secularism, Religion and Multicultural Citizenship*. Cambridge: Cambridge University Press.

Levinson, M. (2012) 'Marginalisation, neglect – or just a matter of misunderstanding? Policy and practice in the education of Gypsy Roma children'. Paper presented at workshop 'Ethnicity and Education: The challenge of diversity and social cohesion', Exeter Centre for Ethno-Political Studies (EXCEPS), 11–12 July.

Lewin, R. (1993) *Complexity: Life at the edge of chaos*. London: Phoenix.

Lilienfeld, S., Ammirati, R., and Landfield, K. (2009) 'Giving debiasing away: Can psychological research on correcting cognitive errors promote human welfare?' *Perspectives on Psychological Science*, 4, 390–8.

Lingis, A. (1994) *The Community of Those who have Nothing in Common*. Bloomington and Indianapolis: Indiana University Press.

Liotta, P.H. (2005) 'Through the looking glass: Creeping vulnerabilities and the reordering of security'. *Security Dialogue*, 36 (1), 49–70.

Locke, R. (2012) *Organized Crime, Conflict, and Fragility: A new approach*. New York: International Peace Institute.

Lolichen, P. (2010) 'Children as research protagonists and partners in governance'. In Cox, S., Robinson-Pant, A., Dyer, C., and M. Schweisfurth, M. (eds) *Children as Decision-Makers in Education*. London: Continuum.

Loorbach, D. (2010) 'Transition management for sustainable development: A prescriptive, complexity based governance framework'. *Governance: An international journal of policy, administration and institutions*, 23 (1), 161–83.

Lundy, L. (2007) '"Voice" is not enough: Conceptualising Article 12 of the United Nations Convention on the Rights of the Child'. *British Educational Research Journal*, 33 (6), 927–42.

Magouirk, J., Atran, S., and Sageman, M. (2008) 'Connecting terrorist networks'. *Studies in Conflict and Terrorism*, 31 (1) 1–16.

Martin, D. (1978) *A General Theory of Secularization*. New York: Harper and Row.

Maruna, S., Porter, L., and Carvalho, I. (2004) 'The Liverpool desistance study and probation practice: Opening the dialogue'. *Probation Journal*, 51 (3), 221–32.

Mason, M. (2008) 'What is complexity theory and what are its implications for educational change?' *Educational Philosophy and Theory*, 40 (1), 35–49.

Mason, P. (2012) *Why It's Kicking Off Everywhere: The new global revolutions*. London: Verso.

McDougall, D. (2012) 'The river that has lost its soul'. *The Sunday Times*, 29 July, Magazine, 42–7.

McGovern, M. (2010) *Countering Terror or Counter-Productive? Comparing Irish and British Muslim experiences of counter-insurgency law and policy. Report of a Symposium held in Cultúrlann McAdam Ó Fiaich, Falls Road, Belfast, 23–24 June 2009*. Ormskirk: Edge Hill University.

McNeill, F. (2003) 'Desistance-focused probation practice'. In Chui, W.H., and Nellis, M. (eds) *Moving Probation Forward: Evidence, arguments and practice*. Harlow: Pearson Longman.

McPherson, J. (1997) *For Cause and Comradeship: Why men fought in the Civil War*. New York: Oxford University Press.

Meah, Y., and Mellis, C. (2009) *Recognising and Responding to Radicalisation: Considerations for policy and practice through the eyes of street level workers*. The RecoRa Institute.

Memarsadeghi, M. (2013) *In the Here and Now: Civic education in advance of democratic transition.* Online. http://tinyurl.com/m9dfz2p (accessed 1 March 2013).

Menefee, T. (2012a) 'Capabilities and Complexity: A response to Owen Barner'. *The Comparativist.* Online. www.comparativist.org/?p=510 (accessed 6 January 2012).

— (2012b) 'Complexity and poverty'. *The Comparativist.* Online. www. comparativist.org/?p=518 (accessed 6 January 2012).

Merry, M., and Karsten, S. (2011) 'Pluralism and segregation: The Dutch experience'. In Ghosh, R., and McDonagh, K. (eds) *Diversity and Education for Liberation: Realities, possibilities and problems* (Canadian Issues). Montreal: Association for Canadian Studies.

Meyer, D. (1999) 'How the Cold War was really won: The effects of the anti-nuclear movements of the 1980s'. In Giugni, M., McAdam, D., and Tilly, C. (eds) *How Social Movements Matter.* Minneapolis: University of Minnesota Press.

Modood, T. (2009) 'Muslims, religious equality and secularism'. In Levey, G.B., and Modood. T. (eds) *Secularism, Religion and Multicultural Citizenship.* Cambridge: Cambridge University Press.

Mohsin, A. (2004). 'Religion, politics and security: The case of Bangladesh'. In Limaye, S.P., Malik, M., and Wirsing, R.G. (eds) *Religious Radicalism and Security in South Asia.* Honolulu, HI: Asia-Pacific Center for Security Studies.

Moisi, D. (2009) *The Geopolitics of Emotion: How cultures of fear, humiliation and hope are reshaping the world.* London: The Bodley Head.

Møller, B. (2003) 'National, societal and human security: Discussion – case study of the Israel–Palestine Conflict'. In Brauch, H.G., Liotta, P.H., Marquina, A., Rogers, P., and El-Sayed Selim, M. (eds), *Security and Environment in the Mediterranean: Conceptualizing security and environmental conflict.* Berlin: Springer.

Morsy, A. (2013) 'Al-Azhar on the Tightrope'. *Sada journal,* 21 February. Online. http://carnegieendowment.org/2013/02/21/al-azhar-on-tightrope/fiqx (accessed 23 February 2013).

NAHT (2010) 'Rights Respecting Schools' (*Leadership Paper 1*). Haywards Heath: National Association of Head Teachers.

National Secular Society (2010) 'Faith school admission briefing'. Online. www. secularism.org.uk/uploads/faith-school-admissions-briefing.pdf (accessed 11 February 2013).

Nawaz, M. (2012) *Radical.* London: W H Allen.

— (2013) 'Lord Ahmed's buffoonery hurts Muslims too'. *The Times,* 15 March. Online. www.thetimes.co.uk/tto/opinion/columnists/article3713908.ece (requires subscription) (accessed 28 August 2013).

NewsThump (2011) 'Top universities a "breeding ground" for Tories, warn Islamic groups'. 7 June. Online. http://newsthump.com/2011/06/07/top-universities-a-breeding-ground-for-tories-warn-islamic-groups (accessed 28 August 2013).

— (2012) 'Creationist school syllabus only takes 7 days, insists Michael Gove'. 18 July. Online. http://newsthump.com/2012/07/18/creationist-school-syllabus-only-takes-7-days-insists-michael-gove (accessed 28 August 2013).

Nordtveit, B. (2010) 'Development as a complex process of change: Conception and analysis of projects, programs and policies'. *International Journal of Educational Development,* 30, 110–17.

Norfolk, A. (2013) 'Profile: Nazir Ahmed'. *The Times*, 14 March. Online. www. thetimes.co.uk/tto/news/uk/article3712992.ece (requires subscription) (accessed 28 August 2013).

Novelli, M. (2010) 'Political violence against education sector aid workers in conflict zones: A preliminary investigation into the possible link between attacks and the increased merging of security and development policy'. In *Protecting Education from Attack: A state of the art review*. Paris: UNESCO.

ODIHR (2007) *Toledo Guiding Principles on Teaching about Religions and Beliefs in Public Schools*. Warsaw: OSCE Office for Democratic Institutions and Human Rights.

— (2011) *Guidelines for Educators on Countering Intolerance and Discrimination against Muslims: Addressing Islamophobia through education*. Warsaw: OSCE Office for Democratic Institutions and Human Rights.

O'Malley, B. (2010) *Education Under Attack*. Paris: UNESCO.

— (2012) 'When schools are casualties of war'. BBC News, 4 July. Online. www.bbc. co.uk/news/business-18509093 (accessed 14 February 2013).

The Onion (2012) 'No one murdered because of this image'. 13 September. Online. www.theonion.com/articles/no-one-murdered-because-of-this-image,29553 (accessed 29 August 2013).

OPM (2010) *Interview with Alyas Karmani, Director, STREET. 14 July 2010*. London: Office for Public Management.

— (2011) *How teaching methods can build resilience to violent extremism*. Report to Department for Education. London: Office for Public Management and NFER.

Osberg, D. (2008) 'The logic of emergence: An alternative conceptual space for theorizing critical education'. *Journal of the Canadian Association for Curriculum Studies*, 6 (1) 133–61.

Osler, A., and Starkey, H. (1996) *Teacher Education and Human Rights*. London: David Fulton.

Owen, P., and Urquhart, C. (2013) 'Woolwich attack: Aftermath and reaction to killing on London street – as it happened'. *The Guardian*, 22 May. Online. www. theguardian.com/uk/2013/may/22/woolwich-two-shot-in-police-incident-live-coverage (accessed 28 August 2013).

Paine, T. (1984) *The Rights of Man*. Originally 1791. Harmondsworth: Penguin .

Paivandi, S. (2012) 'Education in the Islamic Republic of Iran and perspective of democratic reforms'. Working Paper presented at seminar 'Future of Iran: Educational reform', Legatum Institute, London, 12 November.

Pasquale, F. (2012) 'The Social Science of Secularity'. *Free Inquiry*, 32 (2). Online. www.secularhumanism.org/index.php?section=fi&page=pasquale_32_2 (accessed 28 August 2013).

Pinker, S. (2002) *The Blank Slate: The modern denial of human nature*. London: Penguin.

Pinson, H., Levy, G., and Soker, Z. (2012) 'Peace as a surprise, peace as a disturbance: The Israeli-Arab conflict in official documents'. In Schweisfurth, M., and Harber, C. (eds) *Education and Global Justice*. London: Routledge.

Porges, M. (2010) 'The Saudi Deradicalization Experiment'. Online. www.cfr.org/ publication/by_type/region_issue_brief.html (accessed 27 August 2013). New York: Council on Foreign Relations.

Prevent (n.d.) 'One Extreme to the Other'. Online. www.lancsngfl.ac.uk/prevent/index.php?category_id=2 (accessed 28 August 2013).

Pufendorf, S. (1934) *The Laws of Nature and of Nations in Eight Books*, originally 1672. Trans. Oldfather, C.H., and Oldfather W.A. Oxford: Clarendon.

Pye, J., Lister, C., Latter, J., and Clements, L. (2009) *Young People Speak Out: Attitudes to, and perceptions of, full-time volunteering*. London: Ipsos MORI.

Rahman, T. (2008) 'Madrasas, the potential for violence in Pakistan?' In Malik, J. (ed.) *Madrasas in South Asia: Teaching terror?* London and New York: Routledge.

Raihani, R. (2012) 'Report on multicultural education in *pesantren*'. *Compare*, 42 (4), 585–605.

Rapaport, T. (2013) 'Holiness class: Constructing a constructive woman'. In Gross *et al.*, 2013.

Rasool, E. (2010) 'South African Muslims over three centuries: From the jaws of Islamophobia to the joys of equality'. *Arches Quarterly*, 4 (7), 147–54.

Reynaert, D., Bouverne-De-Bie, M., and Vandevelde, S. (2010a) 'Children, rights and social work: Rethinking children's rights education'. *Social Work and Society*, 8 (1), 60–9.

— (2010b) 'Children's rights education and social work: Contrasting models and understandings'. *International Social Work*, 53 (4), 443–56.

Rifkind, H. (2012) 'Political maturity will stop the raging nutter'. *The Times*, 13 September, 21.

Rihani, S. (2002) *Complex Systems Theory and Development Practice*. London: Zed Books.

Ross, T. (2013) 'The implication of the feminization of theology: Deconstructing sacred texts as an educational issue'. In Gross *et al.*, 2013.

Rowe, D., Horsley, N., Breslin, T., and Thorpe, T. (2012) 'Benefit or burden? How English schools responded to the duty to promote community cohesion'. *Journal of Social Science Education*, 11 (3), 88–107.

Rowson, M. (2008) *The Dog Allusion: God, pets and how to be human*. London: Vintage Books.

Ruddock, J., and McIntyre, D. (2007) *Improving Learning through Consulting Pupils*. London: Routledge.

Ruthven, M. (2004) *Fundamentalism: The search for meaning*. Oxford: Oxford University Press.

Sageman, M. (2008) *Leaderless Jihad: Terror networks in the twenty-first century*. Philadelphia: University of Pennsylvania Press.

Sandford-Gaebel, K. (2013) 'Germany, Islam and education: Unveiling the contested meaning(s) of the headscarf'. In Gross *et al.*, 2013.

Save the Children and Davies, L. (2012) *Breaking the Cycle of Crisis: Learning from Save the Children's delivery of education in conflict-affected fragile states*. London: Save the Children.

Sayyid, S. (2009) 'Contemporary politics of secularism'. In Levey, G.B., and Modood, T. (eds) *Secularism, Religion and Multicultural Citizenship*. Cambridge: Cambridge University Press.

Schulz, W., Ainley, J., Fraillon, J., Kerr, D., and Losito, B. (2009) *ICCS 2009 International Report: Civic knowledge, attitudes, and engagement among lower secondary students in 38 countries*. Online. www.iea.nl/fileadmin/user_upload/ Publications/Electronic_versions/ICCS_2009_International_Report.pdf (accessed 28 August 2013). Amsterdam: International Association for the Evaluation of Educational Achievement.

Sebba, J., and Robinson, C. (2010) *Evaluation of UNICEF UK's Rights Respecting Schools Award*. London: UNICEF UK.

Sebestyen, V. (2012) 'A message to Putin: Remember the Plastics'. *The Times*, 18 August, 18.

Sen, A. (1999) *Development as Freedom*. Oxford: Oxford University Press.

Sengupta, K. (2013) 'Woolwich killings suspect Michael Adebolajo was inspired by cleric banned from UK after urging followers to behead enemies of Islam'. *The Independent*, 24 May. Online. http://tinyurl.com/khbb4kl (accessed 28 August 2013).

Shane, S. (2011) 'Killings in Norway spotlight anti-American thought in US'. *The New York Times*, 24 July. Online. www.nytimes.com/2011/07/25/us/25debate. html (accessed 28 August 2013).

Shanks, K. (2012) 'Education and ethno-politics: The alternative role of education in the disputed territories of Iraq' Paper presented at workshop 'Ethnicity and Education: The challenge of diversity and social cohesion', Exeter Centre for Ethno-Political Studies (EXCEPS), 11–12 July.

Shephard, M. (2011) 'Searching for a radical solution to Islamic extremism'. *Toronto Star*, 26 June. Online. www.thestar.com/news./world/article/1014887 (accessed 28 August 2013).

Shermer, M. (2002) *Why People Believe Weird Things: Pseudoscience, superstition, and other confusions of our time*. New York: W.H. Freeman.

Shneour, E. (1998) 'Planting a seed of doubt'. *Skeptical Inquiry*, 22, 40–2.

Sigsgaard, M. (ed.) (2011) *On the Road to Resilience: Capacity development with the Ministry of Education in Afghanistan*. Paris: UNESCO International Institute of Educational Planning.

Singer, P. (2001) 'Pakistan's madrassahs: Ensuring a system of education, not jihad' (Analysis Paper 14). Washington, DC: Brookings Institution.

Skeptic's Annotated Bible (n.d.) 'Cruelty and violence in the Bible'. Online. www. skepticsannotatedbible.com/cruelty/long.html (accessed 28 August 2013).

Slevin, J. (2000) *The Internet and Society*. Cambridge: Polity.

Smith, C. (2008) 'Future directions in the sociology of religion'. *Social Forces*, 86 (4), 1561–89.

Smith, M. (2010) 'Schools as zones of peace: Nepal case study in access to education during armed conflict and civil unrest'. In *Protecting Education from Attack: A state of the art review*. Paris: UNESCO.

Smock, D., and Huda, Q. (2009) *Islamic Peacemaking since 9/11* (USIP Special Report 218). Washington, DC: United States Institute of Peace.

Soans, R. (2004) *The Arab–Israeli Cookbook*. London: Aurora Metro Press.

Spajic-Vrkas, V. (2012) 'Paving the way to self-empowerment through a rights-based education'. In Sleeter, C., Bhushan Upadhyay, S., Mishra, A.K., and Kumar, S. (eds) *School Education, Pluralism and Marginality: Comparative perspectives*. New Delhi: Orient Black Swan.

Spalek, B. (2010) 'Community policing, trust and Muslim communities in relation to "new terrorism"'. *Politics & Policy*, 38 (4), 789–815.

Spalek, B., and Davies, L. (2012) 'Mentoring in relation to violent extremism: A study of role, purpose, and outcomes'. *Studies in Conflict & Terrorism, 35* (5), 354–68.

Spalek, B., Davies, L., and McDonald, L.Z. (2010) *Key Evaluation Findings of the West Midlands (WM) 1-2-1 Mentoring Scheme.* Birmingham: University of Birmingham.

Spalek, B., El-Awa, S., and McDonald, L.Z. (2009) *Police–Muslim Engagement and Partnerships for the Purposes of Counter-Terrorism: An examination.* Birmingham: University of Birmingham.

Spalek, B., and McDonald, L.Z. (2010a) 'Anti-social behaviour powers and the policing of security.' *Social Policy and Society,* 9 (1), 123–33.

— (2010b) *Police–Community Engagement and Counter-Terrorism: Developing a regional, national and international hub.UK–US Workshop Summary Report December 2010.* Birmingham: University of Birmingham.

Stacey, R. (1996) *Complexity and Creativity in Organizations.* San Francisco: Berrett-Koehler.

Stambach, A. (2010) *Faith in Schools: Religion, education and American evangelicals in East Africa.* Stanford, CA: Stanford University Press.

Stares, P. (ed.) (1998) *The New Security Agenda: A global survey.* Tokyo: Japan Centre for International Exchange.

Stark, R., and Finke, R. (2000) *Acts of Faith: Explaining the human side of religion.* Berkeley: University of California Press.

Stark, R., and Iannaccone, L. (1994) 'A supply-side reinterpretation of the "secularization" of Europe'. *Journal of the Scientific Study of Religion,* 33 (3), 230–52.

Starkey, C., and Tomalin, E. (2013) 'Gender, Buddhism and education: *Dhamma* and social transformation within the Theravada tradition'. In Gross *et al.*, 2013.

Stevens, T., and Neumann, P. (2009) *Countering Online Radicalisation: A strategy for action.* London: International Centre for the Study of Radicalisation and Violence.

Svensson, I. (2007) 'Fighting with faith: Religion and conflict resolution in civil wars'. *Journal of Conflict Resolution,* 51, 930–47.

Svensson, I., and Rangdrol, D. (2009). 'Demos or Deus: Patterns of religious dimensions in Asian armed conflicts, 1945–2005'. In Swain, A., Ramses, A., and Öjendal, J. (eds) *The Democratization Project: Opportunities and challenges.* London: Anthem Press.

Tapestry (2013) 'Introduction to "Tapestry"'. Online. http://theplayhouse.org.uk/tapestry/introduction-to-tapestry (accessed 28 August 2013).

Taylor, C. (1999) 'Modes of secularism'. In Bhargava, R. (ed.) *Secularism and its Critics.* Delhi: Oxford University Press.

Taylor, D. (2012) 'US gun lobby calls for more weapons in schools'. *The Times,* 22 December, 39.

Templeton Foundation (2011) *Templeton Report,* 7 September. Online. www.templeton.org/templeton_report/20110907/tr-20110907.pdf (accessed 29 August 2013).

Theis, J. (2010) 'Children as active citizens: An agenda for children's civil rights and civil engagement'. In Percy-Smith, B., and Thomas, N. (eds) (2010) *A Handbook of Children and Young People's Participation: Perspectives from theory and practice*. London: Routledge.

Thomas, P. (2009) 'Between two stools? The government's "preventing violent extremism" agenda'. *The Political Quarterly*, 80 (2), 282–91.

— (2010) 'Failed and friendless: The UK's "'Preventing Violent Extremism" programme'. *British Journal of Politics and International Relations*, 12, 442–58.

The Times (2012a) 'The stakes keep rising in game of revolt and politics, religion and death'. 18 August, 34–5.

— (2012b) 'Protest and punk: Three Russian musicians are a test case for freedom of speech under Putin's regime'. 21 July, 2.

— (2012c) 'Seize This Moment: Pakistan has an historic chance to harness public anger for the public good'. 16 October. Online. www.thetimes.co.uk/tto/opinion/leaders/article3569236.ece (requires subscription) (accessed 29 August 2013).

Times Higher Education (2008) 'Research into Islamic terrorism led to police response'. 22 May. Online. http://tinyurl.com/ke8qlvg (accessed 29 August 2013).

Toft, M. (2007) 'Getting religion? The puzzling case of Islam and civil war'. *International Security*, 31(4), 97–131.

Tomkins, S. (2011) 'If it was good enough for the Apostle Paul, it's good enough for me'. *Ship of Fools*. Online. www.shipoffools.com/features/2011/king_james_only.html (accessed 29 August 2013).

Tomlinson, H. (2011) 'Online dissent has mobilised millions but found no leaders'. *The Times*, 29 July . Online. www.thetimes.co.uk/tto/news/world/middleeast/article3108875.ece (requires subscription) (accessed 29 August 2013).

Tracy, J., Hart, J., and Martens, J. (2011) 'Death and science: The existential underpinnings of belief in intelligent design and discomfort with evolution'. *PLOS ONE*, 6 (3). Online. www.plosone.org/article/info%3Adoi%2F10.1371%2Fjournal.pone.0017349 (accessed 29 August 2013).

Trask, R. (2012) 'Religion spreads the word'. *The Guardian*, 28 November, 10.

Turner, J. (2011) 'It is not racist to say, I will not accept honour killings'. *The Times*, 2 April, 4–5.

Twain, M. (1984). *The Innocents Abroad; Roughing It*. Originally 1872. New York: Library of America.

UNESCO (2010) *Protecting Education from Attack: A state of the art review*. Paris: UNESCO.

UNICEF ROSA (Regional Office of South Asia) (2004) *Wheels of Change: Children and young people's participation in South Asia*. Kathmandu: UNICEF ROSA.

United Nations Assistance Mission to Afghanistan (UNAMA) (2007) *Suicide Attacks in Afghanistan (2001–2007)*. Kabul: UNAMA.

van der Zee, B. (2009) 'Terrorists don't install disabled toilets'. *New Statesman*, 19 November. Online. www.newstatesman.com/economy/2009/11/climate-activists-terrorism (accessed 29 August 2013).

Waever, O., Buzan, B., Kelstrup, M., and Lemaitre, P. (1993) *Identity, Migration and the New Security Agenda in Europe*. London: Pinter.

Waldrop. M. (1992) *Complexity: The emerging science at the edge of order and chaos*. London: Penguin.

Walker, B. (1999) 'Christianity, development and women's liberation'. *Gender and Development*, 7 (1), 15–22.

Walklate, S., and Mythen, G. (2008) 'Terrorism, risk and international security: The perils of asking "what if?"'. *Security Dialogue*, 39 (2), 221–42.

Walzer, M. (1993) *Thick and Thin: Moral argument at home and abroad.* Notre Dame, IN: University of Notre Dame Press.

Warwick, P., Cremin, H., Harrison, T., and Mason, C. (2012) 'The complex ecology of young people's community engagement and the call for civic pedagogues'. *Journal of Social Science Education*, 11 (3), 65–87.

Weber, M. (1958) *The Protestant Ethic and the Spirit of Capitalism.* New York: Charles Scribner's Sons.

Weiman, G. (2006) *Terror on the Internet: The new arena, the new challenges.* Washington, DC: United States Institute for Peace Press.

Wilkinson, T. (2007) *The Lost Art of Being Happy: Spirituality for sceptics.* Forres: Findhorn Press.

Williams, C. (2012) 'Global justice and education: From nation to neuron'. In Schweisfurth, M., and Harber, C. (eds) *Education and Global Justice.* London: Routledge.

Wilson, E.O. (2012) *The Social Conquest of Earth.* New York: W.W. Norton.

Wingrove, J. (2013) 'Gay teen holds the line for Manitoba bullying bill'. *The Globe and Mail*, 17 March. Online. www.theglobeandmail.com/news/national/gay-teen-holds-the-line-for-manitoba-bullying-bill/article9863497 (accessed 29 August 2013).

Winthrop, R., and Graff, C. (2010) *Beyond Madrasas: Assessing the links between education and militancy in Pakistan* (Working Paper 2). Washington, DC: Center for Universal Education at Brookings.

Woodhill, J. (2010) 'Capacities for Institutional Innovation: A complexity perspective'. *IDS Bulletin*, 41, 47–59.

Woolman, S., and Fleisch, B. (2009) *The Constitution in the Classroom: Law and education in South Africa 1994–2008.* Pretoria: Pretoria University Law Press.

World Bank (1998) *Development Report 1998/99: Knowledge for Development.* New York: Oxford University Press.

Yamashita H., and Davies, L. (2010) 'Students as professionals: The London secondary school councils action research project'. In Percy-Smith, B., and Thomas, N. (eds) *A Handbook of Children and Young People's Participation.* London: Routledge.

Yamashita, H., Davies, L., and Williams, C. (2010) 'Assessing the benefits of students' participation'. In Cox, S., Robinson-Pant, A., Dyer, C., and Schweisfurth, M. (eds) *Children as Decision-Makers in Education.* London: Continuum.

Yassine, A. (n.d.) 'Producer/director Ali Yassine'. Online. http://got.uk.net/index.php?option=com_content&view=article&id=94:good-afternoon-prynhawn-da-&catid=35:launch-handout-&Itemid=109 (accessed 29 August 2013).

Yehoshua, Y. (2006) 'Reeducation of extremists in Saudi Arabia'. *Islam Daily.* Online. www.islamdaily.org/en/saudi-arabia/3994.reeducation-of-extremists-in-saudi-arabia.htm (accessed 29 August 2013).

Yurchak, A. (2006) *Everything Was Forever, until it Was no More.* Princeton, NJ: Princeton University Press.

Index